Big Data, Cloud Computing and IoT

Cloud computing, the Internet of Things (IoT), and big data are three significant technological trends affecting the world's largest corporations. This book discusses big data, cloud computing, and the IoT, with a focus on the benefits and implementation problems. In addition, it examines the many structures and applications pertinent to these disciplines. Also, big data, cloud computing, and the IoT are proposed as possible study avenues.

Features:

- Informs about cloud computing, IoT, and big data, including theoretical foundations and the most recent empirical findings
- Provides essential research on the relationship between various technologies and the aggregate influence they have on solving real-world problems
- Ideal for academicians, developers, researchers, computer scientists, practitioners, information technology professionals, students, scholars, and engineers exploring research on the incorporation of technological innovations to address contemporary societal challenges

Big Data, Cloud Computing and IoT

Tools and Applications

Edited by
Sita Rani
Pankaj Bhambri
Aman Kataria
Alex Khang
Arun Kumar Sivaraman

CRC Press
Taylor & Francis Group
Boca Raton London New York

CRC Press is an imprint of the
Taylor & Francis Group, an **informa** business

A CHAPMAN & HALL BOOK

Front cover image: metamorworks/Shutterstock

First edition published 2023
by CRC Press
6000 Broken Sound Parkway NW, Suite 300, Boca Raton, FL 33487-2742

and by CRC Press
4 Park Square, Milton Park, Abingdon, Oxon, OX14 4RN

CRC Press is an imprint of Taylor & Francis Group, LLC

© 2023 selection and editorial matter, Sita Rani, Pankaj Bhambri, Aman Kataria, Alex Khang and Arun Kumar Sivaraman; individual chapters, the contributors

Library of Congress Cataloging-in-Publication Data
Names: Rani, Sita, editor. | Bhambri, Pankaj, editor. | Kataria, Aman,
editor. | Khang, Alex, editor. | Sivaraman, Arun Kumar, editor.
Title: Big data, cloud computing and IoT : tools and applications / edited
by Sita Rani, Pankaj Bhambri, Aman Kataria, Alex Khang, Arun Kumar Sivaraman.
Description: First edition. | Boca Raton : Chapman & Hall/CRC Press, 2023.
| Includes bibliographical references and index. |
Identifiers: LCCN 2022049025 (print) | LCCN 2022049026 (ebook) | ISBN
9781032284200 (hbk) | ISBN 9781032287430 (pbk) | ISBN 9781003298335 (ebk)
Subjects: LCSH: Big data. | Cloud computing. | Internet of things.
Classification: LCC QA76.9.B45 B5537 2023 (print) | LCC QA76.9.B45
(ebook) | DDC 005.7--dc23/eng/20221214
LC record available at https://lccn.loc.gov/2022049025
LC ebook record available at https://lccn.loc.gov/2022049026

ISBN: 978-1-032-28420-0 (hbk)
ISBN: 978-1-032-28743-0 (pbk)
ISBN: 978-1-003-29833-5 (ebk)

DOI: 10.1201/9781003298335

Typeset in Palatino
by SPi Technologies India Pvt Ltd (Straive)

Contents

Preface

The Internet of Things (IoT), big data, and cloud computing are all independent but complementary fields of study. The integration of three technologies provides synergy and a great chance for organizations to reap the enormous benefits of integration. When this combination is properly conceived, built, implemented, and operated, it can unleash a technical force that can propel innovation forward. Big data, the IoT, and the cloud architectures all work together to bring significant economic advantages. In a way, it is a great fit. The IoT captures data in real time. Data management systems benefit from big data's optimization. Rapid data collection, storage, computation, and dissemination are all features of the cloud. Big data solutions linked with IoT andcloud architecture are the key focus of this book, which is based on appealing business propositions. As a result, the book provides a high-level overview of architecture, solution practices, governance, and the underlying technical approach to developing integrated big data, cloud, and IoT solutions.

The security of critical systems and infrastructure is a serious concern for information and communication technology systems and networks. There are a variety of ways to ensure that messages are coming from trustworthy sources. The contributors cover the most recent research and development in authentication systems, including problems and applications for cloud technologies, the IoT, and big data in this edited reference.

Recent advances in micro-electro andmicro-mechanical system innovation, remote intersections, and computerized devices have enabled the creation of low-cost, multifunctional sensor hubs that are simple to operate, waste little power, and send data wirelessly over short distances. Intelligent sensors, when utilized like an IoT segment, convert a predicted reality factor into a digital information stream that may be communicated to a gateway for further processing.

The book illuminates the IoT, the cloud, and big data, as well as other cutting-edge technologies. This book addresses a variety of contemporary scientific and technical issues, including how to transform the IoT concept into a practical, technically feasible, and financially viable product. Big data and cloud computing are presented as important enablers for the sensing and computation backbone of the IoT. We are pleased that CRC Publications offered us the privilege to publish the book. Additionally, we appreciate our families and loved ones for their support. This book is intended for academics, postgraduates, and practitioners interested in cloud computing, the IoT, and big data.

About the Editors

Sita Rani is working in the Deaprtment of Computer Science and Engineering at Guru Nanak Dev Engineering College, Ludhiana. She has completed her B.Tech (CSE) and M.Tech (CSE) in 2002 and 2008 respectively, from Guru Nanak Dev Engineering College, Ludhiana. She earned her PhD in Computer Science and Engineering from I.K.Gujral Punjab Technical University, Kapurthala, Punjab in 2018. She has more than 19 years of teaching experience. She is an active member of ISTE, IEEE, and IAEngg. She is the receiver of ISTE Section Best Teacher Award, 2020, and International Young Scientist Award, 2021. She has contributed to various research activities while publishing articles in renowned journals and conference proceedings. She has published several National and International patents also. She has delivered many expert talks in All India Council of Technical Education (AICTE)–sponsored Faculty Development Programs and organized many international conferences during her 19 years of teaching experience. She is a member of the editorial boards of many international journals of repute. Her research interest includes parallel and distributed computing, machine learning, and the Internet of Things.

Pankaj Bhambri is working in the Department of Information Technology at Ludhiana's Guru Nanak Dev Engineering College. He also serves as the Institute's Coordinator, Skill Enhancement Cell. He has almost 20 years of experience as a teacher. For a long span, he served with the additional duties of an assistant registrar (Academic), member (Academic Council), member (BoS), member (RAC), hostel warden, APIO, and NSS coordinator for his institute. His research has appeared in a variety of prestigious international/national journals and conference proceedings indexed in SCIE, Scopus and UGC-CARE. Dr. Bhambri has contributed numerous textbooks as an editor/author and has filed several patents, too. He is the life member of ISTE, GENCO Alumni Association, I.E. (India), IIIE, IETE, IETA, I2OR and CSI, among others. As a result of his outstanding social and academic/research accomplishments over the past two decades, Dr. Bhambri has been awarded the ISTE Best Teacher Award-2022; I2OR National Award-2020; Green ThinkerZ Top 100 International Distinguished Educators-2020; I2OR Outstanding Educator Award-2019; SAA Distinguished Alumni Award-2012; CIPS Rashtriya Rattan Award-2008; LCHC Best Teacher Award-2007; and countless other accolades from various government and nonprofit organizations. He has supervised many undergraduate/postgraduate research projects/dissertations and is now supervising multiple Ph.D. research works as well. He organized numerous courses while receiving funding from the

AICTE, TEQIP, and others. Machine learning, bioinformatics, wireless sensor networks, and network security are his areas of interest.

Aman Kataria completed his B.Tech in electronics and communication engineering from Malout Institute of Management and Information Technology, Malout (established by state government), in 2010. He did his master's in electronics and instrumentation control engineering and his doctoral degree in 2013 and 2020, respectively, from Thapar Institute of Engineering and Technology, Patiala. Currently, he is working in Council of Scientific and Industrial Research-Central Scientific Instruments Organization as a project associate. He has also served as a lecturer at the Indian Institute of Information Technology, Una, Himachal Pradesh (under mentorship of National Institute of Technology, Hamirpur) in the Electronics and Communication Department. He has contributed to various research activities while publishing papers in the various Science Citation Index Expanded-and Scopus-indexed journals and conference proceedings. He has published three international patents also. His research interest includes are machine learning, artificial intelligence, image processing, cyber-physical systems, the Internet of Things, and soft computing.

Alex Khang, PHDSC, is a professor in information technology at the Universities of Science and Technology in Vietnam and United States, a software industry expert, an artificial intelligence (AI) and data scientist, a workforce development solutions consultant, and the chief of technology (AI and Data Science Research Center) at the Global Research Institute of Technology and Engineering, North Carolina, United States. He has 28-plusyears of nonstop teaching and research experience in information technology (software development, database technology, AI engineering, data engineering, data science, data analytics, Internet of Things (IoT)–based technologies, and cloud computing) at the Universities of Technology and Science in Vietnam, the European Union, India, and United States.

He has beenthe chair of session for 20-plusinternational conferences, an international keynote speaker for more than 25 international conclaves, an expert tech speaker for over 100 seminars and webinars, an international technical board member for 10-plus international organizations,an international editorial board member for more than five journals; a reviewer and evaluator for over 100 journal papers; and an international examiner and evaluator for more than 15 PhD theses in the computer science field.

He is the recipient of the Best Professor of the Year 2021, Researcher of the Year 2021, the Global Teacher Award 2021 (AKS), the Life Time Achievement Award 2021, the Leadership Award 2022 (Educacio World), and many other repute awards. He has contributed to various research activities in fields of AI and data science while publishing many international articles in renowned journals and conference proceedings.

He has published 52 authored books (in computer science between 2000–2010), authored 2 books (software development), edited 4 books, contributed 10 book chapters, and edited 2 books (calling for book chapters) in the fields of AI, data science, big data, IoT, smart city ecosystem, healthcare ecosystem, fintech, and blockchain technology (since 2020).

He has over 28 years of nonstop work as a CEO, a CTO, an engineering director, and a senior consultant in the field of software production and specialized in data engineering for foreign corporations from Germany, Sweden, the United States, Singapore, and multinationals.

Arun Kumar Sivaraman obtained his bachelor's degree in computer science and engineering from Anna University, Chennai, India, and his master's in computer science and engineering in 2010 from the College of Engineering Guindy (CEG) Chennai Campus. He has awarded a PhD, 2017, in computer science and engineering from Manonmaniam Sundaranar University (Govt.), Trinelveli, India. He received a Master of Business Administration, 2020, in education management from Alagappa University, Karaikudi, India. He has more than a decade of professional experience in the industrial, research and development, and academic sectors. He has worked as a lead data engineer for top multinational corporations like Cognizant, Standard Chartered, and Gilead Life Sciences. He worked as project consultant for a healthcare research (R&D) project in "The Research Council, Sultanate of Oman" funded by the Ministry of Health, Oman. He published a book in machine learning titled *Image Processing for Machine Learning* (ISBN: 978-93-5445-509-4). He published many research papers in the Scopus-indexed reputed journal, holds two Indian patents, and got one grant in international patent. For his merit, he got an offer as Lead Data Engineer in Tata Consultancy Services (TCS) 2011, Employment Pass Eligibility Certificate from the government of Singapore in 2012, and the Young Scientist award from the government of Sultanate of Oman 2018. He is currently working as an assistant professor (Sr. Grade) at VIT University, Chennai Campus, India. He is an active coeditor of a couple of special journal issues by TechScience Press (*Computer, Materials and Continua* – IF 4.89). His academic and research expertise covers a wide range of subject areas, including data engineering, data analytics, data science, and machine learning.

List of Contributors

Adalarasu Kanagasabai
SASTRA Deemed to be University
Tamil Nadu, India

Aman Kataria
CSIR-CSIO
Chandigarh, India

Ashish Verma
Military College of Telecommunication
    Engineering (MCTE-MHOW)
Madhya Pradesh, India

B. S. Shylaja
Ambedkar Institute of Technology
Karnataka, India

Bhavesh Borisaniya
Shantilal Shah Engineering College
Gujarat, India

C. Chethana
BMS Institute of Technology and
    Management
Karnataka, India

Charanjeet Singh
Gujranwala Guru Nanak Institute of
    Management and Technology
Punjab, India

Debabrata Sarddar
University of Kalyani
West Bengal, India

Devesh Pratap Singh
Graphic Era deemed to be University
Uttarakhand, India

Enakshmi Nandi
University of Kalyani
West Bengal, India

G. Boopathi Raja
Velalar College of Engineering and
    Technology
Tamil Nadu, India

Ganesh Reddy Karri
VIT-AP University
Andhra Pradesh, India

Gurjot Kaur Walia
Guru Nanak Dev Engineering College
 Punjab, India

Gurwinder Singh
Guru Nanak Dev Engineering College
Punjab, India

Jagannath Mohan
Vellore Institute of Technology
Tamil Nadu

K. P. Maheswari
Fatima College
Tamil Nadu, India

Kailash Kumar Sahu
Pandit Sundarlal Sharma (Open) University
Chhattisgarh, India

Kanagaraj Venusamy
University of Technology and Applied
    Sciences-AI Mussanah
AI Muladdha, Sultanate of Oman

Keerthik Dhivya Rajakumar
Vellore Institute of Technology
Tamil Nadu

Munish Rattan
Guru Nanak Dev Engineering College
Punjab, India

N. Anuradha
Subbalakshmi Lakshmipathy College of
    Science
Tamil Nadu, India

Neelam Sharma
KIET Group of Institutions
Uttar Pradesh, India

Neelam Singh
Graphic Era deemed to be University
Uttarakhand, India

Pankaj Bhambri
Guru Nanak Dev Engineering College
Punjab, India

Parul Dubey
G.H. Raisoni College of Engineering
Maharashtra, India

Payel Ray
University of Kalyani
West Bengal, India

Piyush Kumar Pareek
Nitte Meenakshi Institute of Technology,
    Karnataka, India

Pushkar Dubey
Pandit Sundarlal Sharma (Open) University
Chhattisgarh, India

R. Bhaskar
Ambedkar Institute of Technology
Karnataka, India

R. Nagarajan
Gnanamani College of Technology
Tamil Nadu, India

Rajesh Bodade
Military College of Telecommunication
    Engineering (MCTE-MHOW)
Madhya Pradesh, India

Ramandeep Kaur
Gujranwala Guru Nanak Institute of
    Management and Technology
Punjab, India

Ranjan Kumar Mondal
University of Kalyani
West Bengal, India

S. Kannadhasan
Study World College of Engineering
Tamil Nadu, India

S. Nirmala Devi
Subbalakshmi Lakshmipathy College of
    Science
Tamil Nadu, India

S. R. Deepu
Ambedkar Institute of Technology
Karnataka, India

Sudheer Mangalampalli
VIT-AP University
Andhra Pradesh, India

Saurabh Kumar
The LNM Institute of Information
    Technology
Rajasthan, India

Shefali Kanwar
Amity University
 Uttar Pradesh, India

Shruti Negi
Graphic Era deemed to be University
Uttarakhand, India

Sita Rani
Guru Nanak Dev Engineering College
Punjab, India

Surbhi Gupta
Amity University
Uttar Pradesh, India

Vandana Rawat
Graphic Era deemed to be University
Uttarakhand, India

Vanieka
Vellore Institute of Technology
Madhya Pradesh, India

1

Integration of IoT, Big Data, and Cloud Computing Technologies: Trend of the Era

Sita Rani, Pankaj Bhambri and Aman Kataria

CONTENTS

1.1 Introduction

Today, technology has captured every sphere of day-to-day life. It contributes significantly to providing better services and quality lives to users (Rani et al., 2021b). It has benefited a number of domains, like healthcare, industry, education, agriculture, transportation, banking and finance, among others (Rani et al., 2022c). This technological revolution comprises artificial

DOI: 10.1201/9781003298335-1

intelligence (AI), machine learning (ML), the Internet of Things (IoT), big data analytics, cloud computing, 4G, and 5G. The fundamental aim is to provide all-time connectivity and availability of data (Singh et al., 2021b). Individually as well as together, the IoT, big data, and cloud computing are playing notable roles in many application areas. The development of a strong charging structure network is broadly known as a vital necessity for a huge-scale evolution to electromobility (Bhambri et al., 2022). Kshirsagar et al. (2022) covered research on various methodologies for using neural networks to detect plant leaf diseases. Today, almost every field is making use of neural networks in one or another way (Bhambri et al., 2022).

1.1.1 IoT

The Internet is observed as a communication network that connects people and information (Hussein, 2019). On the other side, the IoT is a network of distributed objects in which each object has the potential to sense data/signals and process them with varying capacities (Soumyalatha, 2016; Rani et al., 2021). Each object/thing has a unique address so it can be located in cyberspace, which helps with the operations and communications among the objects (Singh et al., 2017; Jabraeil Jamali et al., 2020; Rani et al., 2022b). So, the fundamental aim of the IoT is to connect various things and individuals to facilitate all-time connectivity everywhere they are by using various communication networks and services, as shown in Figure 1.1. The IoT is considered one of the phases of the Internet's evolution. The IoT has made it convenient to connect many ordinary devices/gadgets to the Internet and helps achieve many diverse objectives (Kumar et al., 2022; Rani et al., 2022b). Whereas in 2015, only 0.06% of objects were connected to the IoT system, in 2020, approximately 50 billion smart devices have become part of the system and are connected through the Internet, which is a very high number compared to the world's population, shown in Figure 1.2.

With the evolution of the Internet, now it is not only a network of machines but has also emerged as a network of a variety of devices (Rani et al., 2021c; Banerjee et al., 2022). The IoT has become a network of different interconnected objects/things, also called a network of networks (Arya et al., 2022), as depicted in Figure 1.3.

In current times, various devices like smart appliances, vehicles, cyber-physical systems, smartphones, industrial systems, healthcare devices, and many others are using the

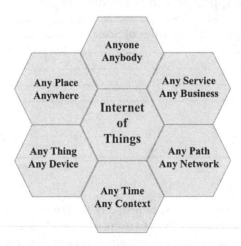

FIGURE 1.1
IoT: anytime, anywhere connectivity (Soumyalatha, 2016).

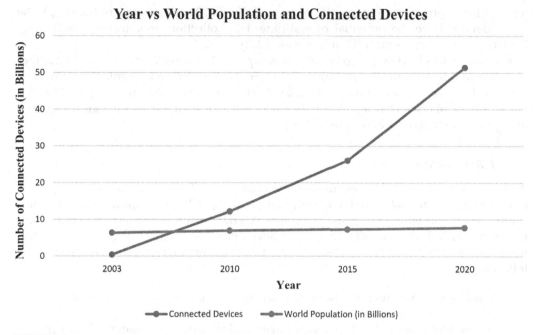

FIGURE 1.2
IoT-connected devices: year/population (Soumyalatha, 2016).

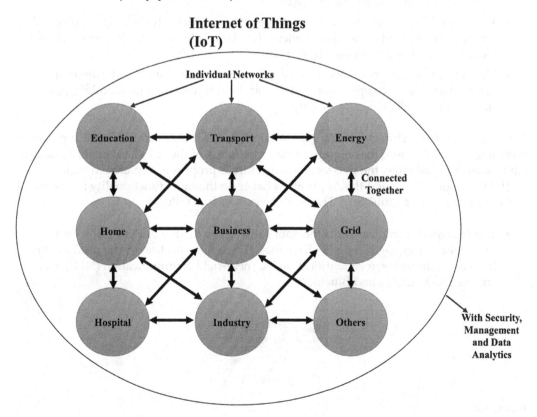

FIGURE 1.3
IoT: network mesh (Hussein, 2019).

Internet for information exchange (Rani et al., 2022a, 2022). Irrespective of the size, these smart devices have the potential of real-time data collection, monitoring, positioning, tracking, and process control (Bhambri et al., 2022).

Keeping all this in view, the IoT platform is supposed to flourish in terms of the number of connected devices and smart objects in a variety of commercial application domains (Rani et al., 2021a; Kothandaraman et al., 2022). The IoT will offer numerous opportunities in the domain of research due to the widespread usage of smart devices in various spheres of day-to-day life (Gupta and Kaur, 2016).

1.1.1.1 Architecture

As the number of smart devices connected through the IoT is increasing rapidly, it needs a flexible and expandable architecture (Aswale et al., 2019). Communication channels should be capable enough to manage voluminous data to avoid congestion (Tandon and Bhambri, 2017). Different IoT models are developed using either of the two architectures, that is, a three-layer architecture or a five-layer architecture, as discussed in the following:

> **Three-Layer Architecture**: It is also called conventional architecture, as shown in Figure 1.4.

- The bottom layer is the Perception Layer, which keeps environmental data sensors. The basic tasks of this layer are to sense the environmental data using sensors and recognize the intelligent devices.
- The second layer, that is, Network Layer interconnects the intelligent objects/devices, servers, and networked devices. The data gathered in the perception layer are transmitted and processed in this layer.
- The Application Layer provides the application-centered services to the users. It caters to a variety of applications, like smart healthcare, intelligent buildings, and smart homes and cities, among others.

The three-layer IoT architecture only gives an overview but is not ample for all application domains, especially those that require the sharper facets of the IoT (Rani et al., 2022d). To administer this challenge, the five-layer architecture is proposed, depicted in Figure 1.5.

The Perception Layer and the Application Layer do the same functionality as discussed earlier in three-layer architecture. The other layers work as follows:

- The Transport Layer transmits the data gathered by the lower Perception Layer to the upper Processing layer and vice versa. The communication media used by this layer are radiofrequency identification, 3G, near-field communication (NFC), local area network (LAN), and Bluetooth.

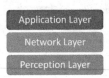

FIGURE 1.4
IoT: three-layer architecture.

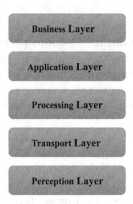

FIGURE 1.5
IoT: five-layer architecture.

- The next layer, that is, the Processing Layer, also known as middleware, stores, analyzes, and processes huge volumes of data received from the Transportation Layer. This layer uses a variety of technologies like databases, big data modules, and cloud computing applications to accomplish its tasks.
- The integrated IoT system is administered by the topmost layer, that is, the Business Layer. It manages the privacy of the users, various applications, and business models.

1.1.1.2 IoT Application Domains

In collaboration with ML and AI, anomaly detection systems are vastly used in behavioral analysis to help identify and predict the prevalence of anomalies (Bhambri et al., 2020). The IoT plays a very significant role in numerous and diverse application domains. Smart devices and gadgets have entered almost all the spheres of day-to-day life for individuals, organizations, and institutions (Rani et al., 2021). Broadly, the IoT has covered many important areas, including healthcare, industry, smart cities, agriculture, and others (Anand and Bhambri, 2018).

- **Smart Cities**

The IoT is contributing significantly to improving the quality of life of residents by improving cities' infrastructure. Some of the prominent applications in the smart city ecosystem consist of intelligent transportation and traffic management, smart buildings, smart parking, smart grids and metering systems, waste management, and smart lighting.

- **Healthcare**

IoT-enabled medical equipment and smart devices are offering many benefits in the healthcare sector, such as monitoring patients remotely, gathering medical data, tracking patient flow, observing the movement of medical staff, and more. Sensor-based devices and smart gadgets significantly enhance the experience of measuring various health parameters, like blood pressure and glucose levels, temperature, cholesterol, and heart rate, among others.

- **Smart Agriculture**

The IoT has the equal potential to improve various processes and services in the agriculture sector. This sensor-based technology is playing a very important role in analyzing various soil parameters and environmental conditions much needed in farming. The IoT has applications in analyzing soil nutrients, sensing microclimatic conditions, analyzing the quantity of vitamins and minerals in various agricultural products, monitoring grazing animals, and so on.

- **Retail and Logistics**

The IoT has made its own place in supply chain management and logistics too. It is used in the domains of product tracking, administering the rotation of articles/products in the warehouses and shelves of the outlets, and more. It also plays an important role in analyzing consignment conditions, studying storage conditions, and even keeping a regular check on gas leakage in industrial environments to ensure safety. Most of these applications are deployed using IoT-facilitated wireless sensor networks.

- **Smart Living**

In this domain, a variety of IoT-equipped smart applications are deployed to provide a better quality of life to residents. Most appliances and equipment can be managed remotely to save time, energy, and other resources. IoT gadgets/devices are also playing a very vital role in the security of individuals and the infrastructure.

- **Smart Environment**

The environment plays a significant role in providing a healthy life to all living beings. There are many factors, like industry waste, vehicle pollution, increasing population, and others, that are continuously damaging the environment. Smart equipment and devices are providing many innovative ways to monitor and manage industrial waste, keep a check on the pollution level in the air, and generate data to regulate government policies (Mohanta et al., 2022).

1.1.2 Big Data

Modern industry revolves around the most vital key term *data*. The rapid development of smart devices, gadgets, sensors, communication networks, computing devices, and storage systems has added a new dimension to data gathering and processing (Yaqoob et al., 2016). The data generated through the various applications in different domains are multiplying each year. *Big data* is a contemporary term initiated from the need of managing voluminous data by big ventures like Facebook, Twitter, Google, Yahoo, and others (Jain et al., 2021). The best way to achieve the balance between energy usage and quality of service is workload-aware energy-efficient virtual machine consolidation (Kaur et al., 2020).

Its key role is to define huge, diversified data, which are usually unstructured and not manageable using traditional techniques and tools. Today, governments, industry, and academia all have become highly attentive toward the unexplored capability of big data (Rodríguez-Mazahua et al., 2016; Rani and Gupta, 2017). The biggest challenge faced by information technology (IT) engineers and data scientists is that the increase in data is very rapid, which makes the administration and analysis of data difficult (Azeem et al., 2021).

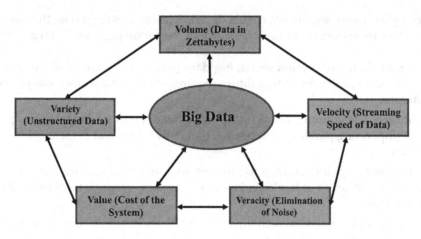

FIGURE 1.6
The big data: 5V model.

Consequently, it becomes important to use standardized tools and techniques to manage, store, and analyze such a voluminous amount of data. Big data models traversed through 3V, 4V, and 5V evolutions, in which each new model is an extension of the previous one (Singh et al., 2021a). The latest development, that is, 5V model (shown in Figure 1.6), is described as follows:

- **Volume**. Due to the rapid development in a variety of domains, the volume of data is increasing tremendously. There is an approximately 40% yearly increase in data and in the size of zettabytes.
- **Velocity**. It describes the timeliness of data. The collection and processing of data must be done rapidly to enhance its commercial utility.
- **Variety**. When the volume of data is huge, it usually comprises semistructured or unstructured data like text, audio, video, and regular structured data.
- **Value**. Today, data are some of the most precious resources. They are administered like commodities that are sold and bought among the parties. Consequently, understanding its value/cost can aid to manage other resources and help in budget planning.
- **Veracity**. As data are gathered from a number of sources, the accuracy of the data is always questionable. Collected data are preprocessed using different techniques and methods before its actual use. It ensures better and more accurate decision-making.

1.1.2.1 Big Data Applications

Big data is an infrastructure that aids in fetching, organizing, and managing huge volumes of data (Chhabra and Bhambri, 2021). It uses various specialized software, methods, and tools to store, sort, access, discover, and process voluminous data (Bhambri and Gupta, 2014). The data, gathered over a long period, are analyzed visually for their value to be administered in various scenarios (Khan and Javaid, 2021). Different software like Hadoop and Apache play a very significant role in deriving inferences from data that are of huge significance to various kinds of industries, such as the following (Shrivastava et al., 2021):

- **Education**. In the education sector, big data plays an important role in grading, restructuring syllabi, predicting future requirements, and in career analysis of the candidates.
- **Healthcare**. The volume of data/samples gathered helps in the detection/prediction of impending pandemic outbreaks, preventive care, and evidence-dependent medicine.
- **Government**. Big data storage techniques and analysis tools are playing a very vital role in the areas of banking, insurance, finance, security from cyber threats, and many more.
- **Media**. Big data analytical techniques are used for customer behavior, audience study and prediction, and more.
- **Transportation**. Big data is used in traffic analysis, rescheduling of traffic routes, ensuring public safety, and so on.
- **Banking**. The study of business statistics, financial security, risk analysis and calculation, forecasting investment funds, and more use big data analytics.

Consequently, big data analytics is aiding many domains for the purpose of analysis and prediction.

1.1.3 Cloud Computing

The concept of cloud computing emerged for the optimal utilization of various computing resources (Nazir et al., 2020). These resources should be paid for only when required/ used like other resources, for example, water, electricity, gas, and so on (Bhambri and Kaur, 2014). The various services provided under this concept are catered to and managed by the various data centers that are located at different geographical locations (Kaur and Bhambri, 2019). A cloud computing service was a long-held fantasy in the domain of information and communication technology (ICT), and it will be realized due to the emergence of economic data centers (Bhambri and Chhabra (2022). Another major challenge arising due to the evolution of computing as a service is the security of data/information (Sinha et al., 2020). From the architectural aspect of cloud computing, the most vital entity is the data center (Sarga, 2012). Basically, data centers provide different categories of cloud services to customers/ users (Kaur et al., 2015). A number of companies like Google, Amazon, Yahoo, Facebook, and many more have already entered the market and provide cloud services to the customers using pay-on-demand/use model (Singh et al., 2021a). As discussed earlier, they have deployed their data centers at different locations to provide economical services to users.

The security of data and the quality of services are managed by cloud service providers. Cloud users have no control over service parameters, like availability of information, quality, and others (Bhambri and Gupta, 2012a). To obtain and ensure committed quality services, consumers usually go for service-level agreements (SLAs). An SLA comprises all the terms and conditions settled between the consumer and cloud provider. The professional image of a cloud service provider is evaluated by their adherence to the SLA (Bhambri and Gupta, 2012b). When large organizations acquire multiple applications to provide the most reliable and efficient services to their clients, the procedure is termed a Hazy Cloud Process (Jasmine and Gupta, 2012).

1.1.3.1 Cloud Service Models

Cloud computing is a framework for fetching customized access to various ICT resources like storage, communication networks, processing units, applications, software, and online services (Paika and Bhambri, 2013). The fundamental aim of the cloud models is to enhance the availability of the resources at affordable cost. The cloud framework comprises five imperative characteristics, three service delivery models, and four deployment models. The delivery models are further classified as follows:

- **Software as a Service (SaaS)**

In this model, a variety of software/services are mounted on the cloud. These software and services are made available to the consumer on a rental basis and are accessed through Internet/email. SaaS provides instant on-demand services to the customer for different kinds of needs like business applications, software, enterprise resource planning (ERP), supply-chain management (SCM), and others. As SaaS and platform as a service (PaaS), both operate on top of infrastructure as a service (IaaS); any infringement in IaaS will surely impact the security mechanism of both delivery models. It depicts the high degree of dependence in the layered architecture, where, on one side, the layered framework strengthens the security and reliability of the model but comprises technical risks too.

- **PaaS**

This model enables the consumer to access a platform to deploy cloud framework and infrastructure using specific applications without acquiring a personal machine. PaaS basically describes the sharing of platforms and software like operating systems and customized application-specific frameworks. PaaS deploys cloud services considering the constraints of the resources. PaaS is usually opted for by consumers who are also using IaaS.

- **IaaS**

This service model provides an infrastructure for consumers on a pay-as-you-go basis. The various resources which become accessible to the consumers are computational resources, servers, and memory storage in cloud. Under IaaS, the service may be provided by an individual physical or virtual vendor or as a conflux of both. In a cloud-based system, the consumers can pay as per usage where all IaaS, PaaS, and SaaS provide layer-specific services in a row one after another.

IaaS facilitates the consumers with a platform where they can have control over physical resources like communication networks, storage devices, and other computer devices (Bhambri and Gupta, 2013). The second cloud layer, that is, PaaS, provides the access to the cloud resources by handing over control at the system administration level, like operating systems and various runtime services. SaaS is the topmost service dependent on end-user applications. Under this model, most of the control is kept by the cloud owner (Kaur and Bhambri, 2015). IBM has depicted the control of the cloud services with a diagram shown in Figure 1.7.

1.1.3.2 Cloud Deployment Models

The cloud deployment models are based on the infrastructure of the communication networks on which it is hosted. They are characterized by the location of the cloud infrastructure (Chopra et al., 2011). The cloud deployment models are categorized as public cloud, private cloud, community cloud, and hybrid cloud:

- **Public Cloud**. The most frequently used cloud is the public cloud. In this model, both individuals and companies can manage their accounts when subscribing to cloud services.

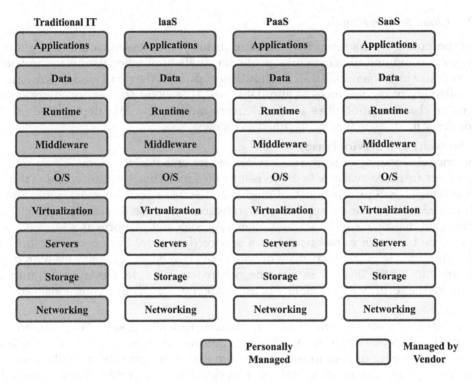

FIGURE 1.7
IBM cloud services: administered by owner and consumer.

- **Private Cloud**. In this model, the cloud services are deployed and administered using a private network for an individual. This type of model can cater to an individual organization or be used in collaboration with some other service provider to cater to the needs of an entity.
- **Community Cloud**. This type of cloud is usually shared by entities with similar requirements. It is used to spread the common policies, employment, promoting the optimal structure and analogy of appliances. Different educational institutions, business organizations, scientific research bodies, health organizations, and many other associations that usually share common interests mostly use community clouds for the exchange of information.
- **Hybrid Cloud**. This model is the confluence of various previously discussed models. It may be the amalgamation of different private clouds, private and public clouds, and so on. This type of cloud model caters the needs of almost all types of consumers. The major challenge faced in this framework is security.

1.1.3.3 Cloud Applications Areas

Today, most organizations, irrespective of their size, benefit from a cloud framework for deploying their data, applications, and software over the cloud. The major objective behind this adoption is to reduce the cost associated with the purchase and maintenance of ICT infrastructure (Harleen, 2016). Cloud computing offers plenty of services to consumers fundamentally through remote access to distant resources. The most prominent cloud computing features are

- on-demand services,
- pooling of available resources,
- better quality services,
- expanded network visibility and availability, and
- quick scalability.

With the preceding features, cloud computing plays a very significant role in different applications domains:

- E-commerce
- Business applications
- Data storage, management, and access services
- Multimedia applications
- Privacy and data security
- Geographical maps and location-dependent applications, among others

Along with this, cloud computing model is used in a number of other domains too.

1.2 Integrated Framework

The three dominating technologies of the current time, that is, big data, the IoT, and cloud computing, are playing significant roles in many real-life applications. The prominent areas that benefit from these technologies are smart cities, Industry 4.0, agriculture, healthcare, transportation, weather forecasting, banking and insurance, and many more (Arunachalam et al., 2021). Applying these technologies in various applications is not done in isolation; the functions integrate with each other, as shown in Figure 1.8. Today,

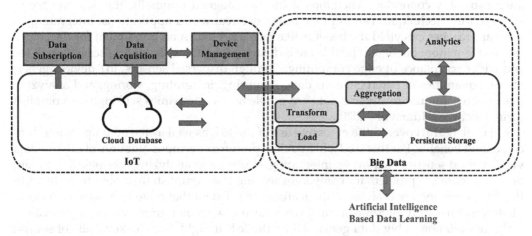

FIGURE 1.8
The integration of the IoT, big data, and cloud computing to realize real-life applications.

the most precious resource is data, and their volume is increasing rapidly in different application domains. In many applications, the data are gathered using IoT-based smart devices, equipment, and gadgets (Bhambri and Gupta, 2012). Because the data gathered are voluminous, they cannot be managed using traditional techniques but are stored, administered, analyzed, and processed using data analytics tools and methods. AI and ML algorithms are applied to draw inferences from this voluminous data to support vital decisions (Bhambri and Kaur, 2014). Many small and medium-sized organizations prefer to use cloud services to manage their data to reduce infrastructure costs. Cloud computing facilitates all-time availability of data, security, and reliable access where consumers have to pay only for the actual use of the resources.

1.3 Application Domains Composed of Amalgamation of Technologies

Although big data, cloud computing, and the IoT are three distinct technologies that have evolved independently over the course of time, they are rapidly becoming more entangled with one another. The increased flexibility and mobility features of wireless are motivating a large number of carriers to take a serious step toward the deployment of wireless technology (Bhambri et al., 2007). The IoT, cloud computing, and big data all work together, creating new opportunities for real-world applications in fields such as medicine, telecommunications, education, business, research, and engineering. The combined use of these methods results in a wide variety of difficulties during the processes of data collection, processing, and administration. Because IoT technologies collect massive volumes of data from a wide variety of networked IoT devices, the IoT serves as a source of data. The administration and storage of these data are provided by the cloud, and the process of extracting useful information from this data is referred to as big data. There is a relationship of complementarity between the IoT and cloud computing. Large amounts of data are produced by the IoT that can be transferred and accessed via the cloud. Additionally, there is a complementary link between IoT and Big Data in which the Big Data system receives IoT sensor data for analysis and report development. Contrarily, CC and Big Data are inextricably connected. Therefore, if they are aligned optimally, the convergence of all these three techniques can improve numerous real-world applications. Integrating all three approaches can yield the benefits like increased return on investment for the corporate sector, a more intelligent healthcare industry, growth in self-catering service analysis, and wider acceptance of edge computing. Through dispersed sensors, IoT devices generate vast quantities of heterogeneous data. Acquiring, integrating, storing, and analyzing this massive amount of diverse data are problems for companies seeking to accomplish their objectives (Humayun, 2020).

Cai et al. (2016) covered the excessive use of the IoT, as well as the accompanying difficulties and benefits. Per this study, IoT devices produce enormous amounts of diverse data via dispersed sensors. Acquiring, integrating, storing, and analyzing this massive amount of diverse data is a problem for companies seeking to accomplish their objectives. In addition to conducting an analysis of the features of IoT data that have been saved on cloud platforms, this study presents a framework for the collection, preservation, assimilation, and interpretation of big data generated by the IoT. It highlights the key traits of several interconnected technical components. Additionally, the possibilities of IoT BGD are discussed along with the accompanying challenges.

Tyagi et al. (2016) discussed that health-related data are extremely sensitive; thus, automation is needed to ensure accuracy. The IoT offers a solution to this problem by connecting individuals, machines, and different types of systems. Additionally, the ability of these networked IoT devices to monitor and transmit patient data makes it much easier for healthcare professionals to deliver prompt treatment to patients. Access to data in a timely manner, the actual monitoring of patients, and the ability to share data in a prompt and timely manner are some of the primary advantages of implementing IoT in healthcare. However, these interconnected IoT sensors produce a significant amount of data on a daily basis; accordingly, the cloud is a perfect choice for preserving these data in order to make them constantly available. This study presents an IoT–cloud infrastructure that facilitates the secure sharing of patient data. All parties participating in the healthcare system are linked via a network that facilitates collaboration. The suggested framework facilitates rapid data transmission, which reduces delivery time and costs. However, these advantages are accompanied by security and trust risks, as well as several technical challenges.

Verma et al., (2018) proposed a framework for monitoring student health by thoroughly assessing received health data. Authors claim that IoT has improved almost every aspect of daily life, including healthcare. The IoT system is now a preventative care system instead of a reactive one, thanks to the integration of mobile computing. In this work, a framework consisting of three stages has been suggested. The first step of the architecture involves the collection of student medical data from a variety of sensors and medical equipment, followed by the transmission of that data stored in the cloud via a gateway. The second phase involves analyzing the obtained data and making cognitive judgments regarding the student's health. In the event of an emergency, Phase 3 alerts parents and caregivers and generates alerts to neighboring hospitals.

A three-part design for an IoT-based ECG surveillance system is suggested by Yang et al. (2016). The first component is just an ECG sensor network as it collects the data. The second component is an IoT cloud that holds the massive amounts of data produced by IoT sensors, specifically BGD, and the third component is a graphical confluence that is a web application that the caregiver uses to access the data and administer treatments. In the suggested framework, wearable ECG sensors are used to capture patient data, which are then wirelessly transferred to the cloud. These cloud-based data can be retrieved by any terminal with intelligent hardware. An experiment was run to test the suggested design, and the findings show that the system is reliable for fast electronic health (ECH) data collection and can therefore help with early diagnosis.

A cloud-based IoT architecture for the syntheses of big data within the healthcare industry was proposed by Ullah et al., (2017). This study reveals that while IoT, cloud, and big data are beneficial in almost every industry, the healthcare sector has undergone a considerable transformation as a result of their integration. The suggested methodology was put into practice on Amazon's cloud provider and produced real-time data utilizing a Raspberry Pi as an IoT device. The ECG application of the system was tested by monitoring and reporting irregularities. By varying the volume and velocity of the processed data, the response time performance of the suggested system was analyzed. The proposed model yields favorable response time outcomes at a minimal cost.

The IoT, CC, and big data are three major ICT paradigms, according to Suciu et al., (2015). The best aspects of such three paradigms can also be integrated to improve the healthcare systems of the next generation. This study explores the convergence of the IoT, CC, and big data paradigms and suggests a decentralized cloud-based machine-to-machine platform for e-health applications. The current approach was developed to handle BGD generated by sensors in a way that allowed data to be pooled for the creation of virtual sensors, and it also included the outcomes of a few measurements.

A cloud-IT architecture for healthcare has been developed by Elhoseny et al. (2018) based on which the most significant difficulty for healthcare is the rapid storage, processing, and retrieval of patient data. The IoT and CC can be combined to solve this problem. The suggested framework's architecture is made up of four main parts: devices of stakeholders, requests of stakeholders, a cloud broker, and a system administrator. The proposed method aims to identify the best virtualization choice in order to reduce implementation time, wait time, and turnaround time for healthcare requests, as well as improve task scheduling and patient data access by optimizing resource utilization.

According to Jiang et al. (2014), IoT devices are employed extensively in several industrial sectors and have a positive influence on performance. These IoT-based gadgets produce a ton of unrelated data. These data's administration, storage, and retrieval present serious challenges. To enable effective data storage and retrieval, this research proposes a structure for data storage within the CC environment. This design, which consists of four parts, offers a way to combine various database types with a single platform for data access. Depending on the type of data, several databases are used to store the data. However, the same application programming interfaces (APIs) can be used to operate it. A real-world case study was used to test the proposed design, and the results in terms of storage and accessibility were favorable. The authors claim that a variety of real-world applications can use the recommended IoT-based data preservation system with the assistance of a cloud platform.

According to Aazam et al. (2014), the majority of real-time apps make extensive use of devices connected to the IoT. For maximum benefit, these IoT devices originate a lot of data that must be processed effectively. This massive amount of data cannot be managed on the IoT end due to the low computational abilities of IoT devices. In this study, the Cloud of Things (CoT), which combines the IoT and computers, is referred to as CC, as the answer to this problem. Connecting the IoT and CC is quite beneficial for optimizing resource usage. Nonetheless, this integration is accompanied by a number of significant obstacles, such as energy economy, resource allocation, protocol support, IPV6 deployment, service discovery, identity management, and, most significantly, security and privacy.

An IoT and cloud-based system for health monitoring was put forth by Muhammad et al. (2017). IoT devices are widely used in a number of practical applications, especially in healthcare, according to this report. Such IoT sensors produce large amounts of data that are insufficient for local servers to retain, making cloud services necessary. This study argues that since both methodologies are complementary, the convergence of IoT and CC is advantageous. The applicability of the proposed approach was examined using the vocal pathology surveillance case study. IoT sensors captured voice signals and sent them to the smart gadgets that housed them. Before processing, these signals were validated by the device housing them. A caregiver has access to the processed data for analysis and decision-making. The correctness of the proposed system was demonstrated; however, some obstacles must be solved. Included among these obstacles are availability, security, scalability, and interoperability.

According to Elhoseny et al. (2018), BGD research, particularly in the realm of healthcare, has gained prominence in recent years. In the realm of healthcare, the deployment of IoT, cloud, and BGD has led to tremendous improvement. In the domain of Industry 4.0 applications, the confluence of CC and IoT contributes significantly to a BGD environment. However, in Industry 4.0, the cloud assets required to manage BGD are insufficient. A model that speeds up the processing time and makes better use of the BGD space and thus provides a real-time situation retrieval procedure for patient records is put forth to get around this problem. The suggested technique improves healthcare services in IoT–cloud and Industrial 4.0 contexts by effectively selecting virtual machines.

According to Manogaran et al. (2018), wearable medical devices produce voluminous data, also known as BGD, which is typically a combination of unstructured and structured data. The analysis and processing with this BGD in healthcare decision-making is difficult because of the large amount and variety of data. To tackle this difficulty, this study presents IoT architecture for storing and processing healthcare BGD. The proposed architecture is made up of two sub-frameworks: meta-for-redirection, which is employed for the collection methods and preserving of BGD generated by IoT sensors, and grouping as well as selecting (GC), which is utilized to secure the inclusion of fog computing with CC. Both of these sub-architectures are used to collect and preserve BGD. Throughput, accuracy, and sensitivity were the determining factors in the evaluation of the suggested structure.

The convergence of the IoT, cloud computing, and big data analytics for e-health apps is presented by Plageras et al. (2017). According to the findings of this research, BGD can be identified using ultraviolet (UV) sensors that are implanted in human bodies. These various pieces of data will be stored, processed, and available on the relevant person's devices via the cloud. The article suggests a system for gathering real-time e-health BGD from numerous IoT actuators and sensors before sending it to the cloud server for processing. The suggested method was tested through simulation, and the secure IoT BGD connection that resulted using CC was found to be satisfactory.

Nepal et al. (2015) claimed that managing the enormous amounts of data big data produced by sensing devices is a substantial challenge in almost all real-world applications. The sensitive and essential nature of health records and their exponential expansion, however, make it far more complex in the healthcare sector. The BGD tied to healthcare is expected to grow to 25,000 petabytes in 2020. Concerns about confidentiality and integrity afflict the operation of such a sizable BGD. For storing backups of BGD, there are three types of clouds: public, private, and hybrid. A mixed nature of cloud solution is preferred for storing healthcare data because confidential information may be placed in a private cloud while sensitive data can be placed in a public cloud where it can be easily accessed by collaborators.

The relevance of CC, IoT, and big data in real-world applications was covered in the section before, with a focus on a health-related application. Three main paradigms of modern ICT—CC, IoT, and BGD—each with advantages and drawbacks of their own. However, these three approaches are complementary to one another. The use of IoT devices has been widely adopted across a varied range of businesses, including healthcare. Most of these IoT gadgets are UV sensors mounted on patients' bodies to track and monitor their health. IoT devices produce massive amounts of data each day. Processing this huge amount of data on IoT devices is not practical due to their low computational power. As a consequence of this, the vast quantities of data that these IoT devices generate are saved in the cloud. Pathways are established by CC in order to facilitate the transmission and processing of the enormous amounts of data produced by IoT devices. IoT devices generate enormous volumes of data, which are stored in the cloud. BGD systems can, however, deal with the issue of effectively processing and analyzing these data to produce usable information. BGD systems are available from a number of service providers, like Google, Amazon Web Services (AWS), and Microsoft, for affordable pricing. Additionally these solutions are scalable and adaptive to organizational needs. This illustrates that in order to attain the best results for current real-time applications, an amalgamation of these three technologies need to be used.

1.4 Advantages

There are several advantages to combining the IoT, big data, and cloud computing technologies; a few of the most important ones are described in the following subsections.

1.4.1 Device Data Scalability

Cloud-based systems may be expanded both vertically and horizontally, allowing them to satisfy the scalability requirements of big data hosting and analytics. For example, you can enhance the capacity of a server by adding more apps, or you can expand your physical resources when necessary. Big data and data analytics can expand due to the cloud.

1.4.2 Scalable Infrastructural Capacity

Big data and cloud data may be used together to accomplish a number of goals, including the storage of vast volumes of data, the facilitation of scalable processing, and the enhancement of real-time data analysis. The lack of physical infrastructure needed to set up and run big data and IoT, as well as the cloud, simultaneously reduces cost and frees you up to concentrate on improving your analytical skills instead of maintaining and providing assistance.

1.4.3 Enhanced Effectiveness in Daily Activities

The IoT and big data generate voluminous amounts of data for which the cloud serves as a conduit.

1.4.4 Global App Usage and Distribution Accelerated

When utilizing the cloud, it is possible to remotely and easily access big data from any part of the world, allowing enhanced collaboration.

1.4.5 Analysis and Appraisal of the Current Situation of IoT-Connected Devices

An Internet connection may be overloaded by a large number of appliances, requiring intelligent devices to transport data to servers rather than using central servers for processing. You may now access data from different network locations, operate on that "edge" of processes, react to interruptions more rapidly, and foresee potential problems. Because regular updates can be sent and any infrastructural breaches can be swiftly notified, using the cloud with the IoT significantly enhances security.

1.4.6 The Advantages of Economies of Scale

Maintain business value by using the cloud, which comes with integrated management tools, processing power, and applications to manage your resources and store and control your big data and IoT in the best possible way.

   The use of big data, the IoT, and the cloud in conjunction with one another enables the most effective and efficient communication, connection, and movement of data from one device to another. In its most basic form, cloud computing serves as a facilitator. It gives users a framework for hosting the IoT and big data, in addition to offering data and process analytics. The provision of a solution that is scalable, trustworthy, and adaptive is the major benefit that businesses receive from the integration of cloud computing, the IoT, and big data. Your company will have access to information that can be put to use thanks to the interplay among the IoT, big data, and cloud computing. This information will be provided in the form of performance and analysis reports.

1.5 Limitations

As discussed previously, these technologies are playing a very vital role in day-to-day applications in a variety of domains. But there are some drawbacks that limit their scalable integration:

- Limited computational power of the IoT-based devices to manage big data
- Limited power backup and technological complexity of smart devices
- A lack of compatible protocols for IoT devices
- The high cost of IoT devices
- The security of data and other services mounted in the cloud
- The availability of a number of big data technologies
- A lack of compatibility/mapping of data gathered through various sources
- The scaling of voluminous data
- Cloud data and applications being prone to different types of attacks
- Unreliable cloud interfaces
- High probability of technological vulnerabilities when infrastructure is shared by many consumers
- Limited control of the consumer on cloud data and services for their organization and management

1.6 Research Directions

There are a few challenges faced in the deployment of these technologies that may be addressed in future research to be carried out by scholars, engineers, and scientists:

- Technology transfer to make various IoT devices function as standalone systems
- Security of data in communication, storage, and processing
- Protocols to map data among various smart devices
- More computational power and backup in IoT devices
- Mapping of data gathered through different devices
- More efficient algorithms to process voluminous data
- Secure APIs for cloud applications

1.7 Conclusion

In today's time, there are many modern technologies that are playing significant roles in diversified application domains. But these technologies do not operate in isolation. In fact, an amalgamation of technologies is making the various applications possible efficiently. In this work, the authors focused on three main technologies, that is, the IoT, big data, and cloud computing. The significant contribution to the integration of these technologies was presented by discussing various application areas. Along with benefits, the authors also highlighted the limitations and challenges faced to make the conflux of the three to work accurately and efficiently.

References

Aazam, M., Khan, I., Alsaffar, A. A., and Huh, E.-N. (2014). Cloud of Things: Integrating Internet of Things and cloud computing and the issues involved. Paper presented at the *Proceedings of 2014 11th International Bhurban Conference on Applied Sciences and Technology (IBCAST)*, Islamabad, Pakistan, 14–18 January 2014.

Anand, A., and Bhambri, P. (2018). Character recognition system using radial features. *International Journal on Future Revolution in Computer Science and Communication Engineering*, 4(4), 599–602.

Arunachalam, P., Janakiraman, N., Sivaraman, A. K., Balasundaram, A., Vincent, R., Rani, S., ... Rajesh, M. (2021). Synovial sarcoma classification technique using support vector machine and structure features. *Intelligent Automation and Soft Computing*, 32(2), 1241–1259.

Arya, V., Rani, S., and Choudhary, N. (2022). Enhanced bio-inspired trust and reputation model for wireless sensor networks. Paper presented at the *Proceedings of Second Doctoral Symposium on Computational Intelligence*.

Aswale, P., Shukla, A., Bharati, P., Bharambe, S., and Palve, S. (2019). An overview of internet of things: Architecture, protocols and challenges. *Information and Communication Technology for Intelligent Systems*, 299–308.

Azeem, M., Haleem, A., Bahl, S., Javaid, M., Suman, R., and Nandan, D. (2021). Big data applications to take up major challenges across manufacturing industries: A brief review. *Materials Today: Proceedings*. Advanced online publication. doi:10.1016/j.matpr.2021.02.147.

Banerjee, K., Bali, V., Nawaz, N., Bali, S., Mathur, S., Mishra, R. K., and Rani, S. (2022). A machine-learning approach for prediction of water contamination using latitude, longitude, and elevation. *Water (Switzerland)*, 14(5), 728.

Bhambri, J., and Gupta, O. P. (2014). Dynamic frequency allocation scheme of mobile networks using priority assignment technique. *International Journal of Engineering and Technology Innovation*, 1(1), 127–134.

Bhambri, L. P., Jindal, C., and Bathla, S. (2007). Future wireless technology-ZigBee. *Proceedings of National Conference on Challenges and Opportunities in Information Technology (COIT)*, pp. 154–156. ACM.

Bhambri, P., Aggarwal, M., Singh, H., Singh, A. P., and Rani, S. (2022). Uprising of EVs: charging the future with demystified analytics and sustainable development. In *Decision Analytics for Sustainable Development in Smart Society 5.0*, pp. 37–53. Springer, Singapore.

Bhambri, P., Bagga, S., Priya, D., Singh, H., and Dhiman, H. K. (2020). Suspicious human activity detection system. *Journal of IoT in Social, Mobile, Analytics, and Cloud*, 2(4), 216–221.

Bhambri, P., and Chhabra, Y. (2022). Deployment of distributed clustering approach in WSNs and IoTs. *Cloud and Fog Computing Platforms for Internet of Things*, pp. 85–98. Chapman and Hall/CRC, USA.

Bhambri, P., and Gupta, O. P. (2012a). Development of phylogenetic tree based on Kimura's Method. *2012 2nd IEEE International Conference on Parallel, Distributed and Grid Computing*, pp. 721–723. IEEE.

Bhambri, P., and Gupta, O. P. (2012b). A novel method for the design of phylogenetic tree. *International Journal of Information Technology, Engineering and Applied Science Research*, 1(1), 24–28.

Bhambri, P., and Gupta, O. P. (2013). Design of distributed prefetching protocol in push-to-peer video-on-demand system. *International Journal of Research in Advent Technology (IJRAT)*, 1(3), 95–103.

Bhambri, P., and Kaur, P. (2014). A novel approach of zero watermarking for text documents. *International Journal of Ethics in Engineering and Management Education (IJEEE)*, 1(1), 34–38.

Cai, H., Xu, B., Jiang, L., and Vasilakos, A. V. (2016). IoT-based big data storage systems in cloud computing: Perspectives and challenges. *IEEE Internet of Things Journal*, 4(1), 75–87.

Chhabra, Y., and Bhambri, P. (2021). Various approaches and algorithms for monitoring energy efficiency of wireless sensor networks. In *Sustainable Development through Engineering Innovations*, pp. 761–770. Springer, Singapore.

Chopra, S., Bhambri, P., and Singh, B. (2011). Segmentation of the mammogram images to find breast boundaries 1. In *International Journal of Computer Science and Technology*, 22(1), 164–167.

Elhoseny, M., Abdelaziz, A., Salama, A. S., Riad, A. M., Muhammad, K., and Sangaiah, A. K. (2018). A hybrid model of internet of things and cloud computing to manage big data in health services applications. *Future Generation Computer Systems*, 86, 1383–1394.

Gupta, O. P., and Kaur, S. (2016). Ortholog and paralog detection using phylogenetic tree construction with distance based methods. In *International Journal of Computer Science and Information Security*, 14(10), 886.

Harleen, B. (2016). A prediction technique in data mining for diabetes mellitus. *Journal of Management Sciences and Technology*, 4(1), 225–234.

Humayun, M. (2020). Role of emerging IoT big data and cloud computing for real time application. *International Journal of Advanced Computer Science and Applications*, 11(4), 56–65.

Hussein, A. H. (2019). Internet of things (IOT): Research challenges and future applications. *International Journal of Advanced Computer Science and Applications*, 10(6), 77–82.

Jabraeil Jamali, M. A., Bahrami, B., Heidari, A., Allahverdizadeh, P., and Norouzi, F. (2020). IoT architecture. *Towards the Internet of Things*, 9–31.

Jain, A., Singh, M., and Bhambri, P. (2021). Performance evaluation of IPv4-IPv6 tunneling procedure using IoT. *Journal of Physics: Conference Series*, 19501, 012010. IOP Publishing.

Jasmine, B. P., and Gupta, O. P. (2012). Analyzing the phylogenetic trees with tree-building methods. *Indian Journal of Applied Research*, 1(7), 83–85.

Jiang, L., Da Xu, L., Cai, H., Jiang, Z., Bu, F., and Xu, B. (2014). An IoT-oriented data storage framework in cloud computing platform. *IEEE Transactions on Industrial Informatics*, 10(2), 1443–1451.

Kaur, G., Kaur, R., and Rani, S. (2015). Cloud computing-a new trend in IT era. *International Journal of Scientific and Technology Management*, 1, 1–6.

Kaur, J., and Bhambri, P. (2019). Various DNA sequencing techniques and related applications. *International Journal of Analytical and Experimental Model Analysis*, 11(9), 3104–3111.

Kaur, K., Dhanoa, I. S., and Bhambri, P. (2020). Optimized PSO-EFA algorithm for energy efficient virtual machine migrations. In *2020 5th IEEE International Conference on Recent Advances and Innovations in Engineering (ICRAIE)*, pp. 1–5. IEEE.

Kaur, P., and Bhambri, P. (2015). To design an algorithm for text watermarking. *The Standard International Journals (The SIJ)*, 3(5), 62–67.

Khan, I. H., and Javaid, M. (2021). Big data applications in medical field: A literature review. *Journal of Industrial Integration and Management*, 6(01), 53–69.

Kothandaraman, D., Manickam, M., Balasundaram, A., Pradeep, D., Arulmurugan, A., Sivaraman, A. K., … Balakrishna, R. (2022). Decentralized Link Failure Prevention Routing (DLFPR) algorithm for efficient Internet of Things. *Intelligent Automation and Soft Computing*, 34(1), 655–666.

Kshirsagar, P. R., Jagannadham, D. B. V., Ananth, M. B., Mohan, A., Kumar, G., and Bhambri, P. (2022, May). Machine learning algorithm for leaf disease detection. *AIP Conference Proceedings*, vol. 2393, no. 1, p. 020087. AIP Publishing LLC.

Kumar, R., Rani, S., and Awadh, M. A. (2022). Exploring the application sphere of the Internet of Things in Industry 4.0: A review, bibliometric and content analysis. *Sensors*, 22(11), 4276.

Manogaran, G., Varatharajan, R., Lopez, D., Kumar, P. M., Sundarasekar, R., and Thota, C. (2018). A new architecture of Internet of Things and big data ecosystem for secured smart healthcare monitoring and alerting system. *Future Generation Computer Systems*, 82, 375–387.

Mohanta, H. C., Geetha, B. T., Alzaidi, M. S., Dhanoa, I. S., Bhambri, P., Mamodiya, U., and Akwafo, R. (2022). An optimized PI controller-based SEPIC converter for microgrid-interactive hybrid renewable power sources. *Wireless Communications and Mobile Computing*, 2022, 1–10.

Muhammad, G., Rahman, S. M. M., Alelaiwi, A., and Alamri, A. (2017). Smart health solution integrating IoT and cloud: A case study of voice pathology monitoring. *IEEE Communications Magazine*, 55(1), 69–73.

Nazir, R., Ahmed, Z., Ahmad, Z., Shaikh, N., Laghari, A., and Kumar, K. (2020). Cloud computing applications: A review. *EAI Endorsed Transactions on Cloud Systems*, 6(17).

Nepal, S., Ranjan, R., and Choo, K.-K. R. (2015). Trustworthy processing of healthcare big data in hybrid clouds. *IEEE Cloud Computing*, 2(2), 78–84.

Paika, E. V., and Bhambri, E. P. (2013). Edge detection-fuzzy inference system. *International Journal of Management and Information Technology*, 4(1), 148–155.

Plageras, A. P., Stergiou, C., Kokkonis, G., Psannis, K. E., Ishibashi, Y., Kim, B.-G., and Gupta, B. B. (2017). Efficient large-scale medical data (ehealth big data) analytics in internet of things. Paper presented at the *2017 IEEE 19th Conference on Business informatics (CBI)*.

Rani, S., and Gupta, O. (2017). CLUS_GPU-BLASTP: Accelerated protein sequence alignment using GPU-enabled cluster. *The Journal of Supercomputing*, 73(10), 4580–4595.

Rani, S., Bhambri, P., and Chauhan, M. (2021a). A machine learning model for kids' behavior analysis from facial emotions using principal component analysis. Paper presented at the *2021 5th Asian Conference on Artificial Intelligence Technology (ACAIT)*.

Rani, S., Kataria, A., Sharma, V., Ghosh, S., Karar, V., Lee, K., and Choi, C. (2021b). Threats and corrective measures for IoT security with observance of cybercrime: A survey. *Wireless Communications and Mobile Computing*, 2021, 1–30.

Rani, S., Mishra, R. K., Usman, M., Kataria, A., Kumar, P., Bhambri, P., and Mishra, A. K. (2021c). Amalgamation of advanced technologies for sustainable development of smart city environment: A review. *IEEE Access*, 9, 150060–150087.

Rani, S., Bhambri, P., and Gupta, O. (2022a). Green smart farming techniques and sustainable agriculture: Research roadmap towards organic farming for imperishable agricultural products. *Handbook of Sustainable Development through Green Engineering and Technology*, pp. 49–67. CRC Press, USA.

Rani, S., Kataria, A., Chauhan, M., Rattan, P., Kumar, R., and Sivaraman, A. K. (2022b). Security and privacy challenges in the deployment of cyber-physical systems in smart city applications: State-of-art work. *Materials Today: Proceedings*, 62, 4671–4677.

Rani, S., Kataria, A., and Chauhan, M. (2022c). Cyber security techniques, architectures, and design. *Holistic Approach to Quantum Cryptography in Cyber Security*, pp. 41–66. CRC Press, USA.

Rani, S., Kataria, A., and Chauhan, M. (2022d). Fog computing in industry 4.0: Applications and challenges—A research roadmap. In R. Tiwari, M. Mittal., and L. M. Goyal (Eds.), *Energy Conservation Solutions for Fog-Edge Computing Paradigms* (pp. 173–190). Springer.

Rodríguez-Mazahua, L., Rodríguez-Enríquez, C.-A., Sánchez-Cervantes, J. L., Cervantes, J., García-Alcaraz, J. L., and Alor-Hernández, G. (2016). A general perspective of Big Data: Applications, tools, challenges and trends. *The Journal of Supercomputing*, 72(8), 3073–3113.

Sarga, L. (2012). Cloud computing: An overview. *Journal of Systems Integration (1804–2724)*, 3(4), 3–14.

Shrivastava, A., Rizwan, A., Kumar, N. S., Saravanakumar, R., Dhanoa, I. S., Bhambri, P., and Singh, B. K. (2021). VLSI implementation of green computing control unit on Zynq FPGA for green communication. *Wireless Communications and Mobile Computing*, 2021, 4655400.

Singh, A. P., Aggarwal, M., Singh, H., and Bhambri, P. (2021a). Sketching of EV network: A complete roadmap. *Sustainable Development Through Engineering Innovations: Select Proceedings of SDEI 2020*, pp. 431–442. Springer, Singapore.

Singh, M., Bhambri, P., Singh, I., Jain, A., and Kaur, E. K. (2021b). Data mining classifier for predicting diabetics. *Annals of the Romanian Society for Cell Biology, 2021*, 6702–6712.

Singh, P., Gupta, O., and Saini, S. (2017). A brief research study of wireless sensor network. *Advances in Computational Sciences and Technology*, 10(5), 733–739.

Sinha, V. K., Jeet, R., Bhambri, P., and Mahajan, M. (2020). Empowering intrusion detection in IRIS recognition system: A review. *Journal of Natural Remedies*, 21(2), 131–153.

Soumyalatha, S. G. H. (2016). Study of IoT: Understanding IoT architecture, applications, issues and challenges. Paper presented at the *1st International Conference on Innovations in Computing and Net-working (ICICN16), CSE, RRCE. International Journal of Advanced Networking and Applications*.

Suciu, G., Suciu, V., Martian, A., Craciunescu, R., Vulpe, A., Marcu, I., … Fratu, O. (2015). Big data, internet of things and cloud convergence–an architecture for secure e-health applications. *Journal of Medical Systems*, 39(11), 1–8.

Tandon, N., and Bhambri, P. (2017). Classification technique for drug discovery in medical image Processing. *International Journal of Advanced Research in Computer Science*, 8(7), 194–197.

Tyagi, S., Agarwal, A., and Maheshwari, P. (2016). A conceptual framework for IoT-based healthcare system using cloud computing. Paper presented at the *2016 6th International Conference-Cloud System and Big Data Engineering (Confluence)*.

Ullah, F., Habib, M. A., Farhan, M., Khalid, S., Durrani, M. Y., and Jabbar, S. (2017). Semantic interoperability for big-data in heterogeneous IoT infrastructure for healthcare. *Sustainable Cities and Society*, 34, 90–96.

Verma, P., Sood, S. K., and Kalra, S. (2018). Cloud-centric IoT based student healthcare monitoring framework. *Journal of Ambient Intelligence and Humanized Computing*, 9(5), 1293–1309.

Yang, Z., Zhou, Q., Lei, L., Zheng, K., and Xiang, W. (2016). An IoT-cloud based wearable ECG monitoring system for smart healthcare. *Journal of Medical Systems*, 40(12), 1–11.

Yaqoob, I., Hashem, I. A. T., Gani, A., Mokhtar, S., Ahmed, E., Anuar, N. B., and Vasilakos, A. V. (2016). Big data: From beginning to future. *International Journal of Information Management*, 36(6), 1231–1247.

2

Cloud Environment Limitations and Challenges

Sudheer Mangalampalli and Ganesh Reddy Karri

CONTENTS

2.1 Introduction

Cloud computing is one of the huge paradigms of the information technology (IT) industry as many companies are shifting their on-premises infrastructure to a cloud environment (Marston et al., 2011). Compared to on-premises infrastructure, cloud computing means the computing, storage, and network infrastructure are done in the cloud. Therefore, when companies shift their infrastructure to a cloud environment, they will be rendered on-demand virtual services from the cloud environment based on the services customers have chosen based on the service-level agreement (SLA). National Institute of Standards and Technology (NIST; Mell & Grance, 2011) defined cloud computing as such a way that "it is a paradigm which is on demand, network access to a shared pool of conigurable computational resources" that gives seamless access to users of the cloud. Users of the cloud paradigm experience the virtual services by just using a browser from their devices; those devices can be any desktop, mobile, and laptop that supports the browser, but it should have internet connectivity (Kaur & Bhambri, 2015; Kaur et al., 2015). The following

DOI: 10.1201/9781003298335-2

subsections discuss the need for cloud computing, the different types of deployment models, and basic types of service models in cloud computing.

2.1.1 Need of Cloud Computing

In the present world, with wide internet connectivity to millions and billions of devices around the world, and many of the devices are generating a huge amount of data that cannot be accommodated with general physical infrastructure in the on-premises environment in terms of storage capacity, which can raise the question of scalability (Josep et al., 2010). This can be one of the important perspectives or reasons for using the cloud paradigm in the current era because when a huge amount of data need to be stored in an on-premises environment or physical infrastructure, it cannot be scaled on demand, but due to the demand of applications in the current era, they should be scalable to any extent on demand whenever it is needed (Rani & Gupta, 2017). This is the primary reason for any user to migrate from an on-premises to a cloud environment. The second reason for any user to go to a cloud paradigm is the kind of computing infrastructure needed for the applications they are using these days as many of the applications need a high-end computing infrastructure, which is high in cost. This infrastructure cannot be useful for the different types of applications, which raises an issue of cost, and procuring the high-end infrastructure in less time and cost is a challenge in an on-premises environment. The third reason for choosing a cloud environment is managing the resources in a physical environment. This is a great challenge for the network administrator who will manage the infrastructure by providing the network and storage to users for their corresponding applications. All these reasons will lead to the need for a cloud-computing paradigm. It is not a new paradigm, and it already existed in the form of SOA, that is, service-oriented architecture (Schaffer, 2009), but the cloud paradigm is much more dynamic in terms of the scalability, flexibility, and agility of services providing to the users (Kaur & Bhambri, 2019). These advantages helped IT people to shift toward the cloud model.

2.1.2 Deployment Models of Cloud Computing

The deployment model is how we can set up a cloud environment, that is, compute, storage, and network infrastructure, as presented by Diaby and Rad (2017). It is of mainly four types: private, public, hybrid, and community cloud models (Shrivastava et al., 2021; Rani et al., 2022a).

Private Cloud—This model services are restricted only to the users in the corresponding organization. Out of the corresponding organization, services cannot be rendered by the private cloud.

Public Cloud—This model renders its services over the internet as its name, public cloud, indicates, and these services can be rendered over the internet through the public IP to the users on demand according to the SLA made between the user and the cloud provider. The major vendors of the public cloud in the market are Amazon Web Services, Google Cloud, Microsoft Azure, and Salesforce, among others.

Hybrid Cloud—This model combines the characteristics of both public and private cloud deployment models. In many organizations, data and resources are to be accessible to some users and restricted to others. Therefore, a hybrid cloud model is necessary for organizations to maintain the security and privacy of the resources they maintain in the cloud paradigm.

Community Cloud—This model can be helpful for the users or companies to work collaboratively on the same cloud environment where users can share resources on the same platform but do not affect the privacy and security of other company resources as every resource that resides on the cloud platform is like an isolated container.

This section described the deployment models in cloud computing, and using those deployment models, we can set up a cloud environment in corresponding organizations (Chhabra & Bhambri, 2021).

2.1.3 Basic Service Models of Cloud Computing

Service models depict how the cloud paradigm renders services to users and how different types of services can be provided to the users (Kavis, 2014). In this section, the basic service models are discussed, and we present a number of services in the cloud paradigm within different vendors:

Infrastructure as a Service—This is a basic service model that renders virtual infrastructure as a service to the users. Typically, it provides virtual storage, network, processors, and memory to users as a service based on the subscription made by the user with the cloud provider. This service model is one of the basic models, as all the users of the cloud will get virtual infrastructure. This virtual infrastructure can be scalable to any extent; that is, it can be scaled up and down at any point of time, but users need to pay for the resources based on their usage. The entire virtual infrastructure can be configured within a span of minutes when compared with an on-premises physical infrastructure.

Platform as a Service—This model will enable cloud users to develop their applications on top of the cloud platform. With this service model, users can develop their applications by using a wide variety of services. The cloud paradigm uses REST APIs and different middleware to hook all types of applications independent of their architecture.

Software as a Service—This service model is for the usage of the corresponding software that is running in the cloud platform. All these are to be used as services by the users, and they need to pay for what they have consumed when they have used that resource.

2.2 Architecture of Cloud Computing

This section discusses mainly the architecture of cloud computing. There are two different types of architectures in the cloud paradigm (Rani & Kaur, 2012; Singh et al., 2021):

1. Generic architecture
2. Market-oriented architecture

2.2.1 Generic Architecture of Cloud Computing

The generic architecture is the generalized version of architecture that represents an overall view of the cloud paradigm. It consists of components, such as front-end, network, and back-end layers (Sudheer et al., 2017). Figure 2.1 clearly represents a generic architecture of the cloud paradigm.

Figure 2.1 represents a generic architecture of cloud computing, which consists of three layers, that is, front end, which is a typical cloud application running from a browser that can reside in any device like desktop, laptop, mobile, and others; the second layer, the network through which the front end, that is, the application, and the back end, that is, the infrastructure, is to be connected; and, finally, the third layer, a virtual infrastructure, which resides on top of physical hosts that reside in different data centers.

2.2.2 Market-Oriented Architecture of Cloud Computing

In a real-time environment, when users need to use a cloud paradigm, they may not use all the services. They will subscribe to the services only they need for their application. In that context, users have to use a customized version of the architecture, that is, market-oriented architecture (Buyya et al., 2008) in cloud computing. In this architecture, there are different components, which can be presented at different layers. At the application level, initially users will give their requests to access resources in the cloud, and brokers, on behalf of users, will take and submit their requests to the task manager. There is a component named as service request examiner in the task manager that will verify the request and whether it is a valid type of request and check the SLA of the user. If the user's request is not valid, then it gives a message to the user that accessibility is not there to the requested resources. If the request is valid and if the user has access to the resources, then it will send the request to the scheduler to give resources to the corresponding user request. The task manager also consists of different components named as a VM monitor, Dispatcher, Accounting, Service request monitor. VM monitor verifies the entire load on VMs, how many of them were free, and how many of them are overloaded and under-loaded to assign requests to resources (Arunachalam et al., 2021; Jain et al., 2021). The functionality of the dispatcher is to take the request from the broker and then verify it with the service request monitor, and if resources are allocated, it dispatches the resources that are allocated to the corresponding user based on the SLA (Rani et al., 2021a).

Figure 2.2 provides an overall representation of a market-oriented architecture in cloud computing.

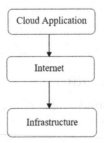

FIGURE 2.1
Generic architecture of cloud computing.

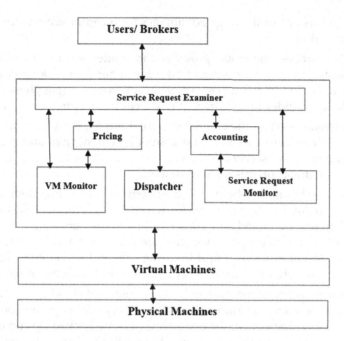

FIGURE 2.2
Market-oriented architecture of cloud computing.

2.3 Characteristics of Cloud Computing

In this section, we discuss the various characteristics of cloud computing presented in Stieninger and Nedbal (2014). There are many characteristics in cloud computing besides those we have mentioned. A few of the characteristics are discussed in the following:

On-Demand Service—The cloud paradigm is on demand as all services that users can subscribe to can be given on demand without any delay. Users can request resources, that is, compute, storage, and network on demand without paying any up-front cost, but it is not possible in an on-premises environment. Therefore, users can benefit from this type of model and reduce their investment in physical infrastructure.

Robust Network Access—Users of the cloud will benefit from the robust and broad network access of the data centers on which they are spinning up the computing and storage equipment virtually that users can access seamlessly. Therefore, the cloud paradigm has a more resilient, broad, and robust network on which all the infrastructure was built.

Scalability—This is one of the important characteristics of the cloud model as we can on-demand scale up our resources without any hesitation. We can also scale down our resources if the resource is not required. This is one of the main advantages of cloud computing. There are two types of scaling techniques are available in a cloud environment: on one side, vertical scaling, which scales up computational resources, and, on the other side, horizontal scaling, which scales up storage resources. This is one of the huge advantages for e-commerce vendors and many other organizations.

Pooling of Resources—The cloud provider can render services to multiple users from the same physical host without affecting other users (Dong et al., 2009). It is also called sharing IT resources with the users from a single physical host. This allows a cloud provider to use efficient resources from a physical host.

Ease of Maintenance—With the cloud computing model, there is no need for users to maintain infrastructure as all the infrastructure will be maintained by the cloud provider, and maintain servers can be easily maintained with less downtime when compared with an on-premises environment.

Economy View—This model helps the user reduce their infrastructure costs and allows them to pay for the resources for which they consume. Users need to pay only based on pricing model they subscribed to. In the perspective (Schniederjans & Hales, 2016) of a cloud provider, they are rendering services through virtual machines on top of a physical host by using different server consolidation techniques in turn, which minimizes energy consumption and other operational costs.

Security—Security is one of the essential characteristics of cloud computing as many servers and data reside in cloud data centers. Every data copy will be backed up, and if any disaster happened, the end points of those backed-up copies will automatically be spun up from the other end. Every cloud computing model follows a high-end security compliance to avoid security breaches.

2.4 Limitations and Challenges of Cloud Computing

Internet Connection—In order to use any cloud service, users need (Mahmood, 2014) to be connected to the internet; without internet connection, cloud services cannot be accessed by users. This is a limitation, as many of countries still need to improve internet connectivity. Hence, it will be a primary limitation for a cloud paradigm.

Management of Costs—It is one of the challenges in the cloud paradigm because if we are using a service or a resource in the cloud, users have to know the exact pricing model that they have currently chosen. For example, elastic IP is one of the services that most users won't release or deallocate that IP address after their usage, which incurs a cost. Therefore, managing the costs of resources in a cloud paradigm is a huge challenge for the user.

Lack of Expertise—Many of employees in IT companies need to be proficient with cloud services, and they also need to have good expertise about how to use cloud services in an efficient manner. Training their employees again to get expertise about the cloud environment is also one of the huge challenges for companies.

Security—Besides being an advantage, it is a limitation too as our data are not in our hands but reside in a data center, which is remotely accessible. Cloud providers (Mahmood, 2014) maintains security with high compliance standards, but still there is a chance that breaches will occur. It should be considered as a top limitation to be prioritized for mitigating risks that poses security threats, and users also should transparently know about the security level of their data in the cloud.

Besides all these challenges and limitations, security in cloud computing is still a limitation, and in this chapter, we have classified various attacks that can occur in a cloud paradigm.

2.5 Classification of Security Attacks in Cloud Computing

Due to communication concerns at four different levels, such as client to internet service provider (ISP), ISP to cloud network, cloud network to virtualization environment (Islam et al., 2016), and virtualization environment to cloud physical servers, the cloud computing environment is vulnerable to numerous attacks (Rani et al., 2022b). We investigated and analyzed potential attacks on cloud connections at four different levels (Hussain et al., 2017), which are shown in Table 2.1.

2.5.1 Security Attacks Against Cloud Consumer Side

To access cloud resources from a remote location, cloud consumers use a graphical user interface (GUI) or a command line interface (CLI). While the consumer is accessing cloud services, attackers disrupt the cloud consumer services (Jamil & Zaki, 2011) by carrying out the following attacks.

Cross-Site Scripting (XSS): This is an injection technique in which an attacker injects malicious scripts into trusted websites. When an attacker gains access to an online program, they can send malicious code to a different end user, typically in the form of a browser-side script. These common issues can be identified whenever a web application receives user input and outputs it without verifying or encoding it. Using this attack, the attacker steals the cloud consumer's web interface, which is then hacked in order to steal the cloud consumer's sensitive data.

TABLE 2.1

Classification of Security Attacks at Various Levels in Cloud Computing

Cloud Consumer–Side Attacks	Internet Service Provider Attacks	Virtualization Attacks	Cloud Application, Storage and Network DoS and DDoS Attacks
• XSS attack	• Man in the middle attack	• Virtual library check-out	• UDP flood
• Virus	• Packet flooding attack	• Migration attack	• ICMP flood
• Worms	• DNS hijacking	• cryptographic attack	• Smurf attack
• trojans	• Packet dropping attack	• Information leakage attack on shared resources	• TCP Syn attack
• Eavesdropping attack	• Packet delay attacks	• Bitcoin mining attack	• Ping of death
• Message Modification attack	• Fake packets inject attack	• Data Integrity attack	• Fragile attack
• SQL injection attack	• Sniffing attack	• Task/job scheduling attack	• HTTP DDoS attack
• DoS attack	• IP Spoofing attack		• XML DDoS attack
• DNS cache poisoning attack	• digital signature forgery attack		• NTP amplification attack
• Non-Repudiation attack	• traffic pattern analysis attacks		• Teardrop attack
• Session Hijacking			• Land attack

Attacks on the integrity and availability of data: In the context of information security, integrity means that when a sender provides data, the receiver must get the same data. While in transit, data must not be altered. The term *availability* refers to the availability of information to authorized individuals at all times. Disaster recovery methods and procedures must be in place to minimize or limit data loss. Unpredictable events, such as natural catastrophes and fires, must be accounted for in a disaster recovery plan. It is strongly advised that you perform backups on a regular basis in order to minimize or lessen the entire data loss from such incidents. Attacks are a risk. Data integrity can be at risk by a variety of attacks, including tampering, masquerading, replaying, and repudiation.

Virus—A virus is a malicious piece of software that spreads from computer to computer, causing data and software harm. Viruses are made to cause problems with the computer system, serious problems with operations, and the loss and exposure of data. Here, the victim system is infected by the attacker's malicious codes, which leads to abnormal system behavior, like a slowdown of the web interface or opening multiple tabs without victim interference.

Worm—Worms are harmful programmers that can replicate and propagate themselves once they get access to a system. Worms do not need to be activated or communicate with humans in order to carry out or follow their instructions or instructions. Using this attack, attacker simply spreads the malicious code in the victim system (cloud consumer) to create a denial-of-service attack.

Trojans—Trojans are a sort of malware that is usually disguised as an email attachment or a free-to-download file before being downloaded and installed on the user's device. After the virus is downloaded, it will do what it was meant to do, like get into business systems, spy on people's online activities, or steal important data.

Eavesdropping—The theft of data transferred across a network by a computer, smartphone, or other connected device is known as "eavesdropping." It is also referred to as "sniffing" or "spying." The attack takes advantage of flaws in network communication to get hold of data while they are being sent or received by the user. Here, the attackers insert the special hardware sniffing components in the victim systems to leak the data at the system level.

SQL injection attack—n a SQL injection attack, the client's input data is used to inject a SQL query into software. A SQL injection attack reads, alters, and conducts database administration operations on sensitive database data, as well as recovering the content of a particular file on the DBMS file system and, in some situations, issuing commands to the operating system. SQL injection attacks take place when SQL commands are inserted into data-plane input to alter the execution of SQL queries. Here, the attacker compromises the legitimate cloud consumer and then successfully installs malicious software in the system to send the malicious codes in the search query to hack the cloud server.

Denial-of-service (DoS) attack: A DoS can take many different forms, including viruses, worms, Trojans, and SQL injection. The attacker's goal is to try various forms of attacks in order to destroy the cloud consumer system's resources. Eventually, the cloud user will be unable to use their resources when they desire. DoS assaults are more widespread in cloud systems because cloud users have limited resources and protection, making them easier to target.

DNS cache poisoning attack: Caching the erroneous information in a DNS cache might result in incorrect results for queries and redirect to the wrong websites. DNS cache poisoning, or "DNS spoofing," is another term for this practice. Allowing web traffic to arrive at the correct locations, IP addresses are the internet's "room numbers." As the "campus directory," DNS resolver caches are responsible for directing traffic to the correct places if the cached information is erroneous. Real websites will not be disconnected from their actual IP addresses by this method. To perform this attack on a cloud consumer site, the attacker tries in all possible ways to insert the malicious code to change the DNS content in the cloud consumer system.

Session hijacking attack: Web users can be hacked by hijacking their sessions using a technique known as session hijacking, which is also known as TCP session hijacking. The user's session ID can be used by an attacker to impersonate the user and execute any network activity that the user is allowed to do. The most valuable outcome of this type of attack is the ability to access a server without having to authenticate it. It is no longer necessary for an attacker to authenticate with the server once they have taken over a session. It's possible for the attacker to get access to all the cloud system's resources in this case because the user who was hacked has already authenticated the server. To perform this attack, first the attacker has to perform the XSS attack or cookie-steeling attack to get the session details of the cloud consumer.

2.5.2 ISP (Cloud Carrier) Side Attacks

Cloud carriers play a crucial role in data transfer between cloud consumers and cloud providers; in most cases, cloud consumers rely on local ISPs (Rani et al., 2021b) to connect to cloud service providers (Cambiaso et al., 2013). Local ISPs, however, are more vulnerable to various attacks like the following:

Man-in-the-middle attack—Man-in-the-middle attacks occur mostly because a compromised ISP provider exists between the cloud consumer and the cloud provider. Both the cloud consumer and the cloud provider are unaware that their ISP provider has been infiltrated and is performing a man-in-the-middle attack. The attacker's purpose is to steal personal information from a computer system, such as usernames, passwords, and credit card numbers. E-commerce websites, as well as SaaS and other firms that require customers to sign in, are typical targets. Cloud security analyzes both the client and the cloud service provider sides but not the cloud carrier side, which attackers exploit to launch a man-in-the-middle attack.

Packet flooding attack—In a packet flood, an attacker delivers IP packets containing user datagram protocol (UDP) packets to random ports on the host in an effort to disrupt service. In this type of attack, the host looks for apps that are linked to these datagrams. A "Destination Unreachable" packet is sent back to the sender if no one is found. As a result of such a flood, the system becomes overburdened and unable to respond to legitimate traffic. The compromised service provider floods the fake packets toward the cloud service provider and the consumer to degrade the cloud services.

Attacks on DNS servers—An attack on a DNS server in which requests are incorrectly resolved in order to send users to a malicious website is called DNS hijacking, also known as DNS redirection. To carry out the attack, hackers may utilize malware installed on user computers, router control is taken over, or DNS communication intercepted or hacked. Malicious local ISPs redirect the cloud consumer traffic to fake web servers.

IP spoofing attack—Spoofing IP packets is the practice of altering the source address of an IP packet to hide one's identity or to impersonate another computer system in order to evade detection. There are many ways to launch a distributed denial-of-service (DDoS) attack against a specified system or its associated functions.

2.5.3 Virtualization Attacks

It is one of the most critical problems with cloud computing that includes one of its core enabling technologies (Gupta et al., 2011; Modi & Acha, 2017). In virtual environments, an attacker can take control of the virtual machines by compromising the bottom-layer hypervisor. An attack vector might be any virtualization layer component. Cloud infrastructure, client data, and system hacking could all be at risk from attacks on various virtualized components in an attack on a virtualized environment.

Migration attack—When a VM is moved from one place to another, a network attack known as a "migration attack" happens. The mobility provided by virtualization is exploited in this attack. Organizations frequently relocate virtual machines based on their usage since VM images can be swiftly transferred between actual systems via the network.

Cryptographic attack—Code, cipher, cryptographic protocol, or key management mechanism flaws can be exploited by a hacker in order to compromise a system's security. "Cryptanalysis" is another name for this process. To find out how the targeted algorithm responds to a variety of data, one can use a differential cryptanalysis attack on block ciphers, which analyses pairs of plaintexts rather than single ones.

Bitcoin mining attack—"Crypto jacking," or malware that mines cryptocurrencies, such as Bitcoin, is a sort of attack that makes use of a target's computing power. An algorithm known as a hash is used by this virus to do complex mathematical operations on a computer's CPU and, in some situations, its GPU.

2.5.4 Cloud Application, Storage, Network, DOS, and DDOS Attacks

The cloud environment offers multiple applications as a service over the internet, and all these services are ultimately run on physical cloud resources. When an attacker attacks the cloud environment to hack the system or application resources, the performance of the underlying resources such as the network, storage, and computing resources suffers. Finally, the previously mentioned attacks affect the entire cloud environment as shown in Gupta and Badve (2017) and Rani et al. (2022a).

UDP flood—Since HTTPv3 uses a UDP connection to transport data, attackers flood the cloud networks with false HTTPv3 packet traffic to bring down the victim web application. DNS and SNMP protocols are also used to flood the cloud networks with fake packets traffic. When numerous attackers carry out this attack at the same time, the severity of the attack increases dramatically.

ICMP flood—In this attack, the attacker/attackers flood the victim's web servers or network with ping messages in order to bring it down.

Smurf attack—This is an amplification attack vector that increases its harm potential by taking use of broadcast networking capabilities.

Fragile attack—This includes sending a huge amount of fake UDP/ICMP traffic to a network router's broadcast address.

TCP SYN attack—An attacker or attackers take advantage of a vulnerability in the TCP three-way handshake protocol to flood the real cloud consumer and the cloud service provider communication with fake TCP SYN packets.

Ping of death—An attacker or attackers use a simple ping command to deliver malicious or bigger packets to the targeted machine or service, causing it to freeze or crash.

Slowloris attack—This is a highly targeted attack that allows one web server to bring down another while leaving other web services and ports on the target network unaffected. It keeps as many links to the target web server as possible. Slowloris repeatedly sends more HTTP headers but never completes your request. Every fraudulent connection is kept, forcing genuine users to reject new connections.

NTP amplification—The attacker or attackers use publicly available NTP servers to flood a targeted server with UDP traffic in NTP amplification attacks. Anyone with access to a list of NTP servers can easily launch a high-volume, high-bandwidth DDoS attack.

Teardrop attack—IP packets are broken down into smaller chunks during network transmission, and each fragment contains the original packet's header, which is useful for reassembling at the destination host. When the TCP/IP stack becomes overburdened with IP fragments, reassembling becomes extremely complex and can fail rapidly.

Land attack—This attack works in the same way as a ping attack in that it sends modified TCP/SYN packets with the victim's IP address in both the source and destination IP fields. As a result, before crashing, the system sends the requests.

The cloud environment is vulnerable mainly at four different levels, and attackers often exploit these vulnerabilities to degrade the cloud performance. We should have a complete security framework that covers all four levels of the cloud environment. However, no such framework is available to secure the cloud environment.

2.6 Conclusion

Cloud computing is one of the highly challenging and dynamic paradigms and leverages services to users on demand by sticking to the SLA between users and cloud provider. Infrastructure, network, and computing services can be given to users through a pay-as-you-go model. This paradigm has many advantages besides that there are limitations that affect the performance of the cloud computing model. In this chapter, initially we have discussed the need for cloud computing, the deployment and service models, and the architectures of cloud computing. Thereafter, we clearly pointed out the characteristics and limitations of the cloud environment. From the limitations, we have identified security as one of the crucial factors for the cloud paradigm, and thereafter, we explored various types of attacks in the cloud at various levels, that is, attacks at the consumer side, ISP, virtualization, and application levels.

References

Arunachalam, P., Janakiraman, N., Sivaraman, A. K., Balasundaram, A., Vincent, R., Rani, S., ... Rajesh, M. (2021). Synovial sarcoma classification technique using support vector machine and structure features. *Intelligent Automation and Soft Computing*, 32(2), 1241–1259.

Buyya, R., Yeo, C. S., and Venugopal, S. (2008). Market-oriented cloud computing: Vision, hype, and reality for delivering it services as computing utilities. In *2008 10th IEEE International Conference on High Performance Computing and Communications* (pp. 5–13). IEEE.

Cambiaso, E., Papaleo, G., Chiola, G., and Aiello, M. (2013). Slow DoS attacks: Definition and categorisation. *International Journal of Trust Management in Computing and Communications*, 1(3–4), 300–319.

Chhabra, Y., and Bhambri, P. (2021). Various approaches and algorithms for monitoring energy efficiency of wireless sensor networks. In *Sustainable Development through Engineering Innovations* (pp. 761–770). Springer, Singapore.

Diaby, T., and Rad, B. B. (2017). Cloud computing: A review of the concepts and deployment models. *International Journal of Information Technology and Computer Science*, 9(6), 50–58.

Dong, B., Zheng, Q., Qiao, M., Shu, J., and Yang, J. (2009). BlueSky cloud framework: An e-learning framework embracing cloud computing. In *IEEE International Conference on Cloud Computing* (pp. 577–582). Springer, Berlin, Heidelberg.

Gupta, B. B., and Badve, O. P. (2017). Taxonomy of DoS and DDoS attacks and desirable defense mechanism in a cloud computing environment. *Neural Computing and Applications*, 28(12), 3655–3682.

Gupta, O., Rani, S., and Pant, D. C. (2011). Impact of parallel computing on bioinformatics algorithms. In *Proceedings 5th IEEE International Conference on Advanced Computing and Communication Technologies* (pp. 206–209). IEEE.

Hussain, S. A., Fatima, M., Saeed, A., Raza, I., and Shahzad, R. K. (2017). Multilevel classification of security concerns in cloud computing. *Applied Computing and Informatics*, 13(1), 57–65.

Islam, T., Manivannan, D., and Zeadally, S. (2016). A classification and characterization of security threats in cloud computing. *International Journal of Next-Generation Computing*, 7(1), 268–285.

Jain, A., Singh, M., and Bhambri, P. (2021, August). Performance evaluation of IPv4-IPv6 tunneling procedure using IoT. *Journal of Physics: Conference Series*, 1950(1), 012010.

Jamil, D., and Zaki, H. (2011). Security issues in cloud computing and countermeasures. *International Journal of Engineering Science and Technology (IJEST)*, 3(4), 2672–2676.

Josep, A. D., Katz, R., Konwinski, A., Gunho, L. E. E., Patterson, D., and Rabkin, A. (2010). A view of cloud computing. *Communications of the ACM*, 53(4), 50–58.

Kaur, G., Kaur, R., and Rani, S. (2015). Cloud computing-A new trend in IT era. *International Journal of Scientific and Technology Management*, 1, 1–6.

Kaur, J., and Bhambri, P. (2019). Various DNA sequencing techniques and related applications. *International Journal of Analytical and Experimental Model Analysis*, 11(9), 3104–3111.

Kaur, P., and Bhambri, P. (2015). To design an algorithm for text watermarking. *The Standard International Journals (The SIJ)*, 3(5), 62–67.

Kavis, M. J. (2014). *Architecting the Cloud: Design Decisions for Cloud Computing Service Models (SaaS, PaaS, and IaaS)*. John Wiley & Sons, UK.

Mahmood, Z. (Ed.). (2014). *Cloud Computing: Challenges, Limitations and R&D Solutions*. Springer.

Marston, S., Li, Z., Bandyopadhyay, S., Zhang, J., and Ghalsasi, A. (2011). Cloud computing—The business perspective. *Decision Support Systems, 51*(1), 176–189.

Mell, P., and Grance, T. (2011). *The NIST Definition of Cloud Computing*, USA.

Modi, C. N., and Acha, K. (2017). Virtualization layer security challenges and intrusion detection/ prevention systems in cloud computing: A comprehensive review. *The Journal of Supercomputing, 73*(3), 1192–1234.

Rani, S., and Gupta, O. P. (2017). CLUS_GPU-BLASTP: Accelerated protein sequence alignment using GPU-enabled cluster. *The Journal of Supercomputing, 73*(10), 4580–4595.

Rani, S., Kataria, A., and Chauhan, M. (2022a). Fog computing in Industry 4.0: Applications and challenges—A research roadmap. In R. Tiwari, M. Mitaal, and L. M. Goyal (Eds.), *Energy Conservation Solutions for Fog-Edge Computing Paradigms* (pp. 173–190). Springer.

Rani, S., Kataria, A., Chauhan, M., Rattan, P., Kumar, R., and Sivaraman, A. K. (2022b). Security and privacy challenges in the deployment of cyber-physical systems in smart city applications: State-of-art work. *Materials Today: Proceedings, 62*(7), 4671–4676.

Rani, S., Kataria, A., Sharma, V., Ghosh, S., Karar, V., Lee, K., and Choi, C. (2021a). Threats and corrective measures for IoT security with observance of cybercrime: A survey. *Wireless Communications and Mobile Computing, 2021*, 1–30.

Rani, S., and Kaur, S. (2012). Cluster analysis method for multiple sequence alignment. *International Journal of Computer Applications, 43*(14), 19–25.

Rani, S., Mishra, R. K., Usman, M., Kataria, A., Kumar, P., Bhambri, P., and Mishra, A. K. (2021b). Amalgamation of advanced technologies for sustainable development of smart city environment: A review. *IEEE Access, 9*, 150060–150087.

Schaffer, H. E. (2009). X as a service, cloud computing, and the need for good judgment. *IT Professional, 11*(5), 4–5.

Schniederjans, D. G., and Hales, D. N. (2016). Cloud computing and its impact on economic and environmental performance: A transaction cost economics perspective. *Decision Support Systems, 86*, 73–82.

Shrivastava, A., Rizwan, A., Kumar, N. S., Saravanakumar, R., Dhanoa, I. S., Bhambri, P., and Singh, B. K. (2021). VLSI implementation of green computing control unit on Zynq FPGA for green communication. *Wireless Communications and Mobile Computing, 2021*, 1–12.

Singh, A. P., Aggarwal, M., Singh, H., and Bhambri, P. (2021). Sketching of EV network: A complete roadmap. In *Sustainable Development Through Engineering Innovations: Select Proceedings of SDEI 2020* (pp. 431–442). Springer, Singapore.

Stieninger, M., and Nedbal, D. (2014). Characteristics of cloud computing in the business context: A systematic literature review. *Global Journal of Flexible Systems Management, 15*(1), 59–68.

Sudheer, M. S., Reddy, K. G., Sree, P. K., and Raju, V. P. (2017). An effective analysis on various scheduling algorithms in cloud computing. In *2017 International Conference on Inventive Computing and Informatics (ICICI)* (pp. 931–936). IEEE.

3

A Guide to Cloud Platform with an Investigation of Different Cloud Service Providers

Parul Dubey, Pushkar Dubey and Kailash Kumar Sahu

CONTENTS

3.1 Introduction

In cloud computing, the term *cloud* refers to networks in the same manner as the term *cloud* refers to networks in nature (Somu et al., 2017; Arunachalam et al., 2021). The user has complete access to all the cloud computing modes of operation at any moment throughout their session (Tandon and Bhambri, 2017). Customers who use cloud computing rather than building their own physical infrastructure frequently choose to work with a third-party mediator provider rather than doing it themselves (Anand and Bhambri, 2018). In the form of "cloud computing," computer power, database storage, application software, and other information technology (IT) resources may be accessible on demand. The user will be able to pay for the service on a pay-as-you-go basis if they utilize a cloud service platform, which is advantageous in this circumstance (Kaur and Bhambri, 2015). Once an individual requests anything, they will only be charged for that item at the time of the request, and they will not be charged again after they have done using it. In other words, we are able to give our clients the precise amount of processing power they need in this manner. The development of a strong charging structure network is broadly known to be a vital necessity for a huge-scale evolution to electromobility (Bhambri et al., 2022).

Because of the cloud, users may customize their requirements with services. Because services are available instantly, there is no need to provide a 24-hour, 72-hour, or even 2-hour notice in order to get all these resources. They may be accessed immediately. Because the majority of service demand is carried by the networks that make up the cloud, executing an application locally is not burdensome on the system. It is an outcome that reduces the number of pieces of hardware and software that are required. Cloud computing may be accessed using a web browser, which is all users need (Kaur and Bhambri, 2015; Kaur et al., 2019).

3.2 Literature Review

Security, service pricing, and multi-cloud management are all things to keep in mind while deciding on a cloud service provider (CSP). The problem of picking a CSP must be addressed in a multi-cloud system. For each online application, a multi-criteria decision-making technique ranks the potential CSP combinations. Solution technique considerations for virtual machines and cloud data centers are included when ranking CSP combinations. From a management and economic standpoint, it is likely that the optimum CSP pairings for various products will not be viable (Ramamurthy et al., 2020). In this way, researchers provide an optimization model for the selection of CSPs for numerous applications inside a company while taking budget and ranking into mind. Experiments using numerical data are used to explain their methods and provide new insights on the topic.

A new study (Jaithunbi et al., 2021) uses intelligent rules in addition to the standard genetic algorithm (SGA) to analyze whether a service provider can be trusted. Among the many factors to consider when assessing trust are things like reputation, accreditation, the accessibility of services, auditing, and self-evaluation. The SGA may be influenced by a single parameter thanks to these creative principles. Because of its dynamic solution-providing methodology based on intelligent rules, the rules are used to foresee unpredictability by offering solutions to complex dynamic systems, where most unpredictability occurs. In order to verify the trustworthiness of cloud servers or instances, intelligence rules and SGA work together. Customers are allowed to utilize the services without limitation because of their reliability.

Cloud service delivery systems, as well as their potential applications for software development, have been examined by Parkhomenk et al. (2021). The SAP Cloud Platform became an enterprise cloud platform when new SAP applications, updates, or add-ons were developed and a hybrid IT environment was built up on the SAP Cloud Platform. DevOps and a new architecture formed the SAP, which was assessed in terms of its strengths and weaknesses. According to the research analyzed, Cloud Foundry is employed in the SAP Cloud Platform development process.

To get the most value for their money, businesses must shop around for the best CSP. A graph-based technique for evaluating CSPs has been devised and was being evaluated, according to Trueman et al. (2021). In the first stage, a correlation between CSP response times is calculated. Using a penalty for each node in the lasso regularization network eliminates unnecessary connections. The degree of centrality is used to determine the order of the service providers. When it came down to rating CSPs, they used a normalized discounted cumulative gain technique.

Li's (2021) review process yielded the following list of the most important contributions. A quantitative method was used to analyze the service quality and pricing since CSPs' income, costs, and profits are all measurable using well-established analytical models. According to the research, there are two types of customer satisfaction: those who are happy with the price of a service and those who are happy with the quality of the service. A closed-form statement of customer satisfaction may be derived from a CSP. In highly competitive cloud computing markets, a noncooperative game model is necessary. As a consequence of this interaction, CSPs reach the Nash equilibrium, which is a result of the market stability mechanism. To find the Nash equilibrium, the researcher has proposed a method.

Based on the premise of user upgrading and switching costs, research has looked at the ideal pricing approaches for a CSP (Nan et al., 2019). Therefore, there isn't a market structure that's perfect for everyone. Upgrade and switch willingness will be altered if the incumbent offers reduced pricing to its present consumers and a lower level at which they must upgrade and switch to suffer a price change. An established business may be obliged to lower its products for new consumers rather than those who have previously bought from it. An on-premises software company may face substantial competition from software-as-a-service (SaaS) suppliers, particularly when it comes to attracting new clients for investment opportunities.

The automation of cloud management services such as traffic monitoring, forecasting, virtual service instance placement, and load balancing has been developed for CSPs. Researchers have employed Autoregressive Integrated Moving Average (ARIMA) models for traffic prediction, randomized weighted majority algorithms for virtual service instance placement, and a threshold-based method for load balancing to instances and anticipating cloud traffic (Dharmapriya et al., 2019; Gupta and Rani, 2010). The cloud management platform was shown to be effective throughout the paper, with a particular focus on the algorithms employed in the modules listed earlier. The modules made accessible to clients were utilized to automate cloud management services with high efficiency and reliability.

In order to make more accurate decisions, cloud professionals and decision-makers modeled and assessed uncertainty using rough sets, which are used to represent and evaluate uncertainty (Rădulescu et al., 2018). Combining two multi-attribute decision-making methodologies, the approach has the following characteristics: the analytic hierarchy process (AHP) and the Simple Additive Weight (SAW). The AHP rough approach, which is explained in the study, was used to calculate the subjective weights associated with each of the criteria. The use of a rudimentary SAW approach in CSP assessments was made to account for the uncertainty in the results. For this case study, they solicited the assistance of a group of cloud professionals who were willing to offer their insights (Gupta and Kaur,

2016). To produce pulse-width modulation pulses for the generator-side converter, a proportional-integral controller is utilized (Mohanta et al., 2022; Rani et al., 2022a).

Because there are so many CSPs to choose from in the cloud market, it may be difficult for customers to choose a provider that fulfills their requirements. CSPs are encouraged to achieve their service-level agreement and enhance service quality by creating a robust service selection framework for quality of service (QoS). QoS attributes should not be assigned weights at random; instead, they should be weighted according to the quality of service they provide (Somu et al., 2017). These models are also quite time-consuming to run. The research paper by Somu et al. (2017) provides a new approach to evaluating CSPs based on the HGCM and MDHP algorithms. It was used to assign weights to attributes and reduce the complexity of the ranking model, while the arithmetic residue and expectation–maximization (EM) approaches were used to fill in the blanks. In several case studies, the ranking method proved to be scalable and computationally attractive in MDHP's experiments (Rani et al., 2022c).

Customers of CSPs assess the quality of their cloud service offerings based on a number of different factors. In order to establish the service quality of the CSP and its own performance metrics, the features of the QoS are examined. In order to ensure the success of customers, it is essential to identify adequate QoS (Lang 2018). By using the Delphi approach, experts from various industries and organizational sizes were asked to assess the significance of QoS in cloud computing environments, and the results were published. In general, we came to a consensus on QoS. When it comes to QoS, we lay the most emphasis on functionality, legal compliance, contracts, server location, and flexibility, among other factors.

3.3 Cloud Computing

Instead of the end user, who gets computer resources as a service, the cloud provider owns and manages the computer resources on their behalf. Cloud-based storage services, web-based applications, and servers located on other people's networks that are used to support a company's computer network or a personal initiative are all instances of this kind of service.

It was formerly necessary for corporations and regular computer users to purchase and maintain their own software and hardware. Applications, storage, services, and equipment delivered via the cloud have made a broad variety of on-demand computing resources available to organizations and individuals worldwide. Because cloud customers do not have to spend their own time or money on acquiring and maintaining these computing resources, they reap the benefits of using distant and distributed resources to do their tasks more efficiently. New enterprises are springing up as a result of this unparalleled access to computing resources, as well as a wide range of ordinary computer-assisted tasks. Communications with colleagues via videoconferencing and other collaboration platforms, accessing entertainment and educational information on demand, interacting with home equipment, calling a taxi, and even renting a vacation room in someone's home have all become possible through cloud computing.

3.3.1 Characteristics

The following characteristics of cloud computing may be observed:

1. Resources Pooling—In order to make computer resources available to a large number of clients, the cloud provider created an architecture with several tenants. Resources, both real and virtual, are allocated and redistributed based on demand. Resource placement is normally out of the client's hands; however, they may be expressed at a higher degree of abstraction if required.

2. Self-Service on the Go—Because cloud computing is able to continually monitor server uptime, capabilities, and allocated network storage, among other things, it is a key factor and a valuable feature. The user may also keep an eye on the machine's overall performance thanks to this function.

3. Simple to Maintain—Administrators often have complete control over the servers; therefore, downtime is rare. Even though there are several iterations of cloud computing, the technology becomes better and better with each new release. Recent upgrades have included bug fixes and other enhancements, as well as better device compatibility.

4. Large-Scale Networking—A user's device and an internet connection are all that are required to access or upload data to the cloud. As a consequence of the technology, these features may be found all over the internet.

5. High Availability—It is possible for the cloud's capabilities to be further extended and customized to match the unique needs of each user. Cloud storage companies may give more storage space to customers at a very cheap cost.

6. Secure—The degree of security offered by cloud computing is yet another major perk. Even if one of the servers goes down, the data may still be accessed because of this feature. It's impossible for anybody else to hack into the data since they have been saved on secure storage devices. Storage facilities are recognized for their speedy and reliable service.

7. Pay as You Go—In cloud computing, clients just pay for the services they use and consume. There are no shady additional costs to be worried about with this deal. As a low-cost alternative, it frequently includes free storage.

3.3.2 Cloud Computing Classifications

There is no one-size-fits-all cloud computing solution that can be applied to every circumstance or every user in the world. In order to assist customers in making the best decision possible for the specific situation, a wide range of models, modifications, and services are offered to us. Prior to moving on to the next step, it is important to choose a cloud deployment model or a cloud computing infrastructure. It is thus possible to implement public, private, and hybrid cloud services simultaneously. Figure 3.1 demonstrates the comparisons of various types of cloud services, including the major differences among infrastructure as a service (IaaS), platform as a service (PaaS), and SaaS.

- IaaS—Cloud computing services based on IaaS give on-demand, fee-based access to computational and storage resources as needed. Serverless computing, PaaS, and SaaS complete the list of cloud services that are now accessible. Moving one's company's infrastructure to an IaaS environment may allow businesses to save money on hardware maintenance while also providing their customers with real-time business data. When we use IaaS solutions, companies have the flexibility to scale up and down their IT resources as needed. Additional advantages include

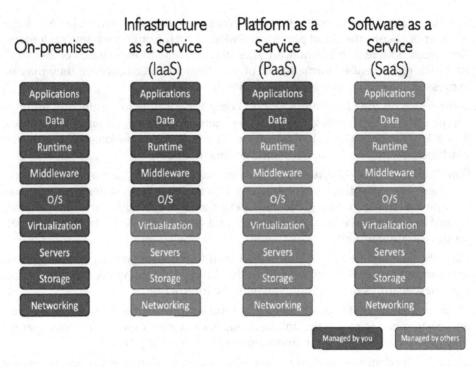

FIGURE 3.1
Comparing the types of cloud services.

making it simpler to deploy applications and improving the general stability of your system. IaaS relieves the burden of purchasing, maintaining, and operating one's own servers and other equipment. The characteristics of each service are unique, and consumers only pay for what they use on a regular basis.

- PaaS—For the design and deployment of cloud-based applications, which might range from basic consumer applications to large corporate systems that are cloud-enabled, just a single location and a little effort are necessary. Users will have access to all the resources they need from CSPs, provided that they have access to a secure internet connection to do so. IaaS (servers, storage, and networking), as well as middleware, development tools, business intelligence, and database management systems, are all included in PaaS. There are several benefits to using a PaaS platform while creating and sustaining web applications. By using PaaS, companies may avoid the expenses and headaches of managing software licenses and middleware, container orchestrators such as Kubernetes, and other resources on their own servers. Cloud computing service providers are often in charge of all other aspects of a company's operations as well.

- SaaS—When employing SaaS, customers may access and utilize cloud-based programs from any place where they have a network connection (SaaS). Technology like email and calendars are common places where this occurs. On a pay-per-use basis, a CSP provides a whole software solution that may be purchased from a CSP. A monthly membership cost is required for corporate users to have access to the app through a web browser. All infrastructure, middleware, application software, and application data are housed at the service provider's data center. To ensure that all the gear and software, as well as any app and any associated data, are taken care of, a company should have a service agreement in place. When we utilize SaaS, we can rapidly and affordably have an app up and running for our business.

- Serverless Computing—Serverless computing reduces the time it takes to build new apps by removing the burden of managing the underlying infrastructure from the developers. It was the CSP's responsibility to build, scale, and maintain the infrastructure needed to operate serverless applications in the cloud. In order to properly enjoy serverless computing, it's important to realize that the code is still running on servers. Developers don't have to worry about maintaining and providing their application's infrastructure in serverless applications. As a result of this approach, developers are better able to concentrate on business logic and so provide greater value to the company's primary function. Serverless computing enables teams to work more efficiently and bring new ideas to market faster while also allowing enterprises to better manage their resources and concentrate on innovation via the use of cloud computing.

3.4 CSPs

Cloud computing is a kind of computing in which scalable and elastic IT-enabled capabilities are provided as a service through the internet, allowing users to use them whenever they choose. According to Gartner [4], the cloud infrastructure and platform services (CIPS) market is composed of standardized, highly automated systems in which infrastructure resources (such as computing, networking, and storage) are backed by integrated platform services (such as disaster recovery). Managed application, database, and functions-as-a-service services are examples of this kind of service. It is possible for resources to be scaled and elastic in near-real time, and they are metered based on their utilization. Customers may self-service interfaces, which are composed of a web-based user interface and an Application Programming Interface, by logging into their accounts. Resource deployments may be either single-tenant or multi-tenant, and they can be hosted either by a service provider or on premises in the customer's data center. Discussed in the following subsections are the strengths and limitations of the vendors:

3.4.1 Amazon Web Services

Amazon Web Services (AWS), a division of Amazon, is positioned as a leader in this magic. AWS aspires to be a one-stop shop for IT services, offering everything from cloud-native to edge computing and mission-critical operations. AWS's long-term aim is to acquire a larger and larger portion of the supply chain that is used to provide cloud services to its clients, according to the company. It has a diverse customer base that includes anything from start-ups to multinational enterprises from all over the globe.

3.4.1.1 Strengths

- The technological competence of AWS is beneficial to certain workloads, particularly in areas such as AWS-designed CPUs, which provide better value for money than their x86 counterparts. Such investments in AWS-designed silicon enable

AWS to provide a long-term supply chain as well as technological advantages to its customers.

- As a result of the size and regularity of large financial commitments made by corporations to AWS, the company has maintained its market share leadership position, which is reflected in the company's market share. AWS is the world's largest cloud computing platform.

- AWS often sets higher standards for itself than its rivals when it comes to technological innovation. When it comes to market attention, AWS commands a disproportionately significant share of it across a diverse range of personae and customer types.

3.4.1.2 Limitations

- When it comes to AWS's very versatile and feature-rich cloud service, there is a steep learning curve to contend with. Consequently, if the internal IT personnel is limited and inexperienced with AWS, it may be challenging to get up and running as rapidly as we would want to. As soon as something goes wrong with their integrations with third-party plugins, the user can contact Amazon and request a variety of levels of technical assistance, depending on how quickly their issues need to be resolved and whether the user requires an account manager who will be assigned specifically to your account.

- There are risks associated with keeping personal and private information in places that are not trustworthy. Despite Amazon's successful use cases, there is a significant amount of bureaucratic red tape involved in moving sensitive data and business-critical settings to the public cloud.

- It is possible that data security may be a challenge when moving to a cloud computing environment. The risk of data breaches rises inexorably as the usage of cloud computing resources becomes more widespread. Data protection and security are inextricably connected. Numerous jurisdictions have strict legislation regarding personal data privacy, and international standards such as ISO-9001 place further restrictions on how firms may conduct their operations. This has a direct impact on the bottom line due to the importance of performance and uptime. Clients may leave a website in a fraction of a second, resulting in a loss of money for the website owner. Even if the site is just down for a few minutes, it might have long-term consequences for your search engine optimization (SEO) and the image of your company.

3.4.2 Microsoft Azure

Microsoft Azure is particularly strong in the fields of extended cloud computing and edge computing. Azure will be a fantastic match for organizations that are heavily reliant on Microsoft products. Microsoft's top objective is to continue to invest in the Azure platform and a broad range of enterprise-focused services, according to the company. It has a diverse customer base that ranges from tiny enterprises to large organizations, and it works in more than 100 countries throughout the globe.

3.4.2.1 Strengths

According to comparisons with other service providers, Microsoft has the broadest and most complete offering for satisfying the information technology needs of organizations across all service types, from cloud computing to on-premises infrastructure management. Microsoft offers a broad variety of IaaS and PaaS capabilities, as well as development tools such as Visual Studio and GitHub, as well as public cloud services.

Because of the long-standing connection that Microsoft has with its clients, Azure is a popular alternative for enterprises to implement. Azure has a competitive advantage in practically every business as a consequence of its tight association with Microsoft.

The efforts of Microsoft Azure in the areas of operational databases and big data solutions have had a successful year. When it comes to customer adoption, Azure's Cosmos DB and its integrated solution with Databricks are the most popular options.

3.4.2.2 Limitations

If we compare Azure cloud computing to on-premises computing, the Azure cloud is a whole other universe. On-premises solutions tend to be more concerned with scaling up, while Azure solutions are more concerned with scaling out.

Any IT professional who has ever had to upgrade to a new piece of hardware will tell you that scaling out is a more flexible and cost-effective alternative than scaling up. Servers will not be moved to Azure; instead, services will. The migration of SQL Server data warehouses to Azure Synapse will take place.

The technique for migrating a service to Azure is more challenging at times than at others, depending on the service being moved. This can be referred to as the "on-premises and Azure overlap," and it is a particularly challenging period. Suppose we have already set up the Azure service, but just a small portion of the information has been relocated. In this case, on-premises storage is used for certain data, while cloud storage is used for other data. Both systems are managed by solution teams, and there has been no cost advantage to the end users as of yet.

Another point to keep in mind is that not every solution will be a great match for Azure. Reporting Services is a wonderful illustration of this. When it comes to Reporting Services, there is no SaaS option in Azure, and there aren't many benefits to using IaaS for this purpose. The capacity of Reporting Services is gradually being moved to Power BI, implying that organizations are now shifting to the cloud while also using Power BI at the same time.

The adjustment in Microsoft's licensing strategy for Azure is just as important as the shift in infrastructure in terms of impact. The fact that IT teams are continually running into licensing difficulties anytime they make progress is a major source of frustration. The Azure license will be significantly different from the licenses that were previously available for on-premises systems, and this is to be anticipated. Companies contemplating a cloud migration, however, would benefit from simplifying the licensing process and decreasing the number of teams engaged.

There may be significant operational variations between the Azure cloud infrastructure and the on-premises infrastructure when comparing the two. Methods that have been in use for a long time may no longer be regarded as best practices in the Azure environment.

3.4.3 Google Cloud

Figure 3.2 demonstrates that Google is a high performer in this space. Fortunately, Google Cloud Platform (GCP) is well suited for the majority of use cases, and the company has been continuously improving its edge capabilities. As Google continues to expand its IaaS and PaaS capabilities, as well as the breadth and depth of its go-to-market operations, the

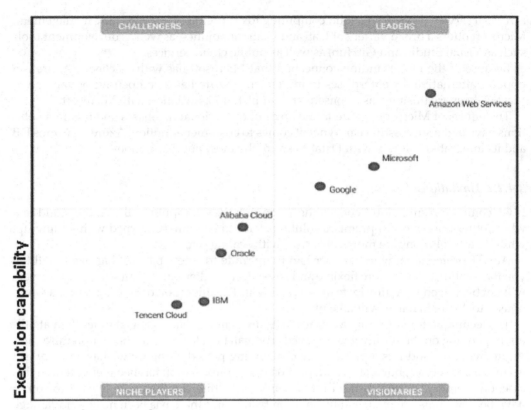

FIGURE 3.2
Magic quadrant for cloud infrastructure as a service.

search engine behemoth is also expanding its go-to-market operations. It serves a diverse range of clients, from tiny enterprises to large organizations, and its operations are dispersed around the world.

3.4.3.1 Strengths

In addition to traditional corporate workloads such as SAP, GCP is gaining popularity in data and analytics due to the company's core competence in these areas.

Business leaders are beginning to see the value of GCP. When infrastructure executives are asked about strategic cloud provider options over the next few years, the company has seen a continuous increase in use and consistently rates at the top of poll results, according to the business.

While AWS and Microsoft Azure have made substantial advancements in CIPS capabilities over 2021, GCP continues to close the gap with AWS and, in some cases, surpasses it in terms of performance. In terms of Kubernetes, for example, GCP offers the most comprehensive solution of any provider in this area (Banerjee et al., 2022; Rani et al., 2021b).

3.4.3.2 Limitations

In order to attract clients, Google is now giving cheaper rates than its rivals; however, it is projected that this discounting will reduce as the company grows in terms of revenue and number of users.

GCP is the only significant company in the CIPS market that is now experiencing financial difficulties. Growth in GCP is eating into Google's overall strong gross margins, yet the cloud business only accounts for a small portion of the parent company's total revenue (Rani and Kaur, 2012; Gupta, 2017).

3.4.4 Alibaba Cloud

Alibaba Cloud (also known as Aliyun in Chinese) is a visionary. During the magic quadrant research (Chand, 2021; Rani et al., 2022d), the researchers focused on Alibaba Cloud's international business, which has its headquarters in Singapore, and our technical assessment was carried out using the international service provided by the company.

The Alibaba Cloud platform is an excellent fit for customers in China or Southeast Asia who want to use Alibaba Cloud's technology to support their ecosystem or who need to locate their cloud infrastructure in China. Alibaba Cloud is also an excellent fit for customers in the United States who want to run cloud-first digital business workloads (Rani and Gupta, 2016). Apart from improving its database PaaS capabilities, Alibaba Cloud is concentrating on achieving more success in the Asian market overall (Gupta et al., 2011).

3.4.4.1 Strengths

Alibaba Cloud has maintained its position as the market leader in China and its neighboring countries in terms of market share and capabilities. Its extensive understanding of the Indonesian and Malaysian markets positions it well to become a favored regional provider in the rapidly expanding cloud computing industries in the area (Rani et al., 2021b).

In recent months, Alibaba Cloud, which has seen significant sales growth, has made a profit for the first time in 2021. Because of Alibaba's success in bringing products to market, both China and Southeast Asia have seen steady growth over 2021 (Kothandaraman et al., 2022).

For enterprises looking to get started with Alibaba Cloud, digital transformation and commerce capabilities are seen as viable options based on the big data and analytics capabilities of Alibaba Cloud, as well as the parent company.

3.4.4.2 Limitations

Despite the fact that Alibaba Cloud is the third-largest cloud computing provider in the world, the company's clientele is virtually completely made up of Chinese-based firms or international organizations with a need for a local presence in China. The firm has been unable to acquire considerable market penetration outside of its home market and does not seem to be on the verge of doing so in the near future.

Established global cloud providers such as AWS and Microsoft compete with China-focused providers such as Tencent Cloud and Huawei for a growing share of the market, putting significant pressure on Alibaba's margins. AWS is the world's largest cloud provider, with a market share of over 80%. Aside from that, Alibaba Cloud is stuck in the heart of a geopolitical battle, which may be a source of concern for international consumers considering Alibaba Cloud's products (Dhanalakshmi et al., 2022).

When it comes to discounts, Alibaba Cloud falls short of its overseas competitors in terms of openness and predictability, as well as in terms of price. Alibaba is still lacking in transparency when it comes to the technical details of service implementations at this point in time Kaur et al. (2018), Kaur and Bhambri (2015).

3.4.5 Oracle

Oracle is positioned as a minority player in the quadrant. Aside from Oracle-specific applications, Oracle Cloud Infrastructure (OCI) is primarily designed for lifting and shifting, high-performance computing, and hybrid workloads. Rather than concentrating on expanding its worldwide presence, Oracle is concentrating on developing capabilities that are similar to those of its more established rivals.

3.4.5.1 Strengths

Oracle's commitment to the industry and its confidence in OCI are shown by the fact that all of Oracle's PaaS and SaaS products are built on top of OCI as its core cloud architecture (Rani et al., 2022d).

Comparing Oracle's strategy to supplying distributed cloud capabilities to the other competitors in the sector, it stands out as being distinctive. Customers may build an OCI private cloud region on premises that has full parity with the public OCI regions, and it can be used without the need for an internet connection.

3.4.5.2 Limitations

Oracle's rapid progress over the preceding 2 years has resulted in the introduction of new and unproven features. Because of the nature of OCI's client base, it is doubtful that cloud-native capabilities have been widely implemented or widely adopted by the community.

Oracle's position among software developers and Independent Software Vendors (ISVs) continues to be a source of contention. Oracle is not regarded as a neutral supplier by ISVs. The negative reputation of Oracle has resulted in the company's grassroots success and enthusiasm being less pronounced than those of larger, more successful vendors.

3.4.6 IBM

IBM is a minority player in this quadrant. The majority of IBM Cloud's revenue is composed of lift and shift and extended corporate use cases, respectively. Approximately 80% of its clients are large and medium-sized enterprises. The hybrid cloud, regulated workloads, and cloud services targeted to certain sectors are just a few of the areas in which IBM intends to make an investment.

3.4.6.1 Strengths

Earlier, IBM announced the start of a spinoff that would see its managed IT services business separated out into a company called Kyndryl, allowing the firm to focus on higher-margin businesses such as IBM Cloud. This may help IBM to devote the necessary resources to IBM Cloud engineering initiatives in order to further improve capabilities.

IBM Cloud is concentrating its efforts on regulated workloads and industries as a primary aim. The firm has a significant amount of expertise in assisting customers with such intricate challenges in a high-touch manner that some consumers find appealing.

IBM has taken innovative approaches to edge computing, with highly visible deployments such as the Mayflower Autonomous Ship project, which demonstrates a pragmatic blend of open-source frameworks and technologies, supplemented by IBM Cloud Satellite and Edge Application Manager.

3.4.6.2 Limitations

When compared to the competitors, IBM's market share and capabilities are well behind the curve. Progress in CIPS capabilities has been noticeable during 2021, but not at the rate that is necessary to keep IBM competitive with its rivals in the marketplace.

For IBM, a vertical strategy started with a concentration on financial services and telecoms sectors, before expanding to other industries. The risk is that these activities will be overshadowed by competitors that are more nimble and have a bigger share of the market, more capabilities, and more reference customers.

3.5 Conclusion

In this study, we looked at a large number of cloud computing service providers. Many additional sources, including the most recent Gartner report, were examined in detail in addition to this one. We've explored CSPs such as AWS, Google Cloud, Azure, and others. The most important goal was to identify the advantages and disadvantages of various service providers.

References

Anand, A., and Bhambri, P. (2018). Character recognition system using radial features. *International Journal on Future Revolution in Computer Science & Communication Engineering*, 4(4), 599–602.

Arunachalam, P., Janakiraman, N., Sivaraman, A. K., Balasundaram, A., Vincent, R., Rani, S., … Rajesh, M. (2021). Synovial sarcoma classification technique using support vector machine and structure features. *Intelligent Automation and Soft Computing*, 32(2), 1241–1259.

Banerjee, K., Bali, V., Nawaz, N., Bali, S., Mathur, S., Mishra, R. K., and Rani, S. (2022). A machine-learning approach for prediction of water contamination using latitude, longitude, and elevation. *Water*, 14(5), 728.

Bhambri, P., Aggarwal, M., Singh, H., Singh, A. P., and Rani, S. (2022). Uprising of EVs: Charging the future with demystified analytics and sustainable development. In *Decision Analytics for Sustainable Development in Smart Society 5.0* (pp. 37–53). Springer, Singapore.

Chand, M. (2021). Top 10 cloud service providers in 2021. https://www.c-sharpcorner.com/article/top-10-cloud-service-providers/

Dhanalakshmi, R., Anand, J., Sivaraman, A. K., and Rani, S. (2022). IoT-based water quality monitoring system using cloud for agriculture use. In *Cloud and Fog Computing Platforms for Internet of Things* (pp. 183–196). Chapman and Hall/CRC, UK.

Dharmapriya, W. A. S. P., Supipi, K. G., Nimesh, G. R., Muhandiram, M. A. B. K., Rankothge, W. H., and Gamage, N. (2019). Smart platform for cloud service providers. In *2019 International Conference on Advancements in Computing (ICAC)* (pp. 434–439). IEEE.

Gupta, O., Rani, S., and Pant, D. C. (2011). Impact of parallel computing on bioinformatics algorithms. In *Proceedings 5th IEEE International Conference on Advanced Computing and Communication Technologies* (pp. 206–209).

Gupta, O. P. (2017). Study and analysis of various bioinformatics applications using protein BLAST: An overview. *Advances in Computational Sciences and Technology, 10*(8), 2587–2601.

Gupta, O. P., and Kaur, S. (2016). Ortholog and paralog detection using phylogenetic tree construction with distance based methods. *International Journal of Computer Science and Information Security, 14*(10), 886.

Gupta, O. P., and Rani, S. (2010). Bioinformatics applications and tools: An overview. *CiiT-International Journal of Biometrics and Bioinformatics, 3*(3), 107–110.

Kaur, A., Raj, G., Yadav, S., and Choudhury, T. (2018). Performance evaluation of AWS and IBM cloud platforms for security mechanism. In *2018 International Conference on Computational Techniques, Electronics and Mechanical Systems (CTEMS)* (pp. 516–520). IEEE.

Kaur, G., Kaur, R., and Rani, S. (2015). Cloud computing-a new trend in IT era. *International Journal of Scientific and Technology Management, 1,* 1–6.

Kaur, P., and Bhambri, P. (2015). To design an algorithm for text watermarking. *The Standard International Journals (The SIJ), 3*(5), 62–67.

Kothandaraman, D., Manickam, M., Balasundaram, A., Pradeep, D., Arulmurugan, A., Sivaraman, A. K., … Balakrishna, R. (2022). Decentralized link failure prevention routing (DLFPR) algorithm for efficient internet of things. *Intelligent Automation and Soft Computing, 34*(1), 655–666.

Lang, M., Wiesche, M., and Krcmar, H. (2018). Criteria for selecting cloud service providers: A Delphi study of quality-of-service attributes. *Information and Management, 55*(6), 746–758.

Li, K. (2021). On the profits of competing cloud service providers: A game theoretic approach. *Journal of Computer and System Sciences, 117,* 130–153.

Mohanta, H. C., Geetha, B. T., Alzaidi, M. S., Dhanoa, I. S., Bhambri, P., Mamodiya, U., and Akwafo, R. (2022). An optimized PI controller-based SEPIC converter for microgrid-interactive hybrid renewable power sources. *Wireless Communications and Mobile Computing, 2022,* 1–10.

Nan, G., Zhang, Z., and Li, M. (2019). Optimal pricing for cloud service providers in a competitive setting. *International Journal of Production Research, 57*(20), 6278–6291.

Parkhomenko, A., Zalyubovskiy, Y., and Parkhomenko, A. (2021). Cloud platform for software development. In *International Conference on Remote Engineering and Virtual Instrumentation* (pp. 343–351). Springer, Cham.

Rădulescu, C. Z., Rădulescu, I. C., Boncea, R., and Mitan, E. (2018). A group decision approach based on rough multi-attribute methods for Cloud Services Provider selection. In *2018 10th International Conference on Electronics, Computers and Artificial Intelligence (ECAI)* (pp. 1–6). IEEE.

Ramamurthy, A., Saurabh, S., Gharote, M., and Lodha, S. (2020). Selection of cloud service providers for hosting web applications in a multi-cloud environment. In *2020 IEEE International Conference on Services Computing (SCC)* (pp. 202–209). IEEE.

Rani, S., and Gupta, O. P. (2016). Empirical analysis and performance evaluation of various GPU implementations of protein BLAST. *International Journal of Computer Applications, 151*(7), 22–27.

Rani, S., and Kaur, S. (2012). Cluster analysis method for multiple sequence alignment. *International Journal of Computer Applications, 43*(14), 19–25.

Rani, S., Mishra, R. K., Usman, M., Kataria, A., Kumar, P., Bhambri, P., and Mishra, A. K. (2021a). Amalgamation of advanced technologies for sustainable development of smart city environment: A review. *IEEE Access, 9,* 150060–150087.

Rani, S., Bhambri, P., and Chauhan, M. (2021b, October). A machine learning model for kids' behavior analysis from facial emotions using principal component analysis. In *2021 5th Asian Conference on Artificial Intelligence Technology (ACAIT)* (pp. 522–525). IEEE.

Rani, S., Arya, V., and Kataria, A. (2022a). Dynamic pricing-based e-commerce model for the produce of organic farming in India: A research roadmap with main advertence to vegetables. In *Proceedings of Data Analytics and Management* (pp. 327–336). Springer, Singapore.

Rani, S., Bhambri, P., and Gupta, O. P. (2022b). Green smart farming techniques and sustainable agriculture: Research roadmap towards organic farming for imperishable agricultural products. In *Handbook of Sustainable Development through Green Engineering and Technology* (pp. 49–67). CRC Press.

Rani, S., Kataria, A., and Chauhan, M. (2022c). Cyber security techniques, architectures, and design. In *Holistic Approach to Quantum Cryptography in Cyber Security* (pp. 41–66). CRC Press, USA.

Rani, S., Kataria, A., and Chauhan, M. (2022d). Fog computing in industry 4.0: Applications and challenges—A research roadmap. In R. Tiwari, M. Mittal., and L. M. Goyal (Eds.), *Energy Conservation Solutions for Fog-Edge Computing Paradigms* (pp. 173–190). Springer.

Somu, N., Kirthivasan, K., and Shankar Sriram, V. S. (2017). A computational model for ranking cloud service providers using hypergraph based techniques. *Future Generation Computer Systems, 68,* 14–30.

Tandon, N., and Bhambri, P. (2017). Classification technique for drug discovery in medical image processing. *International Journal of Advanced Research in Computer Science, 8*(7), 194–197.

Trueman, T. E., Narayanasamy, P., and Ashok Kumar, J. (2021). A graph-based method for ranking of cloud service providers. *The Journal of Supercomputing, 23,* 1–18.

Ucuz, D. (2020). Comparison of the IoT platform vendors, Microsoft Azure, Amazon Web Services, and Google Cloud, from users' perspectives. In *2020 8th International Symposium on Digital Forensics and Security (ISDFS)* (pp. 1–4). IEEE.

4

A Study on the Accuracy of IoT-Sensed Data Using Machine Learning

K. P. Maheswari, N. Anuradha and S. Nirmala Devi

CONTENTS

4.1 Introduction

The Internet of Things (IoT) is a network that connects many physical things to the internet and collects and exchanges data all over the world (Kaur et al., 2020; Kumar et al., 2022). Sensors and the Internet's leading position provide a solution to a wide range of real-world challenges. Smart cities, smart health care systems, smart buildings, smart transportation, and smart environment are examples of such applications (Bhambri and Gupta, 2012; Arya et al., 2022). In collaboration with machine learning and artificial intelligence, anomaly detection systems are vastly used in behavioral analysis to help in identifying and predicting prevalence of anomalies (Kaur et al., 2015; Bhambri et al., 2020). To produce pulse-width modulation pulses for the generator-side converter, a proportional -integral controller is utilized (Chauhan and Rani, 2021; Mohanta et al., 2022).

DOI: 10.1201/9781003298335-4

Machine learning is a sort of data analysis that uses artificial intelligence to create analytical models. Without the need for explicit programming, machine learning algorithms employ training data to create a model that can be used to make predictions or judgments. The majority of IoT applications require machine learning techniques to convert data into something intelligible (Kaur et al., 2013, 2022).

IoT and big data analytics benefit from cloud computing as an infrastructure. It may easily experiment with machine learning capabilities in the cloud. It also allows cognitive capabilities to be accessed without the need for advanced artificial intelligence or data science skills (Kaur et al., 2015; Rani et al., 2022a).

The IoT and machine learning enable the creation of many real-time insights. To make sense, the data handling in this combined system must have a lot of possibilities (Singh et al., 2017, 2021b).

Recently, artificial intelligence has made significant progress in machine learning. To function, machine learning requires huge amounts of data that are being collected by the billions of sensor devices through a network that is part of the IoT (Gupta and Rani, 2013; Kaur et al., 2019).

Using a machine learning algorithm to handle IoT-sensed data is an efficient solution since it leverages previous behavior to detect trends and construct models that help anticipate future behavior and events. To put it another way, the data's nature, correctness, and accuracy may all be analyzed (Bhambri and Gupta, 2014; Rani and Gupta, 2017).

4.2 Proposed Model

4.2.1 Key Factors

For the proposed work, the major criteria must be considered: First is algorithm selection, which is based on IoT applications, IoT data characteristics, and machine learning algorithms' data-driven vision.

Second, because the data are derived from a sensor, the data quality must be carefully checked. The acquired data's quality is critical, as they differ in quality due to the fact that they come from a variety of sources. Each data source's information quality is determined by three factors: (1) inaccuracy in measurements or data collection precision, (2) noise from devices in the environment, and (3) observation and measurements in a discrete manner. To improve quality, more levels of abstraction must be extracted, and actionable information must be provided to other services. The applications and properties of smart data determine the data's quality (Arunachalam et al., 2021).

In the proposed work, an analysis of the accuracy of the data is done by selecting trustworthy sources, which is of key importance. The precision of observations and measurements will be increased by increasing the frequency and density of sampling.

4.2.2 Machine Learning Algorithms

The following are some of the most often used machine learning algorithms for smart data analysis and IoT use cases. In Table 4.1, the available algorithms are listed. From this list, the algorithm selected for the proposed system is a linear regression algorithm (Chhabra and Bhambri, 2021; Rani et al., 2022).

TABLE 4.1

List of Algorithms

Algorithm	Data-Processing Tasks
K-Nearest Neighbors	Classification
Naive Bayes	Classification
Support Vector Machine	Classification
Linear Regression	Regression
Support Vector Regression	Regression

4.2.3 Linear Regression Model

The linear regression algorithm is one of the machine learning algorithms, used to perform predictive analysis.

A linear relationship exists between a dependent (y) and one or more independent (x) variables when using the linear regression algorithm. It helps to determine the strength and character of the relationship between one continuous dependent variable (usually denoted by Y) and a series of other variables (known as independent variables).

Linear regression works based on the equation of a line.

$$Y = mX + C, \tag{4.1}$$

where Y is the dependent variable,

X is the independent variable,

m is the slope, and

C is the y-intercept.

4.3 Development of Machine Learning Model

The machine learning model is developed with the following parameters: The data from the sensors utilized at beach weather stations—automated sensors that collect data in real time for analysis. Weather sensors are installed at beaches along Chicago's Lake Michigan lakefront by the Chicago Park District. While the sensors are in use, they typically take the stated measurements every hour. The data set is created by collecting the gathered data from several sensor locations (Rani and Kaur, 2012; Singh et al., 2021a).

One of the important points from the data is that the sensor's battery life has an impact on effective data collection, which, in turn, reflects data accuracy. The intended work is completed in this dimension, and the accuracy is forecasted using training and testing data (Jain et al., 2021; Rani and Kumar, 2022).

The following are the steps handled for the development of the machine learning model for the prediction of the accuracy level of sensed data through an IoT device:

(1) Data Set and Date Preprocessing

(2) EDA, or Exploratory Data Analysis

(3) Training and Testing of data

4.3.1 Data Set and Data Preprocessing

```
Import Libraries
import pandas as pd
import numpy as np
import matplotlib.pyplot as plt
import seaborn as sns
%matplotlib inline
Check Out the Data
dataset = pd.read_csv('/content/senseddata1.csv')
Reading the Data
dataset.head()
```

Table 4.2 shows the first part of the data set. It retrieves the first few rows from the data set

```
dataset.info().
```

Figure 4.1 shows the information of the data set.

```
dataset.describe()
```

Figure 4.2 describes the data set:
Listing out the columns in the data set

```
dataset.columns
```

Figure 4.3 is the list of columns in the dataset.

4.3.2 EDA

(A) Pair Plot
Using sns.pairplot(dataset), the pair plot is plotted, and Figure 4.4 shows the outcome of the pair plot for the given parameters.
(B) Distribution Plot
The sensed battery life is visualized using sns.distplot(dataset ['Battery Life']), and Figure 4.5 shows the outcome of the distribution plot for the given parameters.
(C) Heatmap – Data Correlation
Using sns.heatmap (dataset.corr ()), the data correlation is visualized in Figure 4.6.

Preprocessing is carried out on the data set by carefully examining all the columns and the data linked with them.

4.3.3 Training and Testing of Data

Data value for X- and Y-axis

```
X = dataset[['Water Temperature','Turbidity','Wave Height','Wave
Period']]
y = dataset['Battery Life']
```

TABLE 4.2

The First Part of the Data Set

	Beach Name	Measurement Timestamp	Water Temperature	Turbidity	Transducer Depth	Wave Height	Wave Period	Battery Life	Measurement Timestamp Label	Measurement ID
0	Montrose Beach	08/30/2013 08:00:00 AM	20.3	1.18	0.891	0.080	3.0	9.4	8/30/2013 8:00 AM	MontroseBeach20130830080
1	Ohio Street Beach	05/26/2016 01:00:00 PM	14.4	1.23	NaN	0.111	4.0	12.4	05/26/2016 1:00 PM	Ohio StreetBeach20160526130
2	Calumet Beach	09/03/2013 04:00:00 PM	23.2	3.63	1.201	0.174	4.0	9.4	9/3/2013 4:00 PM	CalumetBeach20130903160
3	Calumet Beach	05/28/2014 12:00:00 PM	16.2	1.26	1.514	0.147	4.0	11.7	5/28/2014 12:00 PM	CalumetBeach20140528120
4	Montrose Beach	05/28/2014 12:00:00 PM	14.4	3.36	1.388	0.298	4.0	11.9	5/28/2014 12:00 PM	MontroseBeach20140528120

```
<class 'pandas.core.frame.DataFrame'>
RangeIndex: 1136 entries, 0 to 1135
Data columns (total 10 columns):
 #   Column                      Non-Null Count  Dtype
---  ------                      --------------  -----
 0   Beach Name                  1136 non-null   object
 1   Measurement Timestamp       1136 non-null   object
 2   Water Temperature           1136 non-null   float64
 3   Turbidity                   1136 non-null   float64
 4   Transducer Depth            1135 non-null   float64
 5   Wave Height                 1136 non-null   float64
 6   Wave Period                 1136 non-null   int64
 7   Battery Life                1136 non-null   float64
 8   Measurement Timestamp Label 1136 non-null   object
 9   Measurement ID              1136 non-null   object
dtypes: float64(5), int64(1), object(4)
memory usage: 88.9+ KB
```

FIGURE 4.1
Information of the data set.

	Water Temperature	Turbidity	Transducer Depth	Wave Height	Wave Period	Battery Life
count	1136.000000	1136.000000	1135.000000	1136.000000	1136.000000	1136.000000
mean	17.156778	4.164648	1.468042	0.178221	3.514965	11.547095
std	1.545004	5.818532	0.148903	0.083117	1.190915	0.338447
min	13.800000	0.000000	-0.082000	0.013000	2.000000	9.400000
25%	16.000000	1.190000	1.386000	0.120000	3.000000	11.300000
50%	16.900000	2.110000	1.453000	0.154000	3.000000	11.500000
75%	18.100000	4.302500	1.574500	0.215000	4.000000	11.700000
max	27.100000	29.840000	1.818000	0.526000	10.000000	12.800000

FIGURE 4.2
Data set description.

```
Index(['Beach Name', 'Measurement Timestamp', 'Water Temperature', 'Turbidity',
       'Transducer Depth', 'Wave Height', 'Wave Period', 'Battery Life',
       'Measurement Timestamp Label', 'Measurement ID'],
      dtype='object')
```

FIGURE 4.3
Columns details of the data set.

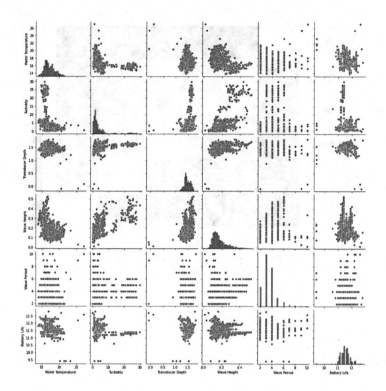

FIGURE 4.4
Outcome of the pair plot for the given parameters.

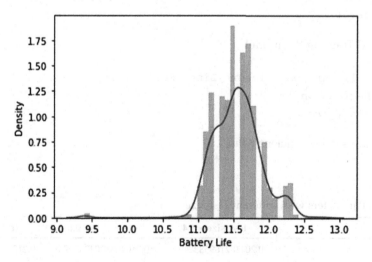

FIGURE 4.5
Outcome of the distribution plot for the given parameters.

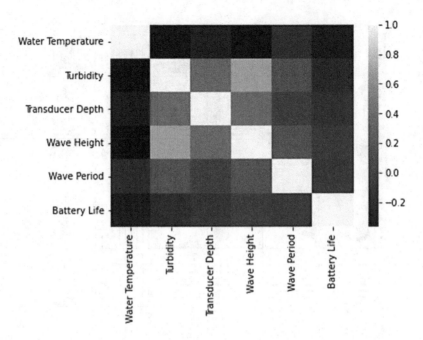

FIGURE 4.6
Visualization of data correlation.

Train Test Split

```
from sklearn.model_selection import train_test_split
X_train, X_test, y_train, y_test = train_test_split(X, y, test_size=0.4,
random_state=101)
```

Creating and Training the model

```
from sklearn.linear_model import LinearRegression
lm = LinearRegression()
lm.fit(X_train,y_train)
```

Table 4.3 shows the coefficient values.

TABLE 4.3

The Evaluation Parameters with Different Test Size

	test_size = 0.4	test_size = 0.5	test_size = 0.6
MAE	0.2041821695338496	0.21046881042339768	0.21311230780983634
MSE	0.08838931474315825	0.10127781183408399	0.10091345835753034
RMSE	0.2973034051993994	0.3182417506143466	0.31766878719435176
Coefficient of determination of the prediction – Test data	0.15159460227098598	0.08881892206036734	0.11607040501568011
Coefficient of determination of the prediction – Train data	0.2013773975073171	0.24219851901492184	0.2444885693125407

4.4 Model Evaluation

The following approach is used to assess the produced model.

```
print(lm.intercept_) gives the result as 13.249035754678275
coeff_df = pd.DataFrame(lm.coef_,X.columns,columns=['Coefficient'])
```

4.4.1 Predictions from the Model

The prediction is done using several visual plots, such as a scatterplot and a residual histogram, with the test and training data.

```
predictions = lm.predict(X_test)
```

(A) Scatterplot

```
plt.scatter(y_test,predictions)
```

Figure 4.7 shows the resultant scatter plot with the given parameters.
Residual Histogram
(B) Distribution Plot

```
sns.distplot((y_test-predictions),bins=50);
```

Figure 4.8 is the resultant of the distribution plot with the given parameters.

4.4.2 Evaluation Metrics

The degree of variation in the actual data is used to calculate the accuracy of a model generated using the linear regression technique. The evaluation metrics taken for the developed model follow:

  (i) MAE – mean absolute error
 (ii) MSE – mean squared error
(iii) RMSE – root mean squared error

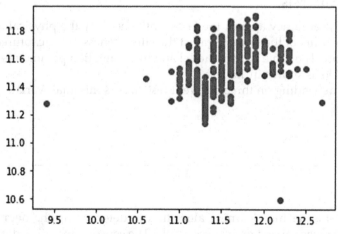

FIGURE 4.7
Outcome of the scatterplot with the given parameters.

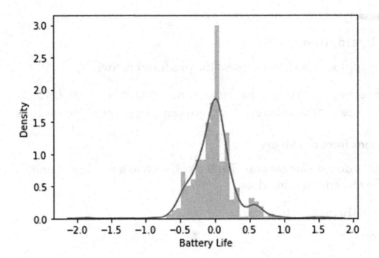

FIGURE 4.8
The resultant of the distribution plot with the given parameters.

```
from sklearn import metrics
print('MAE:', metrics.mean_absolute_error(y_test, predictions))
print('MSE:', metrics.mean_squared_error(y_test, predictions))
print('RMSE:', np.sqrt (metrics.mean_squared_error(y_test, predictions)))
```

The resultant values are

```
MAE: 0.2041821695338496
MSE: 0.0883893147431525
RMSE: 0.2973034051993994
```

4.5 Accuracy Analysis

The analysis of the accuracy against the factor influenced by the physical IoT parameter, which is the battery life of the sensor against the effectiveness of the captured data, cannot be analyzed simply. The same type of model and the evaluation parameters with different test size is recorded as shown in Table 4.3.

The variation depending on three different test sizes is minimal. Variations range from 0.01 to 0.02.

4.6 Conclusion

The application of a machine learning algorithm in determining the degree of accuracy of IoT-sensed data was carried over successfully. The sensor's real-time data are collected and analyzed in order to operate with the linear regression algorithm. The accuracy of the data is anticipated by comparing data sensed through the sensor device to one of the IoT device parameters. The data are tested and trained with the help of the developed linear regression model. The predictive analysis of the model with three distinct test sizes is done to gain a more definite conclusion.

As a result, data accuracy is unaffected by the physical parameter of IoT, and it is insignificant in the range of 0.01 to 0.02.

References

Arunachalam, P., Janakiraman, N., Sivaraman, A. K., Balasundaram, A., Vincent, R., Rani, S., and Rajesh, M. (2021). Synovial sarcoma classification technique using support vector machine and structure features. *Intelligent Automation and Soft Computing*, *32*, 1241–1259.

Arya, V., Rani, S., and Choudhary, N. (2022). Enhanced bio-inspired trust and reputation model for wireless sensor networks. In *Proceedings of Second Doctoral Symposium on Computational Intelligence* (pp. 569–579). Springer, Singapore.

Bhambri, J., and Gupta, O. P. (2014). Dynamic frequency allocation scheme of mobile networks using priority assignment technique. *International Journal of Engineering and Technology Innovation*, *1*, 45–53.

Bhambri, P., Bagga, S., Priya, D., Singh, H., and Dhiman, H. K. (2020). Suspicious human activity detection system. *Journal of IoT in Social, Mobile, Analytics, and Cloud*, *2*, 216–221.

Bhambri, P., and Gupta, O. P. (2012). Development of phylogenetic tree based on Kimura's method. In *2012 2nd IEEE International Conference on Parallel, Distributed and Grid Computing* (pp. 721–723). IEEE.

Chauhan, M., and Rani, S. (2021). Covid-19: A revolution in the field of education in India. In *Learning How to Learn Using Multimedia* (pp. 23–42). Springer, Singapore.

Chhabra, Y., and Bhambri, P. (2021). Various approaches and algorithms for monitoring energy efficiency of wireless sensor networks. In *Sustainable Development through Engineering Innovations* (pp. 761–770). Springer, Singapore.

Gupta, O. P., and Rani, S. (2013). Accelerating molecular sequence analysis using distributed computing environment. *International Journal of Scientific and Engineering Research–IJSER*, *4*, 262–265.

Jain, A., Singh, M., and Bhambri, P. (2021). Performance evaluation of IPv4-IPv6 tunneling procedure using IoT. *Journal of Physics: Conference Series*, *1950*, 012010.

Kaur, G., Kaur, R., and Rani, S. (2015). Cloud computing-a new trend in IT era. *International Journal of Scientific and Technology Management*, *1*, 1–6.

Kaur, J., Bhambri, P., and Gupta, O. P. (2013). Distance based phylogenetic trees with bootstrapping. *International Journal of Computer Applications*, *47*, 6–10.

Kaur, J., Bhambri, P., and Sharma, K. (2019). Wheat production analysis based on Naive Bayes classifier. *International Journal of Analytical and Experimental Model Analysis*, *11*, 705–709.

Kaur, K., Dhanoa, I. S., and Bhambri, P. (2020). Optimized PSO-EFA algorithm for energy efficient virtual machine migrations. In *2020 5th IEEE International Conference on Recent Advances and Innovations in Engineering (ICRAIE)* (pp. 1–5). IEEE.

Kaur, P., and Bhambri, P. (2015). To design an algorithm for text watermarking. *The Standard International Journals (The SIJ)*, *3*, 62–67.

Kaur, S., Kumar, R., Kaur, R., Singh, S., Rani, S., and Kaur, A. (2022). Piezoelectric materials in sensors: Bibliometric and visualization analysis. *Materials Today: Proceedings*, *65*, 3780–3786.

Kumar, R., Rani, S., and Awadh, M. A. (2022). Exploring the application sphere of the internet of things in industry 4.0: A review, bibliometric and content analysis. *Sensors*, *22*, 4276.

Mohanta, H. C., Geetha, B. T., Alzaidi, M. S., Dhanoa, I. S., Bhambri, P., Mamodiya, U., and Akwafo, R. (2022). An optimized PI controller-based SEPIC converter for microgrid-interactive hybrid renewable power sources. *Wireless Communications and Mobile Computing*, 2022, 1–10.

Rani, S., Arya, V., and Kataria, A. (2022b). Dynamic pricing-based e-commerce model for the produce of organic farming in India: A research roadmap with main advertence to vegetables. In *Proceedings of Data Analytics and Management* (pp. 327–336). Springer, Singapore.

Rani, S., and Gupta, O. P. (2017). CLUS_GPU-BLASTP: Accelerated protein sequence alignment using GPU-enabled cluster. *The Journal of Supercomputing*, 73, 4580–4595.

Rani, S., Kataria, A., and Chauhan, M. (2022a). Fog computing in industry 4.0: Applications and challenges—A research roadmap. *Energy Conservation Solutions for Fog-Edge Computing Paradigms*, 1, 173–190.

Rani, S., and Kaur, S. (2012). Cluster analysis method for multiple sequence alignment. *International Journal of Computer Applications*, 43, 19–25.

Rani, S., and Kumar, R. (2022). Bibliometric review of actuators: Key automation technology in a smart city framework. *Materials Today: Proceedings*, 60, 1800–1807.

Sheth, A. (2013) Transforming big data into smart data deriving value via harnessing volume, variety and velocity using semantics and semantic web. In Keynote at the *21st Italian Symposium on Advanced Database Systems*.

Sheth, A. (2014). Transforming big data into smart data deriving value via harnessing volume, variety, and velocity using semantic techniques and technologies. In *IEEE 30th International Conference on Data Engineering (ICDE)* (pp. 2–2). IEEE.

Sheth, A. (2016). Internet of things to smart iot through semantic, cognitive, and perceptual computing. *IEEE Intelligent Systems*, 32, 108–112.

Singh, A. P., Aggarwal, M., Singh, H., and Bhambri, P. (2021a). Sketching of EV network: A complete roadmap. In *Sustainable Development Through Engineering Innovations: Select Proceedings of SDEI 2020* (pp. 431–442). Springer, Singapore.

Singh, M., Bhambri, P., Singh, I., Jain, A., and Kaur, E. K. (2021b). Data mining classifier for predicting diabetics. *Annals of the Romanian Society for Cell Biology*, 2021, 6702–6712.

Singh, P., Gupta, O. P., and Saini, S. (2017). A brief research study of wireless sensor network. *Advances in Computational Sciences and Technology*, 10, 733–739.

5

Cloud-Based Remote Sensing: Developments and Challenges—Research Point of View

G. Boopathi Raja

CONTENTS

5.1 Introduction

The concept of remote sensing is nothing but the collection of data regarding things or wonder without arriving at the object and, along these lines, instead of on-the-spot observation, especially the Earth. Remote sensing is otherwise known as faraway recognition. The utility of services provided by remote sensing is found in several fields, such as geology, land reviewing, and all other earth science disciplines. For example, it provides services to hydrology, condition, meteorology, oceanography, glaciology, and topography. Also, it is used in areas such as the military, information, business, and monetary, orchestrating, and magnanimous applications (https://www.nrcan.gc.ca/).

DOI: 10.1201/9781003298335-5

In the present scenario, the word *remote sensing* corresponds to only the use of satellite- or plane-based sensor progressions to capture and portray forests on Earth. It consolidates the surface and the air and oceans, considering the spread finished paperwork (for instance, electromagnetic radiation; Tempfli, 200). It may be part of the "dynamic," far away from identifying (when a sign is delivered by a satellite or plane to the thing and its appearance is perceived by the sensor), and "idle" removed distinguishing (when the impression of light is recognized by the sensor).

Remote sensing is a way to identify and evaluate existing domain credits by examining their radiant displays in a dignified manner, usually from satellite or aircraft. High-resolution cameras collect distant images, helping professionals understand things about the world (Wang et al., 2014; Singh et al., 2017). The role of artificial intelligence (AI) and the Internet of Things (IOT) plays a major role in remote sensing (Gupta and Rani, 2013; Raja, 2021).

A few models include the following:

- Satellite and aircraft cameras capture images of large regions across the globe, allowing us to see beyond the surface.
- Sonar systems on ships can be used to create sea-level images without reliance on the sea.
- Satellite cameras can be used to take pictures of sea temperature changes.

Some specific occupations of remotely recognized photos of the Earth include the following:

- Extreme forest fires can be seen in the atmosphere, allowing authorities to monitor a much larger area than in the first phase (Manikiam, 2003).
- Cloud tracking can help predict the atmosphere or update volcanic launches and detect dust storms.
- Tracking of urban development and changes in farms or forests over a critical period or decades.
- Discovery and arranging of the unpleasant geography of the ocean bottom (e.g., tremendous mountain ranges, significant gorges, and the "alluring striping" on the ocean depths; Boopathi Raja, 2021).

The overview of this work follows: Section 5.1 provided an introduction to remote sensing. Section 5.2 discusses the motivation of the study as well as the definition of remote sensing. Section 5.3 describes the pathway of remote sensing, and Section 5.4 explains the working principle of remote sensing with a simple illustration. The classification of remote sensing is described in Section 5.5, and the concept of cloud-based remote sensing is outlined in Section 5.6. Section 5.7 explains the various challenges faced by remote sensing.

5.2 Motivation

5.2.1 Definition

Remote sensing refers to the acquisition of data about any items or areas by utilizing electromagnetic (EM) radiation. This is done without any direct contact with an object or region.

It records the reflected or transmitted EM waves from the Earth. The total amount of radiated energy emitted by an object is known as brilliance. Both the characteristics of the target or object and the radiation that strikes the target may affect the performance of remote sensing (https://www.wamis.org).

However, the normal human eye of a healthy adult is limited to a narrow range of the EM spectrum. For example, it ranges approximately from the wavelength of 400–700 nm. For remote access (remote sensing), different types of metals and gadgets are utilized in the design (Bhambri and Kaur, 2014). The EM radiation beyond this range, especially in the near-infrared (NIR) range, the midpoint of infrared (IR) waves, warm IR, and microwaves, are visible to normal human eyes (Davis and Marshak, 2002). Remote discovery currently performs an excellent role in the broad field of natural sciences, for example, geography, geography, zoology, agriculture, ranger services, botany, meteorology, oceanography, and architecture (Van Westen, 2000; Eguchi et al., 2008; Rani and Gupta, 2017).

Remote sensing is viewed as an essential method for procuring spatial information. The interaction of EM waves with the environment and the object can be measured by this remote-sensing technique. The EM radiation obtained from the outer surface of the Earth describes not only the information from the sensory medium and the target but also the intensity, frequency, classification, direction, and duration of the radiation. This estimation can provide statistical data on materials and techniques about geological features (Zhu et al., 2017; Arunachalam et al., 2021).

Remote sensing is also known as far-off sensing. It has helped researchers expand their understanding of the behavior of the Earth under different circumstances (Bhambri and Gupta, 2012). Remote observations have helped researchers find the magnitude of the ozone layer in the climate, detect natural ozone differences in the north and south hemispheres, and know the effects of ozone depletion. Remote sensing is assuming an essential part in the endeavors to comprehend the unpredictable elements of sea course (Steven, 2004; Rani et al., 2022).

The concept of remote sensing is utilized in precision farming. In this capacity, it follows crop cultivation and distinguishes water or supplement shortfalls. Far-off sensing is utilized to gather data essential for supporting woodlands and preserve nature (Rani and Kaur, 2012; Kaur et al., 2013).

5.3 History of Remote Sensing

The notable achievements and journey of remote sensing are shown in Table 5.1 (Steven, 2004).

5.4 Remote Sensing–Working Principle

5.4.1 Concepts of Remote Sensing

Sometimes, the concept of remote sensing was referred to as far-off detection, Earth observation, or Earth perception. The term refers to an overall perspective of the instruments, strategies, and techniques to sense, track, or monitor the land or water surface, as a rule by

TABLE 5.1

Road Map of Remote Sensing (modified from Campbell, 1996)

Year	Notable Milestone
1800	Sir W. Herschel discovered infrared rays.
1839	Photography practices were initiated.
1847	J.B.L. Foucault describes the infrared spectrum.
1859	The images were taken from balloons.
1873	J.C. Maxwell proposed the theory of electromagnetic (EM) spectrum.
1909	Images of the Earth surfaces were obtained from airplanes.
1916	Aerial Reconnaissance was introduced in the First World War.
1935	Germany introduced the radar technique.
1940	Nonvisible part of EM spectrum was used in the Second World War.
1950	Research and development in the military field expands.
1959	Explorer-6 has captured the first earth photography taken from the space.
1960	The TIROS meteorological satellite was introduced the first time.
1970	Observations of Earth from space were made through Skylab remote sensing.
1971	ERTS-1 (Landsat-1) was launched. The multimedia messaging service (MSS) sensor was included in it.
1972	The digital image processing field underwent rapid development.
1973	The first satellite-based navigation system named GPS was introduced by the United States.
1978	The Seasat satellite was launched.
1982	Landsat-4 was launched successfully. Advanced Landsat sensors were included.
1982	GLONASS was launched successfully by the Soviet Union for global navigation services.
1986	The first French commercial satellite SPOT was launched.
1986	The hyperspectral sensors were developed.
1990	High-resolution spaceborne systems were introduced. The first commercial development was included in the field of distant sensing.
1991	ERS1 was considered as the first European remote-sensing satellite. An active radar was included in this project and launched successfully.
1998	One-goal satellite missions were started at a cheaper rate.
1999	The satellite EOS-TERRA was launched.
1999	The very high spatial resolution sensor system IKONOS was launched.
2001	A new ETM+ sensor was launched along with the Landsat-7 satellite.
2001	The QuickBird was launched with VHSRSS. It stands for very high spatial resolution sensor system.
2002	The ESA's Envisat was introduced with 10 advanced payloads.
2008	GeoEye was launched.
2008	Chandrayan 1 was successfully launched by India.
2009	WorldView-2 was introduced by DigitalGlobe.
2013	Landsat-8 was launched by NASA/USGS.
2013	Region-based navigation system IRNSS was introduced by India.
2013	Mars Orbit Mission Mangalyaan was launched by India.
2015	Sentinel-1 was introduced by ESA.
2016	Sentinel-2 was started by ESA.
2016	Sentinel-3 was launched by ESA.

the arrangement of a picture in a position, fixed or versatile, at a specific separation far off from that surface (Chopra et al., 2011; Rani and Kumar, 2022). In remote sensing, the EM radiation originates from an object; if there should arise an occurrence of Earth perception, this item is the world's surface. It is estimated and converted into data about the item or measures identified with the item. In the previous estimation stage, the accompanying segments are applicable:

- The source that provides EM radiance
- Atmospheric path
- Communication with object
- Capturing the radiation by a sensing element

The remote sensing setup comprising these modules are described in Figure 5.1.

The subsequent stage may be described to include the accompanying components:

- Transferring, gathering, and preprocessing of the stored radiance
- Interaction, as well as the examination, of the far-off sensing information
- Advances in the development of the desired framework (Steven, 2004; Kaur et al., 2015)

5.4.2 Sensors

The sensors are nothing but devices or instruments that are capable of measuring or capturing radiation in the form of EM waves (Steven, 2004; Gupta and Rani, 2010):

This may be categorized into two types:

a. Passive sensors
b. Active sensors

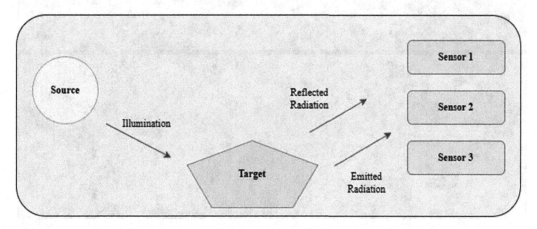

FIGURE 5.1
Remote sensing system.

Figure 5.2 shows the remote sensing in forest services. The images can be captured by SPOT 6 satellite under the Aerial Photography Vegetation index and in true color and be native and pan-sharpened (https://www.gps.gov/cgsic/meetings/2020/hinkley-1.pdf).

a. **Passive sensors**

Passive sensors depend on radiation from other sources. These sensors are highly sensitive to radiation from a natural source. It is generally reflected sunlight or the vitality discharged by a natural object.

Mostly it handles radiation from the sun to illuminate the surface of the earth. Also, it detects the reflected waves from the region of the earth. Typically, it records the EM spectrum in both visible and IR waves. It senses visible light in the range of about 420–740-nm wavelength and NIR light in the range of about 750–950 nm.

The best example for a conventional or traditional case of a passive sensor is a camera. The dispersion of radiation from an object is recorded by the passive sensors on a photographic film (Kaur and Bhambri, 2015; Rani and Gupta, 2016). There are different models available in practice. Some of them are the thermal scanner, microwave radiometer, and multispectral scanner. In this setup, both objects and sensors are passive (Steven, 2004; Gupta et al., 2011). The acquiring images in middle-IR (MIR) waves is done by a few frameworks, including SPOT 5, in the range of 1580–1750 nm. The sensed information of the passive sensor has to be converted into an electrical parameter, such as voltage or power. It primarily depends on the physical temperature, surface roughness, composition, and other geographical features of the Earth. Examples of such types of sensors in this category include the Pleiades, GeoEye, EROS, SPOT, Landsat, and WorldView satellites (Zhu et al., 2017).

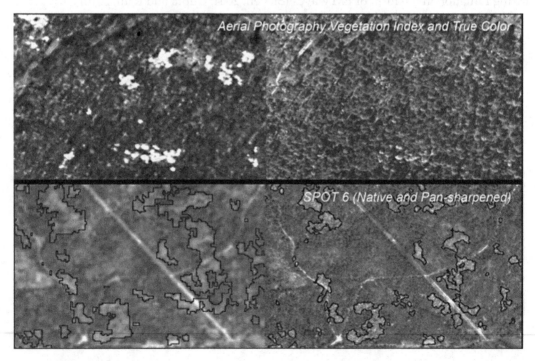

FIGURE 5.2
Images provided by USDA Forest Service, remote-sensing applications center, http://fsweb.rsac.fs.fed.us.

b. Active Sensors

Active sensors have an in-built source of electromagnetic radiation. Almost all the objects are passive. RADAR and LIDAR are the major categories that fall under the case of active sensors. The word RADAR stands for RAdio Detection And Ranging, and LIDAR stands for Light Detection And Ranging (Albinet and Borderies, 2012; Hale, 2016). Specific absorption rate (SAR) utilizes microwaves to enlighten a target on the Earth's surface. It also estimates the traveling period of the transmitted waves reflected back from the targets on the Earth's surface. It must be placed on a moving stage, for example, spaceborne and airborne stages (Zhu et al., 2017; Rani et al., 2022).

Based on the frequency bands, sensors are classified as

- single frequency, including X-band, L-band, or C-band, and
- multiple frequencies, which are the combination of two or more frequency bands.

Based on the polarization modes, sensors are classified into

- single polarization, which consists of VV, HH, or HV, and
- multiple polarizations, which are nothing but the integration of two or more polarization modes (Zhu et al., 2017; Banerjee et al., 2022).

The responses obtained by the sensor can be recorded only in analog form. The airborne images are a specific model, or radiation may be stored in a binary image format (i.e., in a digital format). The set of signals are recorded in CD-ROM, magnetic device, or DVD (Bhambri and Gupta, 2013; Kumar et al., 2022). The visualized images or pictures might be obtained from computerized information of imaging sensors. Before preceding the operation, it is advised to test the fit to demonstrate which features permit the perception and acknowledgment of an item.

The five fundamental classes can sum up the many item attributes (Steven, 2004; Rani et al., 2021):

1. *Size and shape of the object or item*: The most significant reason for any sensor is the geometric or spatial resolution. Normally, in the case of landscape measurements, the pixel size is utilized as an important parameter.

2. The dynamic range and the radiometric resolution, reflective as well as emissive properties of the object are significant for all types of sensing element. This is characterized as the number of digital levels wherein the recorded reflection and emission should be monitored.

3. *Characteristics of the spectrum*: These traits include such as frequency, wavelength, and color of the object or an item; the spectral resolution, for example; and the bandwidth are significant factors for any type of sensor.

4. *Impact of polarization of the target or item*: The determination of polarization is significant for the sensing element, that is, (HH) horizontally polarized transmission and gathering, (VV) vertical polarization, and (HV) or (VH) cross-polarization. It may be applicable, especially to a microwave-based application.

5. *Temporal impacts of the object or item*: It is an important parameter to measure the changes concerning time or area. The temporal resolution is nothing but a potential period among the progressive distant detecting overviews of a similar locale that is significant for remote sensing.

Remote sensing is the utilization of reflected and emitted radiation to determine and analyze the physical or geographical properties of inaccessible items and their environmental factors (Wardlow et al., 2012; Bello and Aina, 2014; Roopa, 2014). Far-off detection, or remote sensing, also incorporates the more seasoned studies of photography, photograph grammetry, and airborne geophysical reviewing just with up-to-date procedures for the different bands of the EM range (Singh et al., 2013; Sudevan et al., 2021).

The plan and utilization of far-off detection frameworks ought to be gone through before with numerous contemplations that rely on explicit applications (Singh et al., 2020; Arya et al., 2022).

5.5 Classification of Remote Sensing

5.5.1 Types of Remote Sensing

Based on the sensors used, the remote-sensing area is categorized into two major classes. They are active remote sensing and passive remote sensing. Dynamic or active frameworks have their own source of radiation. Radar is a suitable example of active remote sensing. However, the passive frameworks rely on an external source of radiation. The sun or self-discharge for remote-sensing acts as a passive type of remote sensing (https://www.wamis.org).

5.5.2 Passive Microwave Remote Sensing

Passive microwave remote sensing includes all-climate work abilities, but atmospheric media have various impacts on satellite microwave brilliance temperature under various meteorological conditions and situations. Atmospheric media, for example, water fume and cloud fluid water, impacted the land surface parameters inversion utilizing inactive (passive) microwave satellite information. Precisely ascertaining environmental data in satellite brightness temperature and remedying brightness temperature are the fundamental ways to improve the surface parameters inversion accuracy (https://www.remote-sensing-solutions.com).

The environment media, which can impact the satellite microwave signals, are principally dry air (oxygen, nitrogen) and water fume under clear sky conditions, and most cloudy fluid water content under mists secured zone (Lijuan Shi et al., 2015; Chauhan and Rani, 2021).

5.5.3 Satellite Remote Sensing

Satellite remote sensing is one of the well-established techniques in the field of far-off detection. It is composed of a few or more sensing instruments that are included along with a satellite. This framework consists of only one satellite or a group of satellites as a satellite constellation for gathering data about an object or the surface of the earth. This is achieved without making any physical contact directly with that target or object. This is contrasted with an airborne and terrestrial platform; spaceborne stages are the steadiest carrier.

The satellites were planned to launch based on their orbital parameters such as latitude, longitude, elevation, transit time, geometry, and all other parameters. Three different categories of satellite orbits are preferred in remote-sensing techniques, namely, sun-synchronous, geostationary, and equatorial orbits.

The high inclination angles were maintained in the sun-synchronous satellites. These types of orbits are preferred so that the satellite consistently ignores the equator at a similar sun local time. Similarly, such types of satellites keep up a uniform relative position with the sun for entire orbits. Most of the remote-sensing satellites are planned to launch to sun-synchronous orbits. The important reason is to guarantee the sun illumination conditions repeatedly during explicit seasons.

A geostationary satellite has a time equivalent to that of Earth so that it consistently remains over a similar area on Earth. Telecommunication, broadcasting, and weather forecasting satellites frequently utilize geostationary orbits, with a considerable lot of them situated over the equator. A satellite revolves around the planet at a low inclination in the case of equatorial orbit, that is, the edge between the orbital plane and the tropical plane.

The sensor and orbital features decide the frequency of the satellite sensor at which it can get information on the entire planet. Most of the satellites provide the entire coverage of the Earth; it is done by two times per day to once every 16 days. Another important orbital parameter is height. The space transport has a low orbital height of 300 km, although other regular distant detection or remote-sensing satellites normally keep up higher orbits going from 600 to 1000 km (Zhu et al., 2017; Bhambri et al., 2022). The image obtained for weather forecasting of India was utilized by the Department of Meteorology, Ministry of Earth Sciences under the Government of India (https://mausam.imd.gov.in/imd_latest/contents/satellite.php).

5.6 Cloud-Based Remote Sensing

The operating principle involved in Cloud-based remote sensing is shown in Figure 5.3. It comprises a light source, a sensor, cloud storage, a processor, and a storage device.

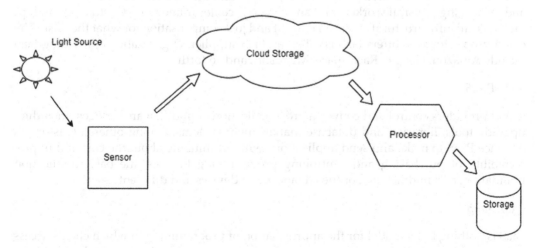

FIGURE 5.3
Cloud-based remote sensing.

5.6.1 Cloud Computing

Cloud computing has risen as an intriguing issue among information technology (IT) ventures, academics, and individual clients because of its capacity to offer adaptable unique IT foundations, QoS-ensured computing, and configurable software or programming services (Dong et al., 2011; Lin et al., 2013; Yan et al., 2017).

As per the statement of the National Institute of Standards and Technology (NIST), cloud computing is viewed as a framework for empowering pervasive, convenient, on-request network access to a common pool of configurable computing resources, for example, networks, workers, stockpiling, applications, and administrations that should be immediately provisioned and delivered with insignificant management exertion or specialist organization cooperation.

The five fundamental qualities of cloud computing are broad network access, fast versatility, asset pooling, on-request self-administration, and estimated administration. Based on the statement of the NIST, there are three different service models and four deployment models present in cloud computing (Gaolisu et al., 2009; SavasOzkan, 2009; Zou et al., 2017).

5.6.2 Cloud Service Models

Cloud computing utilizes a service-driven model. The cloud service models are categorized into three major categories:

- Infrastructure as a service (IaaS)
- Platform as a service (PaaS)
- Software as a service (SaaS)

(1) *IaaS*

IaaS receives virtualization techniques to provide a customer's on-request provisioning of infrastructural assets, for example, networks, stockpiles, virtual workers, and so on. IaaS assists customers with staying away from the cost and multifaceted nature of purchasing and overseeing physical workers and another data center framework. Customers can rapidly scale all infrastructural assets on request and just compensation for what they use. The cloud proprietor who offers IaaS is called an IaaS supplier. Organizations providing IaaS include Amazon, Google, Rack space, Microsoft, and so forth.

(2) *PaaS*

Cloud providers control and convey a broad collection of middleware services (including upgrade tools, libraries, and database management systems, among others). Customers embrace PaaS to make and send applications without thinking about the cost and unpredictability of purchasing and controlling programming licenses, the basic application foundation, and middleware, or the advancement devices and different assets.

(3) *SaaS*

SaaS is nothing but a model for the appropriation of programming in which clients access programming over the Internet on a pay-only-as-costs-arise premise. Regularly, customers access programming utilizing a thin client through an Internet browser.

5.6.3 Cloud Deployment Models

Cloud deployment refers to a cloud that is intended to offer explicit types of assistance depending on the requests of clients. A deployment model may hold onto enhanced boundaries, for example, storage size, availability and ownership, and so forth (Wang et al., 2020; Rani et al., 2021).

Four normal cloud organization models contrast altogether:

- Public clouds
- Private clouds
- Community clouds
- Hybrid Clouds

(1) *Public Cloud*

The public cloud corresponds to the cloud that the service providers provide their resources as services to the public or a large enterprise group. In order to guarantee the nature of cloud services, service-level agreements are provided to specify the number of various prerequisites between a cloud services provider and a client. However, public clouds lack fine-grained authority over information among the communication network and privacy settings.

(2) *Private Cloud*

Private clouds are intended for use based on the selection by a specific establishment, association, or undertaking. On comparing with the public cloud, private cloud offers the furthest extent of control over execution, reliability, and considerable security for services (storage, applications, other resources) provided by service providers.

(3) *Community Cloud*

Community clouds are assembled and worked explicitly for a particular group that has comparable cloud prerequisites (security, consistency, purview, and so forth).

(4) *Hybrid Cloud*

A hybrid cloud is nothing but the integration of at least two clouds to provide the benefits of multi-deployment models. It may be public, private, or community. These hybrid clouds also provide more adaptability than both public and private clouds.

5.6.4 Cloud Service Providers

Cloud-assisted remote sensing allows for distributed sensory data processing, data sharing, and global resources, real-time data remote sensing and connectivity, dynamic resource provisioning and scaling, and pricing models for paying as you go (Ghaffar and Vu, 2015).

Smart cloud infrastructure is a paradigm for allowing easy and on-demand network access to a common pool of configurable computing services that can be easily provisioned and released with minimal maintenance effort or interaction between service providers.

Amazon, Microsoft, and CloudSigma are the most frequently deployed cloud services. We considered flexibility, scalability, management, and pricing depending on the limiting factors that the satellite image-processing mission demands:

TABLE 5.2

Comparison of Features Provided by Cloud Service Providers

Parameter/Service Provider	OS Flexibility	Monitoring Accessories	Graphics Processing Unit	High-Performance Computing
CloudSigma	Yes	No	No	Yes
Microsoft	Yes	Yes	No	Yes
Amazon	Yes	Yes	Yes	Yes

- Flexibility ensures the hardware infrastructure is adaptable.
- Scalability explains how the program can leverage the available computational power and continue to work well.
- Management looks at the availability of cloud resources management dashboards and control panels.
- Pricing covers the expense of designing and operating the service on the top of the cloud platform.

The comparison of the world's top three cloud services providers—Cloudsigma, Microsoft, and Amazon—is shown in Table 5.2. Among these, in terms of graphics processing unit support, high-performance computing service, OS versatility, and tracking accessories, Amazon offered the greater connectivity.

The other leading cloud-service providers include Google, Alibaba Cloud, Oracle, IBM, and Tencent Cloud, among others.

5.7 Challenges Faced by Remote Sensing

Over the past decade, the remote-sensing network has made gigantic steps in advancing remote sensing. However, a few difficulties need to be discussed to more fully coordinate the remote-sensing data into continuous observing and follow the energy set up by the innovative instruments and tools that have recently developed. Among these, a few of the key difficulties in establishing remote sensing as credible, and valuable, the information source is highlighted next (Wardlow et al., 2012).

a. *Engagement of the User Community*

Dynamic commitment and communication between the remote-sensing network and the experts throughout the development of a new technique are significant for the fruitful incorporation of satellite observation items into the expected item. There is a requirement for a more grounded linkage between remote-sensing researchers and end clients to more readily characterize the information/data prerequisites for any application.

b. *Accuracy Assessment*

Based on the spatiotemporal complexity and varying sectoral definitions, the accuracy assessment of information received in remote sensing is more complicated. The "convergence of evidence" technique that collectively analyzes the discoveries from a few evaluation techniques is expected to increase a more complete viewpoint of the accuracy and utility of a particular far-off detection device or remote-sensing tool. The considerable work in the area of the zone of precision evaluation is as yet required to all the more completely understand the commitment of distant detecting for this application.

c. *Spatial Resolution and Scale*

Higher spatial goal data are, as a rule, progressively requested in endeavors to comprehend and address local-scale impacts on the ground.

d. *Long-Term Data Continuity*

Long-haul, or long-term, sustained information records are fundamental for observing to give a meaningful historical context. Likewise, long-term data continuity is a challenge given the budgetary limitations of many space offices and different associations liable for supporting the assortment of satellite-based Earth observations.

5.8 Conclusion and Future Scope

The innovation in remote sensing started with balloon photography, continued with aerial photography, and was developed with several advanced techniques, including satellite imaging under multi-spectrum. The features of radiation by the interaction of both land surface and climate in several locales of EM range are useful for distinguishing and portraying the Earth and environmental highlights.

The present trend-setting innovations in remote sensing or Earth distant-detection frameworks raise a few issues, remembering the part of the government for distinguishing and advancement in research and development for remote-sensing techniques to analyze the surface of the Earth. The way of finding a harmony between the dangers and likely advantages of specialized advancement is a specific issue in satellite-based far-off detection frameworks because these frameworks are portrayed by long lead times and significant expenses. The dangers in building up another sensor framework have two parts: the specialized development of segment innovations (e.g., the identifier framework), and the plan development. A specific plan that has not been utilized before might be a moderately dangerous endeavor for an operational program, regardless of whether it depends on demonstrated innovation.

References

Albinet, C., and Borderies, P. (2012). Radar and optical modelling of forest remote sensing. *IEEE Conference, IGARSS* (pp. 7181–7184).

Arunachalam, P., Janakiraman, N., Sivaraman, A. K., Balasundaram, A., Vincent, R., Rani, S., ... Rajesh, M. (2021). Synovial sarcoma classification technique using support vector machine and structure features. *Intelligent Automation and Soft Computing*, 32(2), 1241–1259.

Arya, V., Rani, S., and Choudhary, N. (2022). Enhanced bio-inspired trust and reputation model for wireless sensor networks. In *Proceedings of Second Doctoral Symposium on Computational Intelligence* (pp. 569–579). Springer, Singapore.

Banerjee, K., Bali, V., Nawaz, N., Bali, S., Mathur, S., Mishra, R. K., and Rani, S. (2022). A machine-learning approach for prediction of water contamination using latitude, longitude, and elevation. *Water, 14*(5), 728.

Bello, O. M., and Aina, Y. A. (2014). Satellite remote sensing as a tool in disaster management and sustainable development: Towards a synergistic approach. *Procedia – Social and Behavioral Sciences, 120*, 365–373. https://doi.org/10.1016/j.sbspro.2014.02.114.

Bhambri, P., Aggarwal, M., Singh, H., Singh, A. P., and Rani, S. (2022). Uprising of EVs: Charging the future with demystified analytics and sustainable development. In *Decision Analytics for Sustainable Development in Smart Society 5.0* (pp. 37–53). Springer, Singapore.

Bhambri, P., and Gupta, O. P. (2012). Development of phylogenetic tree based on Kimura's method. In *2012 2nd IEEE International Conference on Parallel, Distributed and Grid Computing* (pp. 721–723). IEEE.

Bhambri, P., and Gupta, O. P. (2013). Design of distributed prefetching protocol in push-to-peer video-on-demand system. *International Journal of Research in Advent Technology (IJRAT), 1*(3), 95–103.

Bhambri, P., and Kaur, P. (2014). A novel approach of zero watermarking for text documents. *International Journal of Ethics in Engineering and Management Education (IJEEE), 1*(1), 34–38.

Boopathi Raja, G. (2021). *Impact of IIOT in Future Industries Opportunities and Challenges, Internet of Things*. CRC Press, USA.

Chauhan, M., and Rani, S. (2021). Covid-19: A revolution in the field of education in India. In *Learning How to Learn Using Multimedia* (pp. 23–42). Springer, Singapore.

Chopra, S., Bhambri, P., and Singh, B. (2011). Segmentation of the mammogram images to find breast boundaries 1. *International Journal of Computer Science and Technology, 22*(1), 164–167.

Davis, A. B., and Marshak, A. (2002). Optical remote sensing of dense isolated clouds with high-resolution satellite- and ground-based imagers. In *IEEE International Geoscience and Remote Sensing Symposium* (pp. 2817–2819). Penguin.

Dong, J., Xue, Y., Chen, Z., Xu, H., and Li, Y. (2011). Analysis of remote sensing quantitative inversion in cloud computing. In *IEEE International Geoscience and Remote Sensing Symposium, IGARSS* (pp. 4348–4351). IEEE.

Eguchi, R. T., Huyck, C. K., Ghosh, S., and Adams, B. J. (2008). The application of remote sensing technologies for disaster management. *The 14th World Conference on Earthquake Engineering*, October 12–17, Beijing, China.

Gaolisu, X. X., Liu, Q., and Zhou, B. (2009). Remote Sensing of Cloud Cover in the High Altitude region from MTSAT-1R data during the HEI'HE experiment. In *2009 IEEE International Geoscience and Remote Sensing Symposium IEEE, IGARSS* (pp. III-623–III-626). IEEE.

Ghaffar, M. A. A., and Vu, T. T. (2015). Cloud computing providers for satellite image processing service: A comparative study. In *International Conference on Space Science and Communication (IconSpace)* (pp. 61–64). Langkawi, Malaysia. https://doi.org/10.1109/IconSpace.2015.7283781.

Gupta, O., Rani, S., and Pant, D. C. (2011). Impact of parallel computing on bioinformatics algorithms. In *Proceedings 5th IEEE International Conference on Advanced Computing and Communication Technologies* (pp. 206–209). IEEE.

Gupta, O. P., and Rani, S. (2010). Bioinformatics applications and tools: An overview. *CiiT-International Journal of Biometrics and Bioinformatics, 3*(3), 107–110.

Gupta, O. P., and Rani, S. (2013). Accelerating molecular sequence analysis using distributed computing environment. *International Journal of Scientific and Engineering Research–IJSER, 4*(10), 262–265.

Hale, R. (2016). Multi-channel ultra-wideband radar sounder and imager. In *IEEE International Geoscience and Remote Sensing Symposium, IGARSS* (pp. 2112–2115). IEEE.

Indian Meteorological Department Database. https://mausam.imd.gov.in/imd_latest/contents/satellite.php

Kaur, G., Kaur, R., and Rani, S. (2015). Cloud computing-a new trend in IT era. *International Journal of Scientific and Technology Management, 1*, 1–6.

Kaur, J., Bhambri, P., and Gupta, O. P. (2013). Distance based phylogenetic trees with bootstrapping. *International Journal of Computer Applications, 47*, 6–10.

Kaur, P., and Bhambri, P. (2015). To design an algorithm for text watermarking. *The Standard International Journals (The SIJ), 3*(5), 62–67.

Kumar, R., Rani, S., and Awadh, M. A. (2022). Exploring the application sphere of the internet of things in Industry 4.0: A review, bibliometric and content analysis. *Sensors, 22*(11), 4276.

Lijuan Shi, Y. Q., Shi, J., and Zhao, S. (2015). Atmospheric influences analysis in passive microwave remote sensing. In *IEEE International Geoscience and Remote Sensing Symposium, IGARSS* (pp. 2334–2337). IEEE.

Lin, F. C., Chung, L.-K., Ku, W.-Y., Chu, L.-R., and Tien-Yin, C. (2013). The framework of cloud computing platform for massive remote sensing images. In *27th International Conference on Advanced Information Networking and Applications* (pp. 621–628). IEEE Publications.

Manikiam, B. (2003). Remote sensing applications in disaster management. *Mausam, 54*(1), 173–182. https://doi.org/10.54302/mausam.v54i1.1501.

Natural Resources Canada. *Fundamentals of Remote Sensing. A Canada Center for Remote Sensing Remote Sensing Tutorial (E-book).* https://www.nrcan.gc.ca/

Ozkan, S., Efendioglu, M., and Demirpolat, C. (2018). Cloud detection from RGB color remote sensing images with deep pyramid networks. In *IEEE International Geoscience and Remote Sensing Symposium, IGARSS* (pp. 6939–6942). IEEE.

Raja, G. B. (2021). Impact of Internet of things, artificial intelligence, and blockchain. In R. Y. W. Kumar, T. Poongodi, and A. L. Imoize (Eds.), *Technology Interface Industry 4.0. Internet of Things, Artificial Intelligence and Blockchain Technology.* Springer. https://doi.org/10.1007/978-3-030-74150-1_8.

Rani, S., Bhambri, P., and Chauhan, M. (2021). A machine learning model for kids' behavior analysis from facial emotions using principal component analysis. In *2021 5th Asian Conference on Artificial Intelligence Technology (ACAIT)* (pp. 522–525). IEEE.

Rani, S., and Gupta, O. P. (2016). Empirical analysis and performance evaluation of various GPU implementations of protein BLAST. *International Journal of Computer Applications, 151*(7), 22–27.

Rani, S., and Gupta, O. P. (2017). CLUS_GPU-BLASTP: Accelerated protein sequence alignment using GPU-enabled cluster. *The Journal of Supercomputing, 73*(10), 4580–4595.

Rani, S., Kataria, A., and Chauhan, M. (2022a). Fog computing in industry 4.0: Applications and challenges—A research roadmap. *Energy Conservation Solutions for Fog-Edge Computing Paradigms, 1*, 173–190.

Rani, S., Kataria, A., Chauhan, M., Rattan, P., Kumar, R., and Sivaraman, A. K. (2022b). Security and privacy challenges in the deployment of cyber-physical systems in smart city applications: State-of-art work. *Materials Today: Proceedings, 62*, 4671–4676.

Rani, S., and Kaur, S. (2012). Cluster analysis method for multiple sequence alignment. *International Journal of Computer Applications, 43*(14), 19–25.

Rani, S., and Kumar, R. (2022). Bibliometric review of actuators: Key automation technology in a smart city framework. *Materials Today: Proceedings, 60*, 1800–1807.

Rani, S., Mishra, R. K., Usman, M., Kataria, A., Kumar, P., Bhambri, P., and Mishra, A. K. (2021). Amalgamation of advanced technologies for sustainable development of smart city environment: A review. *IEEE Access, 9*, 150060–150087.

Remote Sensing: Environment Monitoring. https://www.remote-sensing-solutions.com/

Roopa, V. (2014). Remote sensing and its applications in disaster management like earthquake and Tsunamis. *International Journal of Scientific and Engineering Research, 3*(6), 1710–1715.

Service, F., & National Remote Sensing Program. https://www.gps.gov/cgsic/meetings/2020/hinkley-1.pdf

Singh, M., Bhambri, P., Singh, I., Jain, A., and Kaur, E. K. (2021). Data mining classifier for predicting diabetics. *Annals of the Romanian Society for Cell Biology, 2021*, 6702–6712.

Singh, P., Gupta, O. P., and Saini, S. (2017). A brief research study of wireless sensor network. *Advances in Computational Sciences and Technology, 10*(5), 733–739.

Sinha, V. K., Jeet, D. R., Bhambri, P., and Mahajan, M. (2020). Empowering intrusion detection in Iris recognition system: A review. *Journal of Natural Remedies, 21*(2), 131–153.

Sudevan, S., Barwani, B., Al Maani, E., Rani, S., and Sivaraman, A. K. (2021). Impact of blended learning during Covid-19 in Sultanate of Oman. *Annals of the Romanian Society for Cell Biology, 2021,* 14978–14987.

Tempfli, K., Kerle, N., Huurneman, G. C., and Janssen, L. L. F. (2009). *Principles of Remote Sensing* (4th ed). International Institute for Geo-Information Science and Earth Observation (ITC).

Van Westen, C. 2000 (1609–17). Remote sensing for natural disaster management. *International Archives of Photogrammetry and Remote Sensing, B7,* p. XXXIII.

Wang, Lizhe, Yan, J., and Ma, Y. (2020). *Cloud Computing in Remote Sensing.* Taylor & Francis, CRC Press.

Wang, Zongbo et al. (2014). Wideband imaging radar for cryogenic remote sensing. In *IEEE International Geoscience and Remote Sensing Symposium, IGARSS,* (pp. 4026–4029). IEEE.

Wardlow, B. D., Anderson, M. C., Sheffield, J., Doorn, B. D., Verdin, J. P., Zhan, X., and Rodell, M. (2012). Drought mitigation center faculty. Future opportunities and challenges in remote sensing of drought. *Publications, 103.* http://digitalcommons.unl.edu/droughtfacpub/103

Yan, J., Ma, Y., and Wang, L. (2017). A cloud-based remote sensing data production system. *Future Generation Computer Systems, 86,* 1154–1166.

Zhu, L., JuhaSuomalainen, J. L., JuhaHyyppä, H. K., and Haggren, H. (2017), Chapter 2. A review: Remote sensing sensors. In *Multi-purposeful Application of Geospatial Data* (pp. 19–43). IntechOpen, USA.

Zou, Q., Li, G., and Yu, W. (2017). An integrated disaster rapid cloud service platform using remote sensing data. In *IEEE International Geoscience and Remote Sensing Symposium, IGARSS* (pp. 5221–5224). IEEE.

6

Recent Trends in Machine Learning Techniques, Challenges and Opportunities

S. Kannadhasan, Kanagaraj Venusamy and R. Nagarajan

CONTENTS

6.1 Introduction

Everything you see on Netflix, Amazon, Google, and other sites is based on what you search for. Recommendations from these websites are available on a variety of platforms, devices, and applications. The increased flexibility and mobility features of wireless are motivating a large number of carriers to take a serious step toward the deployment of wireless technology [1]. Our online experiences are vastly improved by the use of automated systems that connect buyers and sellers, and digital material with people that are interested in viewing it. Using Amazon's machine learning (ML) algorithms, it is possible for the company to accurately forecast what you will purchase and when you will make the purchase [2]. Anticipatory shipping is an invention owned by the corporation that allows you to place an order and have your order arrive at the warehouse of your choice. Randomness, constantly changing data, and a variety of other elements are all part of the algorithmic trading process. Machine learning algorithms, however, are able to anticipate all that behavior, and they do it far more quickly than humans can. Based on market conditions during the past three years, we would be able to predict what a certain region's median house price will be in the coming year [3–7]. Feed the model data such as recent market home prices, interest rates, and wage rates. The end result would be the next year's house price forecast. The process by which a model learns to comprehend the world around it. Input data are referred to as "model training." ML relies heavily on the concept of training. In order to understand the potential of ML, it is necessary to look at the ways in which individuals and organizations are already making use of this technology [8, 9]. The following are some examples.

Input from users, such as new terms and syntax, is fed into Google Translates ML algorithms, which continually improve the service. Natural language processing is used by

DOI: 10.1201/9781003298335-6

Siri, Alexa, Cortana, and, most recently, Google Assistant to detect speech and synthesize words they have never heard before. A large number of machine learning applications are in the educational sector. The following are a few worth exploring: analyzing and predicting student achievement and student performance prediction are an excellent use for ML. The ML algorithm can identify students' deficiencies and provide strategies to improve (such as more lectures or reading additional books) by "learning" about each student's test and grade students fairly (computerized adaptive tests can be created with the help of machine learning).The ML-based evaluation offers teachers and students continual feedback on how the student learns, the help they need, and the progress they are making toward their learning goals [10]. Retention rates can also be improved via ML, such as the use of learning analytics. It is possible to aid "at-risk" students by identifying and reaching out to those students and provide aid to educators and institutions. Algorithms based on ML can aid in the classification of students' handwritten evaluation papers [11–15].

Computing on one's own, World Wide Web, or just the Internet. Computing on the go. With computing in the cloud, the primary applications that are a part of the software industry shift at least once every decade. As the domain changes, in the future, more software engineering goals will be set, which will make software companies change their advancement methods to suit these new needs. Artificial intelligence (AI) skills that are based on ML breakthroughs are the next big thing in the software industry. AI encompasses technology for reasoning, problem-solving, planning, and learning, among others. There has been significant interest in the software and services sector for statistical modeling techniques known as machine learning. Bing Search, Cortana virtual assistant, Microsoft Translator, Cognitive Services, and the Azure AI platform are all examples of Microsoft product teams using machine learning to create application suites and platforms such as Microsoft Translator, Microsoft Cognitive Services, Microsoft Translator, and the Azure AI platform. Microsoft has built on its existing AI capabilities while also developing new areas of knowledge across the organization to generate these software solutions.

There is a lot of interest in big data analytics and deep learning in data science. As a result, many public and commercial organizations are amassing enormous amounts of domain-specific information that can be used to solve challenges such as national intelligence, cybersecurity and fraud detection, marketing, and medical informatics. For example, Google and Microsoft evaluate enormous volumes of data in order to make commercial decisions that have an impact on present and future technological developments. Algorithms that use deep learning to extract high-level, complex abstractions from raw data do so via a hierarchical learning process.

Complex abstractions are learned by building on lesser abstractions defined at a previous level in the hierarchy. Deep learning is a strong technique for big data analytics when raw data is unlabeled and uncategorized, because it can analyze and learn from vast volumes of unsupervised data. Some of the hardest problems in big data analytics, such as extracting complex patterns from vast volumes of data, semantic indexing, tagging, rapid information retrieval, and simplifying discriminative tasks are addressed in this work. We also look at several parts of deep learning research that require further investigation to include particular big data analytics concerns, such as streaming data, high-dimensional data, model scalability, and distributed computing. Establishing data sampling criteria, domain adaption modeling, defining criteria for generating usable data abstractions, enhancing semantic indexing, semi-supervised learning, and active learning are some of the topics we pose at the end of the chapter.

6.2 ML Techniques

An investigation into how various Microsoft software teams create apps with customer-focused AI elements is described in this chapter. In order to do this, Microsoft has combined its existing Agile software engineering procedures with AI-specific workflows influenced by its previous experiences developing early AI and data science products. While conducting our research, we spoke with Microsoft employees to learn more about their approaches to dealing with the increasing difficulties of developing AI-specific software on both a daily basis and the larger, more critical issues associated with building out a large-scale AI infrastructure and application.

Many of the difficulties raised by newer teams have diminished in importance as the teams mature, but others have remained critical to large-scale AI practice, as evidenced by our observations that teams across the organization have varying levels of AI work experience [16–19]. We have attempted to construct a process maturity meter to help teams identify how far they have progressed in their paths to producing AI apps. For example, we observed three basic differences in designing ML applications and platforms compared to previous application domains. It is important to note that ML relies heavily on data. Data discovery, sourcing, management, and versioning are all fundamentally more difficult tasks and in a way that is distinct from that of writing code. Building models that can be customized and extended requires teams to have both software engineering and extensive expertise of ML, which is virtually always required [20–24]. Third, explicit unit limits among ML elements can be more difficult to maintain than in software engineering modules. Models can be "entangled" in sophisticated ways that affect one another during training and tweaking, even when the software teams building them intended for them to remain independent.

It is common in many real-world situations for a supervised algorithm to be used to learn a family of related functions rather than a single function (Figure 6.1). The diagnostic is expected to have certain commonalities even if it is applied to various places (e.g., Kolkata and London). Hierarchical Bayesian techniques, a type of ML algorithm, postulate

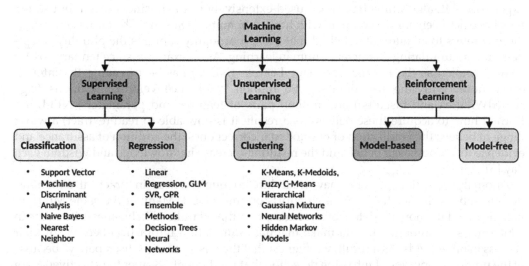

FIGURE 6.1
Techniques of ML.

that the parameters for learning are data from several city hospitals can override irrelevant priors because they share certain similar prior probabilities in both functions, say, for Kolkata and London. The intricacy rises even more as the transfer between functions is multiplied. Multiple ML algorithms have been invented and used in a variety of fields. There is a study path aimed at discovering the probable correlations between the existing ML algorithms and the appropriate cases or scenarios for using a certain method [25–28]. Take a look at naive Bayes and logistic regression as two examples of supervised classification methods. It is possible to establish their equivalence by applying them to specific types of training data (i.e., when the criteria of naive Bayes classifier are fulfilled, and the number of examples of trying to set tends to infinity). There is still much to learn about the conceptual underpinnings of ML algorithms, as well as their convergence characteristics, effectiveness, and limitations as they stand now. An emerging field of border research focuses on learning systems that do not just employ data collected by others in a mechanical way.

Actively acquires information for its own processing and learning through various means. Finding the best way to entirely delegate control of the learning algorithm is the focus of the project. A drug testing system, for example, tries to learn about the drug's success while also monitoring patients for probable negative effects and attempting to minimize them. Successfully implementing data mining without abusing the underlying information is drawing interest from a wide range of academic disciplines. Medical diagnosis routines taught using data from hospitals throughout the world are an example. As a result, this type of application is not widely pursued because of privacy concerns. Data mining and data privacy may seem to be at odds here, but new research shows that they are not mutually exclusive [29, 30]. A shared learning algorithm, rather than a central database, has been offered as a solution to the previously mentioned problem. To ensure patient privacy, the algorithm will only be used in specific circumstances and then passed on to the next facility. Combining statistical analysis of data with the most contemporary cryptography algorithms is a hot study area. It is common for ML jobs to involve training the learner with a specific data set, then storing the learner's results, and using the output instead, whereas, in contrast, humans and other animals continuously adapt and employ their talents and abilities in a synergistic manner, adopting different skills sequentially as they gain experience. ML algorithms have been used extensively in the business sector, but so far, they have not been able to compete with human or animal learning. The term *never-ending learning* refers to an alternate method that more thoroughly captures the plurality, adeptness, and accumulating character of human learning. As an example, since January 2010, a student known as the Ending Language Learner (NELL) has been reading the internet every hour. With the use of about 80 million confidence-weighted opinions (e.g., servedWith(tea and biscuits)) and million pairs of features and parameters, NELL has learned how to acquire these beliefs. As a result, it is now able to read (extract) a wider range of beliefs: the eradication of outmoded incorrect ones, the addition of assurance and evidence to support each belief, and the resulting increase in knowledge and wisdom each day [31–35].

Anomaly detection systems have had limited effectiveness in practical situations, despite substantial academic research efforts on the subject. Many of the same ML technologies used in anomaly detection systems are routinely utilized in business situations in which massive amounts of data make manual examination impractical because of their success in other fields. As a result, we suggest that there is a "success discrepancy" because of the unique properties of intrusion detection that fundamentally alter the effectiveness of ML systems. To help the community better understand the challenges anomaly detection faces while working in network traffic, we outline these modifications in the following sections. Our examples from different fields are mostly for demonstration reasons because many of the traits mentioned have a wide range (e.g., spam detection faces a similarly adversarial environment as intrusion detection does). We want to make it clear that we are not specialists in ML as a network security research team.

Thus, we argue mostly on an intuitive level rather than attempting to express our thoughts in ML formalisms. These intuitive reasons hold water, however, because we have talked to coworkers who use ML on a daily basis. Allowing a system to analyze data and extract knowledge is the goal of ML. It involves more than just acquiring information; rather, it involves putting that information to good use and refining it through practice. Hidden patterns in "training" data must be discovered and exploited as the primary purpose of ML. In order to classify or map new data to previously identified categories, the previously learned patterns are applied to the unknown data. Programming paradigm shifts as a result of this development, whereby programs are created to perform a certain goal. ML develops a program (i.e., model) that is based on the data it analyzes. Recently, ML has reemerged as a popular topic. There was no flexibility in the early ML approaches, which were unable to accommodate any deviations from the training data.

For example, cloud computing provides almost limitless computation and storage resources, while graphics processing units and tensor processing units accelerate training and inference for large datasets. To emphasize, a trained ML model can be used for inference on devices with lower processing power, such as smartphones. Human error still accounts for the vast majority of network failures in spite of these improvements. Faults in the network can lead to financial losses and damage to the reputation of the companies that supply the network service. Building networks that are self-configuring, self-healing, self-optimizing, and self-protecting is of particular interest because of this. Cognitive control in network operations and management necessitates a distinct set of obstacles for ML, even though it is critical. To begin with, no standards are enforced to ensure uniformity between networks, so each one is distinct. For instance, the company network of one company differs greatly from that of another. Therefore, the patterns that have worked in one network may not function in another. A second problem is that the network is always changing, making it difficult to rely on a set of preestablished patterns to keep track of and manage it. Network administration is nearly hard to maintain manually because of the rapid expansion of network applications and the types of apps running on the network.

Following the "AI winter" of the 1980s and 1990s, interest in the use of data-driven AI approaches in a variety of technical domains, such as voice and image analysis and communications has gradually increased. The newfound faith in data-driven approaches is prompted by the results of pattern recognition tools based on ML, as opposed to the logic-based expert systems that dominated previous AI research These tools combine a number of recent algorithmic innovations, such as innovative regularization approaches and adaptive learning rate schedules, with decades-old algorithms, such as backpropagation, the Expectation Maximization (EM) algorithm, and Q-learning. In many technical disciplines, their success is predicated on the unparalleled availability of data and computational power.

While the current wave of promises and successes in ML may fall short, at least for the time being, of the criteria that propelled early AI research learning algorithms have proved effective in a number of critical applications—and more are on the way.

An outline of ML for communication systems is provided in this chapter. However, this is a departure from past reviews in that it concentrates on the situations in which ML is allowed in engineering difficulties and the specific classes of learning algorithms that are acceptable for addressing them. Following an introduction to fundamental technical concepts, the lecture proceeds to a discussion of communication network applications. These applications were selected to demonstrate broad design criteria and techniques rather than to provide a thorough overview of the state of the art and the historical history of improvements in the field.

This section begins by answering the question, "What is machine learning?" and then moves on to a taxonomy of ML techniques before addressing the question, "When should machine learning be used?" Furthermore, as deep learning [12] grows more popular, more training data are required. Feature engineering is one of the most difficult processes in classical ML, where the user must understand the application and contribute features for training models. Deep learning, on one hand, can produce features automatically, saving us the time and effort of feature engineering, which is an important element of data preparation. Deep learning, on the other hand, may need more training data to function effectively [13].

As a result, in the age of big data, there is a real need for accurate and scalable data-gathering methods. This is why we want to do a complete review of the data-gathering literature from a data management point of view. It is possible to get data in one of three ways (Figure 6.2). The first thing to do is look into data acquisition techniques. They can be used to find, add to, or make new sets of data if the primary objective is really to start sharing and searching new datasets. Second, when the datasets are available, different ways can be used to label each individual instance. Finally, instead of labeling new sets of data, it will be more efficient to improve old data or train on top of models that have already been trained, not start from scratch. These three methods are not all the same and can be used together. For example, new data points might be searched and tagged, and old datasets could be improved.

They have been studied for years by people in the data management field, mostly under the names of data science and data analytics. They come from both the machine learning community and the data management community, which both use machine learning a lot.

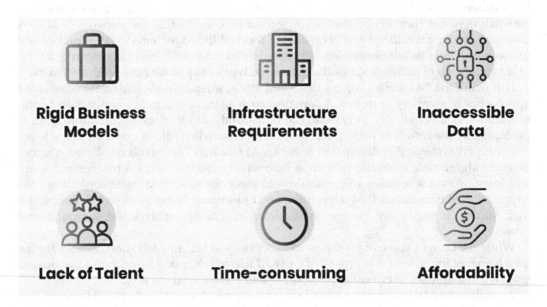

FIGURE 6.2
Business challenges—ML.

Data augmentation may be thought of as a subset of data integration, particularly if we are supplementing current data sets with new ones. We refer readers to several great surveys, since this field is well established. More recently, an intriguing line of ML research reports that many organizations in reality employ relational databases with training data separated into smaller tables. Most ML toolkits, however, assume that a training dataset is a single file and overlook the fact that, owing to normalization, most databases include several tables. The main question is whether connecting the tables and adding more data is good for model training. The Hamlet++ system addresses this issue by defining whether Key–Foreign Key joins are necessary for improving model accuracy for different classifiers (linear, decision trees, artificial neural networks) and recommending decision rules to predict when it is safe to avoid joins and, as a result, significantly reduce total runtime. Hamlet and Hamlet++ are both open source. Joins can usually be left out of a model without affecting its precision, which is a surprise. A primary key, on the surface, tells you everything about the record in the table you are joining. The features added by a join do not give you much more information.

If there are no suitable datasets for training, another alternative is to create them manually or automatically. Crowdsourcing is the conventional approach for manual creation, in which human employees are assigned jobs to collect the essential pieces of data, which are then combined to form the resulting dataset. Automatic approaches, however, may be used to create synthetic datasets. It is worth noting that data production may also be considered data augmentation if there is already data that have to be supplemented.

Crowdsourcing is utilized to address a broad variety of issues, and numerous surveys have been conducted. Amazon Mechanical Turk is one of the first and most prominent systems, where human workers are given tasks (known as HITs) and paid for completing them. Many more crowdsourcing platforms have been built since then, and crowdsourcing research has exploded in the fields of data management, ML, and human–computer interface. Crowdsourcing projects vary from basic ones like picture categorization to more sophisticated ones like collaborative writing that need numerous processes. In this part, we concentrate on crowdsourcing strategies that are specifically designed for data-generating activities. A recent report goes into great detail about the problems of data crowdsourcing. Another study looks at the theoretical underpinnings of data crowdsourcing [4]. According to both studies, crowdsourcing data generating may be separated into two stages: data collection and data preparation (Figure 6.3).

Data collection activities are procedural or declarative, which is one approach to characterize data collection strategies. The task creator creates clear stages and assigns them to employees in a procedural job. One may, for example, create computer software that assigns assignments to employees.

TurKit enables users to develop HIT-containing scripts using a crash-and-return programming approach, which allows a script to be rerun without rerunning expensive routines with side effects. AUTOMAN is a Scala-based domain-specific language that allows crowdsourcing jobs to be called like regular functions. In DOG, a high-level programming language, you can write code that turns into MapReduce jobs for people and computers to do. When a task creator gives high-level data needs, the workers give them the data that meets them. Declarative tasks are the type of tasks that do this. Database users can run a SQL query like "SELECT title, director, genre, rating FROM MOVIES WHERE genre is action." This query will get movie ratings data for a recommendation system. DECO is a simple extension of SQL that makes it possible to make queries on both stored data and data made by the crowd. CrowdDB is a database that talks about how to use crowdsourcing to answer questions that cannot be answered automatically.

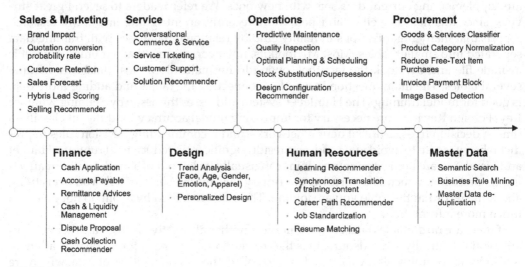

FIGURE 6.3
Opportunities and value chain of ML.

6.3 Conclusion

As a result of recent advancements in machine learning, these techniques may now be applied to a wide range of real-world circumstances, from remarkable to routine. Medical imaging and computer-aided diagnosis, for example, have benefited substantially from the use of ML in healthcare. ML-based technology is frequently employed in our daily lives. Nontrivial activities like query suggestions, spelling correction, web crawling, and page ranking are all handled by ML in search engines. Indeed, as our lives become increasingly automated, ML approaches will play an increasingly essential role in many systems that aid in decision-making, analysis, and automation, such as home automation and self-driving cars. ML's resurgence is not solely due to technological advancements. The success of ML approaches is largely dependent on the quality of the data used. Existing networks, such as the Internet of Things, with billions of connected devices, already contain enormous amounts of data that will only continue to rise in the future. In this way, it stimulates the use of ML that not only finds hidden and unexpected patterns but can also be used to learn and comprehend the processes that generate the data. ML models can be trained and tested on massive amounts of data to recent breakthroughs in computation.

ML is a technique for teaching computers how to handle data more effectively. We may be unable to comprehend the pattern or extract information from the data after examining them. Users use ML in this case. ML has become more popular because there are so many datasets to choose from. ML is used in a wide range of industries, from medicine to the military, to find useful data.

In ML, the goal is to learn from the data that is given. A lot of people have looked into how to make robots learn on their own. A type of ML algorithm that needs help from outside sources is called supervised ML. The testing and training datasets are not mixed with the input dataset at all. People using the training dataset need to figure out what the output variable is going to be or categorize it. All algorithms learn patterns from the training dataset and apply them to the test dataset when they make predictions or classify data, which is why they work so well for this. Decision trees are trees that organize qualities by sorting them according to their values. The decision tree is mostly used for categorization. Nodes and branches make up each tree. Each branch indicates a value that the node may take, and each node represents qualities in a group that needs to be categorized.

To solve this challenge, mathematicians and programmers use a variety of ways.

Semi-supervised learning algorithms combine the benefits of both supervised and unsupervised learning techniques. It may be useful in fields like ML and data mining if there is existing unlabeled data, and acquiring labeled data is a time-consuming procedure. Semi-supervised learning is divided into many groups. The following are a few of them:

1) Generative Models: One of the earliest semi-supervised learning methods, generative models have a structure like $p(x,y) = p(y)p(x|y)$, where $p(x|y)$ is a mixed distribution, such as Gaussian mixture models. The mixed components may be identified within the unlabeled data. To check the mixture distribution, one labeled sample per component is sufficient.

2) Self-Training: A classifier is trained using a part of labeled data in self-training. After that, the classifier is supplied with unlabeled data. In the training set, the unlabeled points and predicted labels are combined together. After then, the operation is performed once again. The term *self-training* refers to the classifier's ability to learn on its own.

3) Transductive Support Vector Machine (TSVM): The TSVM is a support vector machine extension. Both labeled and unlabeled data are considered in TSVM. It is used to label unlabeled data in such a manner that the margin between the labeled and unlabeled data is as small as possible. Using TSVM to find an exact answer is a nondeterministic polynomial–hard problem.

References

[1] Gupta, O. P. (2017). Study and analysis of various bioinformatics applications using protein BLAST: An overview. *Advances in Computational Sciences and Technology, 10*(8), 2587–2601.

[2] Gupta, O., Rani, S., and Pant, D. C. (2011). Impact of parallel computing on bioinformatics algorithms. In *Proceedings 5th IEEE International Conference on Advanced Computing and Communication Technologies* (pp. 206–209). IEEE.

[3] Kothandaraman, D., Manickam, M., Balasundaram, A., Pradeep, D., Arulmurugan, A., Sivaraman, A. K., ... Balakrishna, R. (2022). Decentralized link failure prevention routing (DLFPR) algorithm for efficient internet of things. *Intelligent Automation and Soft Computing, 34*(1), 655–666.

[4] Arunachalam, P., Janakiraman, N., Sivaraman, A. K., Balasundaram, A., Vincent, R., Rani, S., ... Rajesh, M. (2021). Synovial sarcoma classification technique using support vector machine and structure features. *Intelligent Automation & Soft Computing, 32*(2), 1241–1259.

[5] Banerjee, K., Bali, V., Nawaz, N., Bali, S., Mathur, S., Mishra, R. K., and Rani, S. (2022). A machine-learning approach for prediction of water contamination using latitude, longitude, and elevation. *Water, 14*(5), 728.

[6] Rani, S., Bhambri, P., and Gupta, O. P. (2022). Green smart farming techniques and sustainable agriculture: Research roadmap towards organic farming for imperishable agricultural products. In *Handbook of Sustainable Development through Green Engineering and Technology* (pp. 49–67). CRC Press, Singapore.

[7] Rani, S., Mishra, R. K., Usman, M., Kataria, A., Kumar, P., Bhambri, P., and Mishra, A. K. (2021). Amalgamation of advanced technologies for sustainable development of smart city environment: A review. *IEEE Access, 9*, 150060–150087.

[8] Rani, S., Bhambri, P., and Chauhan, M. (2021). A machine learning model for kids' behavior analysis from facial emotions using principal component analysis. In *2021 5th Asian Conference on Artificial Intelligence Technology (ACAIT)* (pp. 522–525). IEEE.

[9] Wang, H. C., Chang, C. Y., and Li, T. Y. (2008). Assessing creative problem-solving with automated text grading. *Computers & Education, 51*(4), 1450–1466.

[10] Watkins, C. (1989). Learning form delayed rewards. *Ph.D. Thesis*, King's College, University of Cambridge.

[11] Bhambri, L. P., Jindal, C., and Bathla, S. (2007). Future wireless technology-ZigBee. In *Proceedings of National Conference on Challenges & Opportunities in Information Technology (COIT)* (pp. 154–156). ACM.

[12] Bhambri, P., and Kaur, P. (2014). A novel approach of zero watermarking for text documents. *International Journal of Ethics in Engineering & Management Education (IJEEE), 1*(1), 34–38.

[13] Harleen, B. (2016). A prediction technique in data mining for diabetes mellitus. *Journal of Management Sciences and Technology, 4*(1), 1–12.

[14] Rani, S., and Kaur, S. (2012). Cluster analysis method for multiple sequence alignment. *International Journal of Computer Applications, 43*(14), 19–25.

[15] Rani, S., and Kumar, R. (2022). Bibliometric review of actuators: Key automation technology in a smart city framework. *Materials Today: Proceedings, 60*(3), 1800–1807.

[16] Abbott, R. G. (2006). Automated expert modeling for automated student evaluation. In *International Conference on Intelligent Tutoring Systems* (pp. 1–10). Springer, Berlin, Heidelberg.

[17] Bhambri, P., Aggarwal, M., Singh, H., Singh, A. P., and Rani, S. (2022). Uprising of EVs: Charging the future with demystified analytics and sustainable development. In *Decision Analytics for Sustainable Development in Smart Society 5.0* (pp. 37–53). Springer, Singapore.

[18] Delen, D. (2010). A comparative analysis of machine learning techniques for student retention management. *Decision Support Systems, 49*(4), 498–506.

[19] Rani, S., Arya, V., and Kataria, A. (2022). Dynamic pricing-based e-commerce model for the produce of organic farming in India: A research roadmap with main advertence to vegetables. In *Proceedings of Data Analytics and Management* (pp. 327–336). Springer, Singapore.

[20] Bhambri, P., and Gupta, O. P. (2012). Development of phylogenetic tree based on Kimura's method. In *2012 2nd IEEE International Conference on Parallel, Distributed and Grid Computing* (pp. 721–723). IEEE.

[21] Gupta, O. P., and Rani, S. (2010). Bioinformatics applications and tools: An overview. *CiiT-International Journal of Biometrics and Bioinformatics, 3*(3), 107–110.

[22] Kaur, G., Kaur, R., and Rani, S. (2015). Cloud computing-a new trend in IT era. *International Journal of Scientificand Technology Management, 1*, 1–6.

[23] Kaur, J., Bhambri, P., and Gupta, O. P. (2013). Distance based phylogenetic trees with bootstrapping. *International Journal of Computer Applications, 47*, 6–10.

[24] Rani, S., Kataria, A., and Chauhan, M. (2022). Fog computing in Industry 4.0: Applications and challenges—A research roadmap. In R. Tiwari, M. Mittal., and L. M. Goyal (Eds.), *Energy Conservation Solutions for Fog-Edge Computing Paradigms* (pp. 173–190). Springer.

[25] Chai, K. E., and Gibson, D. (2015). *Predicting the Risk of Attrition for Undergraduate Students with Time Based Modelling*. International Association for Development of the Information Society.

[26] Goodfellow, I., Bengio, Y., Courville, A., and Bengio, Y. (2016). *DeepLearning*. MIT Press, Cambridge, vol. 1.

[27] Lykourentzou, I., Giannoukos, I., Nikolopoulos, V., Mpardis, G., and Loumos, V. (2009). Dropout prediction in elearning courses through the combination of machine learning techniques. *Computers & Education, 53*(3), 950–965.

[28] Ram, S., Wang, Y., Currim, F., and Currim, S. (2015). *Using Big Data for Predicting Freshmen Retention*. ICIS.

[29] Đambić, G., Krajcar, M., and Bele, D. (2016). Machine learning model for early detection of higher education students that need additional attention in introductory programming courses. *International Journal of Digital Technology & Economy, 1*(1), 1–11

[30] Wu, J. Y., Hsiao, Y. C., and Nian, M. W. (2018). Using supervised machine learning on large-scale online forums to classify course-related Facebook messages in predicting learning achievement within the personal learning environment. *Interactive Learning Environments*. Advanced online publication. doi:10.1080/10494820.2018.1515085.

[31] Dempster, A. P., Laird, N. M., and Rubin, D. B. (1977). Maximum likelihood from incomplete data via the em algorithm. *Journalof the Royal Statistical Society. Series B (Methodological), 39*(1), 1–38.

[32] Hinton, G., Deng, L., Yu, D., Dahl, G. E., Mohamed, A.-R., Jaitly, N., Senior, A., Vanhoucke, V., Nguyen, P., Sainath, T. N., et al. (2012). Deep neural networks for acoustic modeling in speech recognition: The shared views of four research groups. *IEEE Signal Processing Magazine, 29*(6), 82–97. doi:10.1109/MSP.2012.2205597.

[33] Ibnkahla, M. (2000). Applications of neural networks to digital communications–A survey. *Signal Processing, 80*(7), 1185–1215.

[34] Levesque, H. J. (2017). *Common Sense, the Turing Test, and the Questfor Real AI: Reflections on Natural and Artificial Intelligence*. MIT Press.

[35] Rumelhart, D. E., Hinton, G. E., and Williams, R. J. (1985). Learning internal representations by error propagation. California University San Diego, La Jolla Institute for Cognitive Science, *Tech. Rep.*

7

Heart Disease Prediction Using Machine Learning and Big Data

Vandana Rawat, Devesh Pratap Singh, Neelam Singh and Shruti Negi

CONTENTS

7.1 Introduction

Heart disease claims the lives of approximately 17.8 million individuals each year, which includes several diseases that harm or affect your heart. One of the most severe is coronary heart disease (Rani and Gupta, 2017; Gavhane et al., 2018). It is developed when the arteries that carry blood to the heart get blocked with plaque. This makes the arteries narrow and hard. Plaque contains cholesterol and other substance (Sowmya Sundari et al., 2021). Due to this, the supply of blood is reduced, a result of which is the heart receives less oxygen and nutrient (Rahman et al., 2022). In comparison, a congenital heart defect is when a person is born with this heart defect, which may include a hole in the wall between the lower and upper chamber or valves may not open properly or miss. Then there is another heart disease called cardiomyopathy, which has several types as well, such as dilated cardiomyopathy, which weakens the heart by any previous injuries to the heart, such as

DOI: 10.1201/9781003298335-7

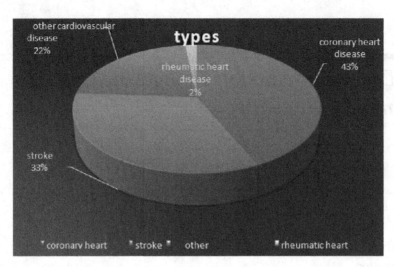

FIGURE 7.1
Types of heart disease (%).

drugs, infection, or heart attack. It can also be inherited (Sharma and Mounika Vemula, 2021). The increased flexibility and mobility features of wireless technology are motivating a large number of carriers to take a serious step toward the deployment of wireless technology (Bhambri et al., 2007; Arunachalam et al., 2021). Hypertrophic cardiomyopathy, which leads to a thicker heart muscle, is generally inherited from your family (Haq et al., 2018). Restrictive cardiomyopathy is caused due to abnormal protein buildup or any scar tissue that results in rigid heart walls (Bhambri and Kaur, 2014; Rani et al., 2022).

The most common heart disease symptoms can be pain and tightness in the chest, shortness of breath, neck jaw pain, throat, dizziness, slow or fast heartbeat, swelling in legs, pale gray or blue skin color, easily getting tired while doing any work, and swelling in hands, ankle or feet, among others (Bhambri and Gupta, 2012b; Gupta and Rani, 2013).

Due to the changes happening over such a short period, our changing environmental and social factors, such as an increase in the intake of junk food instead of healthy food and a lack of exercise or yoga, are causing these changes. These unhealthy practices over time are causing heart issues (Nikhar and Karandikar, 2016; Rani and Kaur, 2012).

Machine learning techniques gather all the data and detect a common pattern to predict disease risk and outcome (Gupta, 2017; Sharma and Rizvi, 2017). Types of Heart Diseases are shown in Figure 7.1.

7.2 Machine Learning

Machine learning uses algorithms and data to imitate the way that human learns, which then improves accuracy. It is also used in the field of data science, which is one of the most interesting concepts of the computer science field (Rani and Gupta, 2016; Bharti et al., 2021). Machine learning uses statistical methods and algorithms, and it is trained to make predictions and make decisions (Guptaet al., 2011; Harleen, 2016).

In the past few years, machine learning has given us self-driving cars, web searches, and practical speech recognition. It is a part of artificial intelligence (Kaur et al., 2013; Rani et al., 2022). There are different kinds of machine learning approaches, which are discussed in the following subsections (Rawat and Suryakant, 2019; Banerjee et al., 2022).

7.2.1 Supervised Machine Learning

From the name, supervised machine learning means a supervisor as a teacher. When we use data that is well labeled to teach or train a machine, this is what we called as machine learning. After that supervised learning algorithm analysis, the training data bring out a correct output from labeled data (Hussain et al., 2021).

Suppose you have a vegetable bag with sauteed vegetables. Then the very first step is to train the machine using the various vegetables, meaning if the object is round or oval with purple color, then it will be labeled as onion. Now, after training the data, if you give the machine a vegetable to identify, it will first identify the shape and color and confirm it as an onion (Kaur and Bhambri, 2015; Rani et al., 2021).

7.2.2 Unsupervised Machine Learning

Training machines using information that is not classified or labeled. It allows algorithms to identify the patterns in the dataset that are not labeled without any supervision. For example, there are both cats and dogs that the machine has never seen (Kaur and Bhambri, 2015; Sudevan et al., 2021) Hence, the machine can categorize them as dogs or cats, but it can categorize them based on pattern differences and similarities.

7.2.3 Big Data

The term *big data* refers to a set of massive data collections if a given analytic approach may give a similar pattern, or relationship among the data points (Bhambri and Gupta, 2013; Kumar et al., 2022). Since the traditional data management system fails to store and process large and complex data, here big data can be used. It is characterized by

- volume,
- variety,
- velocity, and
- variability.

Figure 7.2 depicts the flow from source to storage in big data. We have a large data set of heart disease patients. So to manage these data, we have to use the concept of big data analytics.

7.3 Materials and Methods

7.3.1 Data Source

Heart disease prediction is gathered from the Heart Disease Dataset, that is, the UCI machine repository. The dataset contains 303 records (Ramalingam et al., 2018; Kothandaraman et al., 2022). There are 13 attributes that are in a dataset where only one

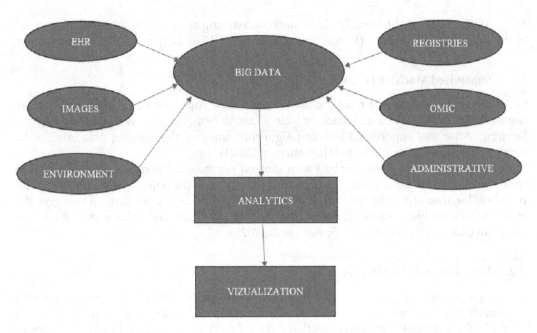

FIGURE 7.2
Flow from source to storage in big data.

TABLE 7.1

Data Set Attributes for Heart Disease

Attribute/Features	Description	Type
AGE	Patient's age (in years)	Numeric
SEX	Gender	Nominal
CP	Chest pain (Types)	Nominal
TRESTBPS	Level of blood pressure (mm/hg)	Numeric
CHOL	Serum cholesterol in mg/dl	Numeric
RESTING	ECG outcome during rest	Nominal
THALI	Obtaining the highest heart rate possible	Numeric
EXANG	Strength training angina	Nominal
OLDPEAK	ST depression caused by exercise	Numeric
SLOPE	ST-segment measured in terms of slope	Nominal
CA	Fluoroscopy colored major vessel	Numeric
THAL	Status of heart	Nominal
FBS	Blood sugar level on fasting	Nominal

attribute is an output. A confusion matrix is used for generating the accuracy for different machine learning methods. Table 7.1 shows the dataset attributes for heart diseases.

The model's accuracy is measured using a confusion matrix. Multiple machine learning approaches' real objective properties are calculated by the matrix. Accuracy, Precision,

F1-Score, Recall, as well as other parameters, can be evaluated by using a confusion matrix (S. Mohan et al., 2019; Rani et al., 2021).

Accuracy specifies the computation forecasting ability cases (Kumar et al., 2022). The model's accuracy could be assessed by looking for the median value that lies on the diagonal.

$$\text{Accuracy} = (\text{TP} + \text{TN}) / (\text{TP} + \text{TN} + \text{FP} + \text{FN})$$

Recall means exactness and attentiveness are evaluated by the recall (Dewan and Sharma, 2015). It is written like this:

$$\text{Recall} = \text{TP} / (\text{TP} + \text{FN})$$

Precision is the act of determining the appropriateness of something. It is depicted as

$$\text{Precision} = \text{TP} / (\text{TP} + \text{FP}).$$

The F1-score is the mean of recall and precision. F1-score is defined as a measurement of [0, 1]. It specifies both the accuracy and the strength of your classifier. It is depicted as

$$\text{F1 Score} = 2 * ((\text{precision} * \text{Recall}) / (\text{Precision} + \text{Recall})).$$

7.3.2 Methods

For cardiac diseases, many forms of machine learning algorithms are applied. These algorithms are support vector machine (SVM), K-nearest neighbor (KNN), naïve Bayes, decision tree, and random forest, among others.

7.3.2.1 SVM

SVM is a type of algorithm that would be used to tackle both classification and regression issues. The distinct classes are distinguished using a hyperplane in this approach. SVM classifies both linear and nonlinear data (Jasmine and Gupta, 2012; Rani et al., 2022). An SVM classifier determines the plane with a maximum margin between two data classes. The main advantage of the SVM algorithm is that it gives better precision and recall values (Limbitote et al., 2020).

7.3.2.2 KNN

A KNN algorithm finds the similarities between new data and the existing data and put the new data into a group that is most similar to the existing data. This algorithm does not learn from training data, and during the classification process, it stores the dataset. It is utilized in the segmentation and extrapolation of data. The input is a data set with the k-nearest training instances in both circumstances. This is one that trains a function from labeled data input and then implements it to new unseen data and generates a valid result (Bhambri and Gupta, 2012; Rani et al., 2021).

7.3.2.3 Decision Tree

A decision tree is used for both classification and regression. Here the internal nodes are the dataset's features, and the leaf node is the outcome. The tree could be described by two entities: decision nodes and leaves. The leaves represent the decisions or final results. The data are separated at the points (Kumar et al., 2022).

7.3.2.4 Naïve Bayes

Naïve Bayes is a supervised machine learning technique, based on the probability of an object it is used to predict the outcome (Iyer et al., 2020). This technique is based on Bayes' theorem. Naïve Bayes consists of two words – *naïve*, because it assumes that the occurrence of one characteristic is independent of other characteristics, and *Bayes*, because it is based on Bayes' theorem for calculating posterior probability.

7.3.2.5 Random Forest

In this algorithm, multiple classifiers are grouped together to solve the complex problem to improve the accuracy in terms of time and performance. It consists of several decision trees of given data and then takes the average in order to attain maximum accuracy (Bashir et al., 2019; Venkatesh et al., 2019).

7.4 Results

Table 7.2 lists the most effective classification algorithm. This table compares the accuracy, precision, and F-measure. The highest accuracy is achieved by naïve Bayes in comparison with all the other techniques. Comparative chart for machine learning algorithms is shown in Figure 7.3.

TABLE 7.2

Comparative Analysis with Various Machine Learning Algorithms

Author Name	Source	Algorithm	Accuracy
Senthi Kumar Mohan et al.	UCI repository	NAÏVE BAYES	75.7
Senthi Kumar Mohan et al.	UCI repository	DECISION TREE	85
Purushotamsharma et al.	UCI repository	RANDOM FOREST	86.1
Chandrasegartirumalai et al.	UCI repository	SVM	86.1
Senthi Kumar Mohan et al.	UCI repository	LOGISTIC REGRESSI ON	82.8
Neeraj Sharma et al.	UCI repository	Decision Tree	75.88
Neeraj Sharma et al.	UCI repository	Linear Regression	85.49
V. v. Ramalinguam et al.	UCI repository	NAÏVE BAYES	98
Neeraj Sharma et al.	UCI repository	ANN	85
Sirabih.mujawar et al.	UCI repository	HRFLM	88.4

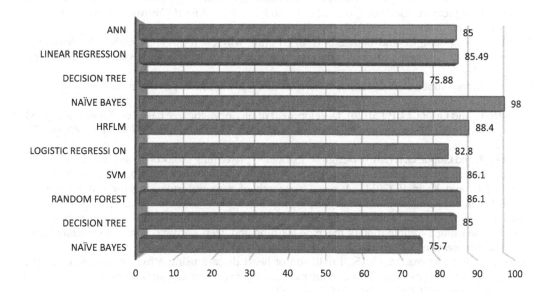

FIGURE 7.3
Comparative chart with machine learning algorithms.

7.5 Conclusion and Future Plans

One of the deadliest problems in human society is heart disease (Ed-Daoudy and Maalmi, 2019). This chapter covers different studies, and a comparative study has been performed with different machine learning algorithms using the concept of big data on the Heart Disease Dataset. In the end, several machine learning techniques were compared to see their accuracy and precision. Based on the foregoing research, machine learning algorithms offer great potential in recognizing heart-related disorders, according to research. Each of the algorithms discussed has performed excellently in some situations while failing miserably in others. Various machine learning algorithms have been applied, such as naïve Bayes, decision tree, random forest, SVM, logistic regression, linear regression, naïve Bayes classifier, ANN (Artificial Neural Network), and HRFLM (Hybrid Random Forest Linear Model), among others, and giving accuracy levels of 75.7%, 85%, 86.1%, 86.7%, 82.8%, 85.99%, 98%, 85%, and 88.9%, respectively. Of these algorithms, the naïve Bayes classifier provides the best accuracy. In the future, some other techniques like particle swarm optimization and ant colony optimization can be applied for better results and accuracy.

References

Arunachalam, P., Janakiraman, N., Sivaraman, A. K., Balasundaram, A., Vincent, R., Rani, S., … Rajesh, M. (2021). Synovial sarcoma classification technique using support vector machine and structure features. *Intelligent Automation and Soft Computing, 32*(2), 1241–1259.

Banerjee, K., Bali, V., Nawaz, N., Bali, S., Mathur, S., Mishra, R. K., and Rani, S. (2022). A machine-learning approach for prediction of water contamination using latitude, longitude, and elevation. *Water*, *14*(5), 728.

Bashir, S., Khan, Z. S., Khan, F. H., Anjum, A., and Bashir, K. (2019). Improving heart disease prediction using feature selection approaches. In *2019 16th International Bhurban Conference on Applied Sciences and Technology (IBCAST)* (pp. 619–623). IEEE.

Bhambri, L. P., Jindal, C., and Bathla, S. (2007). Future wireless technology-ZigBee. In *Proceedings of National Conference on Challenges and Opportunities in Information Technology (COIT)* (pp. 154–156).

Bhambri, P., and Gupta, O. P. (2012a). A novel method for the design of phylogenetic tree. *International Journal of Information Technology Engineering in Applied Science Research*, *1*(1), 24–28.

Bhambri, P., and Gupta, O. P. (2012b). Development of phylogenetic tree based on Kimura's method. In *2012 2nd IEEE International Conference on Parallel, Distributed and Grid Computing* (pp. 721–723). IEEE.

Bhambri, P., and Gupta, O. P. (2013). Design of distributed prefetching protocol in push-to-peer video-on-demand system. *International Journal of Research in Advent Technology (IJRAT)*, *1*(3), 95–103.

Bhambri, P., and Kaur, P. (2014). A novel approach of zero watermarking for text documents. *International Journal of Ethics in Engineering and Management Education (IJEEE)*, *1*(1), 34–38.

Bharti, R., Khamparia, A., Shabaz, M., Dhiman, G., Pande, S., and Singh, P. (2021). Prediction of heart disease using a combination of machine learning and deep learning. *Computational Intelligence and Neuroscience*, *2021*, 1–11.

Dewan, A., and Sharma, M. (2015). Prediction of heart disease using a hybrid technique in data mining classification. In *2015 2nd International Conference on Computing for Sustainable Global Development (INDIACom)* (pp. 704–706). IEEE.

Ed-Daoudy, A., and Maalmi, K. (2019). Real-time machine learning for early detection of heart disease using big data approach. In *2019 International Conference on Wireless Technologies, Embedded and Intelligent Systems (WITS)* (pp. 1–5). IEEE.

Gavhane, A., Kokkula, G., Pandya, I., and Devadkar, K. (2018). Prediction of heart disease using machine learning. In *2018 Second International Conference on Electronics, Communication and Aerospace Technology (ICECA)* (pp. 1275–1278). IEEE.

Gupta, O., Rani, S., and Pant, D. C. (2011). Impact of parallel computing on bioinformatics algorithms. In *Proceedings 5th IEEE International Conference on Advanced Computing and Communication Technologies* (pp. 206–209). IEEE.

Gupta, O. P. (2017). Study and analysis of various bioinformatics applications using protein BLAST: An overview. *Advances in Computational Sciences and Technology*, *10*(8), 2587–2601.

Gupta, O. P., and Rani, S. (2013). Accelerating molecular sequence analysis using distributed computing environment. *International Journal of Scientific and Engineering Research–IJSER*, *4*(10), 262.

Haq, A. U., Li, J. P., Memon, M. H., Nazir, S., and Sun, R. (2018). A hybrid intelligent system framework for the prediction of heart disease using machine learning algorithms. *Mobile Information Systems*, *2018*, 3860146.

Harleen, B. (2016). A prediction technique in data mining for diabetes mellitus. *Journal of Management Sciences and Technology*, *4*(1), 1–12.

Hussain, S., Nanda, D., Kumar, S., Barigidad, S., Akhtar, S., and Suaib, M. (2021). Novel deep learning architecture for heart disease prediction using convolutional neural network. *arXiv* preprint *arXiv*:2105.10816.

Iyer, S., Thevar, S., Guruswamy, P., and Ravale, U. (2020). Heart disease prediction using machine learning. *International Research Journal of Modernization in Engineering Technology and Science*, *2*(07), 1598–1603.

Jasmine, B. P., and Gupta, O. P. (2012). Analyzing the phylogenetic trees with tree-building methods. *Indian Journal of Applied Research*, *1*(7), 83–85.

Kaur, J., Bhambri, P., and Gupta, O. P. (2013). Distance based phylogenetic trees with bootstrapping. *International Journal of Computer Applications*, *47*, 6–10.

Kaur, P., and Bhambri, P. (2015). To design an algorithm for text watermarking. *The Standard International Journals (The SIJ)*, *3*(5), 62–67.

Kothandaraman, D., Manickam, M., Balasundaram, A., Pradeep, D., Arulmurugan, A., Sivaraman, A. K., … Balakrishna, R. (2022). Decentralized link failure prevention routing (DLFPR) algorithm for efficient internet of things. *Intelligent Automation and Soft Computing*, 34(1), 655–666.

Kumar, R., Rani, S., and Awadh, M. A. (2022). Exploring the application sphere of the internet of things in industry 4.0: A review, bibliometric and content analysis. *Sensors*, 22(11), 4276.

Limbitote, M., Damkondwar, K., Mahajan, D., and Patil, P. (2020). A survey on prediction techniques of heart disease using machine learning. *International Journal of Engineering Research and Technology (IJERT)*, ISSN 2278–0181.

Mohan, S., Thirumalai, C., and Srivastava, G. (2019). Effective heart disease prediction using hybrid machine learning techniques. *IEEE Access*, 7, 81542–81554.

Nikhar, S., and Karandikar, A. M. (2016). Prediction of heart disease using machine learning algorithms. *International Journal of Advanced Engineering, Management and Science*, 2(6), 239484.

Rahman, M. M., Rana, M. R., Nur-A-Alam, M., Khan, M. S. I., and Uddin, K. M. M. (2022). A web-based heart disease prediction system using machine learning algorithms. *Network Biology*, 12(2), 64–80.

Ramalingam, V. V., Dandapath, A., and Raja, M. K. (2018). Heart disease prediction using machine learning techniques: A survey. *International Journal of Engineering and Technology*, 7(2.8), 684–687.

Rani, S., Arya, V., and Kataria, A. (2022). Dynamic pricing-based E-commerce model for the produce of organic farming in India: A research roadmap with main advertence to vegetables. In *Proceedings of Data Analytics and Management* (pp. 327–336). Springer, Singapore.

Rani, S., Bhambri, P., and Chauhan, M. (2021). A machine learning model for kids' behavior analysis from facial emotions using principal component analysis. In *2021 5th Asian Conference on Artificial Intelligence Technology (ACAIT)* (pp. 522–525). IEEE.

Rani, S., Chauhan, M., Kataria, A., and Khang, A. (2021). IoT equipped intelligent distributed framework for smart healthcare systems. *arXiv* preprint *arXiv*:2110.04997.

Rani, S., and Gupta, O. P. (2016). Empirical analysis and performance evaluation of various GPU implementations of protein BLAST. *International Journal of Computer Applications*, 151(7), 22–27.

Rani, S., and Gupta, O. P. (2017). CLUS_GPU-BLASTP: Accelerated protein sequence alignment using GPU-enabled cluster. *The Journal of Supercomputing*, 73(10), 4580–4595.

Rani, S., Kataria, A., and Chauhan, M. (2022). Fog computing in industry 4.0: Applications and challenges—A research roadmap. In R. Tiwari, M. Mittal., and L. M. Goyal (eds.), *Energy Conservation Solutions for Fog-Edge Computing Paradigms*, (pp. 173–190). Chapman and Hall/CRC, Singapore.

Rani, S., Kataria, A., Chauhan, M., Rattan, P., Kumar, R., and Sivaraman, A. K. (2022). Security and privacy challenges in the deployment of cyber-physical systems in smart city applications: State-of-art work. *Materials Today: Proceedings*, 62(7), 4671–4676.

Rani, S., and Kaur, S. (2012). Cluster analysis method for multiple sequence alignment. *International Journal of Computer Applications*, 43(14), 19–25.

Rani, S., Mishra, R. K., Usman, M., Kataria, A., Kumar, P., Bhambri, P., and Mishra, A. K. (2021). Amalgamation of advanced technologies for sustainable development of smart city environment: A review. *IEEE Access*, 9, 150060–150087.

Rawat, V., and Suryakant, S. (2019). A classification system for diabetic patients with machine learning techniques. *International Journal of Mathematical, Engineering and Management Sciences*, 4(3), 729–744.

Sharma, H., and Rizvi, M. A. (2017). Prediction of heart disease using machine learning algorithms: A survey. *International Journal on Recent and Innovation Trends in Computing and Communication*, 5(8), 99–104.

Sharma, N. K., and Mounika Vemula, V. T. (2021). An experimental study of heart disease prediction using different supervised machine learning algorithms. *International Journal of Engineering Research and Technology*, 14(3), 227–240.

Sowmya Sundari, L. K., Ahmed, S. T., Anitha, K., and Pushpa, M. K. (2021). COVID-19 outbreak based coronary heart diseases (CHD) prediction using SVM and risk factor validation. In *2021 Innovations in Power and Advanced Computing Technologies (i-PACT)* (pp. 1–5). IEEE.

Sudevan, S., Barwani, B., Al Maani, E., Rani, S., and Sivaraman, A. K. (2021). Impact of blended learning during Covid-19 in Sultanate of Oman. *Annals of the Romanian Society for Cell Biology*, 25(4), 14978–14987.

Venkatesh, R., Balasubramanian, C., and Kaliappan, M. (2019). Development of big data predictive analytics model for disease prediction using machine learning technique. *Journal of Medical Systems*, 43(8), 1–8.

8

Analysis of Credit Card Fraud Data Using Various Machine Learning Methods

C. Chethana and Piyush Kumar Pareek

CONTENTS

8.1 Introduction

In this era, customers are doing online transactions for various purposes. Again, the transactions can be done using various possibilities like ATMs, Phone Pay, Google Pay, or through any online banking system, among others. All these applications require credit card details to be used for the transaction purpose (Kaur et al., 2013; Gupta, 2017). This user information and card details have to be kept secret so that the details are not stolen by the third-party customer. If the details of the actual customers were taken by fraud, then such transactions need to be identified to secure the details. In collaboration with machine learning and artificial intelligence, anomaly detection systems are vastly used in behavioral analysis to help identify and predict the prevalence of anomalies (Rani and Gupta, 2016; Bhambri et al., 2020; Kshirsagar et al., 2022) covers research on various methodologies for the use of neural networks to detect plant leaf diseases.

Many machine learning and deep learning algorithms have been used on the available dataset or for the raw data during the transaction time for analysis purposes. A machine learning model is proposed to recognize the emotional state of kids, that is, toddlers and preschoolers (Rani et al., 2021a). The increased flexibility and mobility features of wireless technology are motivating a large number of carriers to take a serious step toward deploying it (Bhambri et al., 2007; Gupta et al., 2011).

The identification of a fraudulent transaction has been done by using supervised learning or unsupervised learning methods (Bhambri and Kaur, 2014). The performance of the models can be evaluated by using various performance metrics like accuracy, precision,

DOI: 10.1201/9781003298335-8

recall and specificity, F1 score, area under the curve, and others (Bhambri and Gupta, 2012; Rani et al., 2022).

The objective of this chapter is to study the performance measure of different machine learning methods in predicting the accuracy and other measures on European credit card details (Harleen, 2016; Banerjee et al., 2022).

8.2 Algorithms

We have various machine learning algorithms. They can be categorized as supervised, unsupervised, semi-supervised, and reinforcement learning.

Supervised machine learning methods: Use the historical data for training the model. The instances, along with the target values, are given. Once the model is trained then the testing of the model can be done by giving new instances without the target values for the predictions.

The different supervised learning algorithms available are

- regression,
- logistic regression,
- classification,
- support vector machine (SVM),
- decision tree,
- naïve Bayes classifiers, and
- K-nearest neighbors (KNN).

a) Regression: It is used to find the relationship between the target and the predictor variables. The model applies this to predict the output of continuous or real values, such as the price of a house, the salary of a person, age, temperature, and so on.

b) Logistic regression: This type of regression uses the sigmoid function to model the data, which outputs the values between 0 and 1.

$$\text{sig}(x) = \frac{1}{1+e^{-x}} \tag{8.1}$$

c) Classification algorithm: These algorithms are used to find the output of the categorical values. The two types of classification are
  - binary classifier—only two possible outcomes are predicted, for example, spam email or not spam email.
  - multiclass classifier—more than two possible outcomes are predicted, for example, the classification types of flowers.

d) Support vector machine: Can be used to solve regression and classification types of problems.

e) Support vector regression: Predicts continuous valued output.

f) Decision tree: A tree-like structure is constructed to represent the independent attributes as root/internal nodes and the dependent variables as leaf nodes. It can be used as a classification or regression type of problem-solver.

g) Naïve Bayes classifier: It uses Bayes' theorem and is applied to solving classification problems.

Bayes' theorem is given by

$$P(A/B) = \frac{P(B|A)P(A)}{P(B)} \tag{8.2}$$

h) K-nearest neighbors: It can be used as a regression or a classification. It is a non-parametric and lazy learner algorithm. Various distance measurements can be used to find the category of the new instance. Basically, it uses the Euclidean distance between the two points.

If $A = (X1, Y1)$ and $B = (X2, Y2)$ are the two points in space, then the Euclidean distance between A and B is given by

$$\sqrt{\sqrt{(X2-X1)^2 + (Y2-Y1)^2}} \tag{8.3}$$

1. **Unsupervised algorithms**: The given data set is grouped into various categories based on the characteristics of the data. The data instances will not be associated with the target values. The categories are clustering and associations. **K-means algorithm**: It is one of the clustering methods. This algorithm partitions the given unlabeled data instances into k number of groups until the centroid of the clusters converges. **Minkowski distance, and** Euclidian **distance are used to measure** the distance between the data points and the centroid of the clusters. The various applications are as follows: marketing, biology, libraries, Insurance and banking, **image segmentation, and docume**nt clustering.

2. **Semi-supervised learning algorithms**: It uses the smaller fractions of data instances with target values and larger fractions of data without the target values. It falls between supervised and unsupervised learning methods. The various applications of the algorithms can be found in speech analysis, internet content classification, and protein sequence classification.

3. **Reinforcement learning**: This method does not use the target concepts for the data instances. The agent (software) learns by itself to get the experience by interacting with the environment. It tries to get the maximum reward to improve performance. The various applications can be found in robotics, marketing, healthcare, and finance, among others.

8.3 Related Works

Chen and Lai (2021) proposed a "credit card fraud detection using artificial neural network," which compared the accuracy values obtained by using SVM, KNN, and artificial neural network (ANN), in which ANN has obtained better accuracy compared with other models approximately near to 100% (Asha and Suresh Kumar, 2021).

The research paper "Credit Card Fraud Detection" by Sailusha et al. (2020) used a publicly available data set for predicting model performance (Kanchana et al., 2020; Rani et al., 2021).

"Deep Convolution Neural Network Model for Credit-Card Fraud Detection and Alert" by Chen (Chen and Lai, 2021a) used a deep convolutional neural network, compared the existing system with a real-time credit card fraud data set and found an accuracy of about 99%.

"Credit Card Fraud Detection Using Machine Learning: A Survey" by Sharma et al. (2021) discussed the task of detection and approaches used to capture the transactions (Sailusha et al., 2020; Arya et al., 2022).

"Credit Card Fraud Detection using machine Learning Algorithms," by Varun Kumar et al., describes the confusion matrix of various machine learning algorithms used and its accuracy (Sharma et al., 2021; Kumar et al., 2022). The authors also showed interest in using time-series analysis by using various methods.

Kumar et al. (2022), in "Credit Card Fraud Detection using Machine Learning Methodology" proposed that an accuracy of about 95% was achieved after preprocessing the data. Logistic regression with different options link oversampling (98.01%), vanilla logistic regression (99.8%), and balanced weights (97.5%). K-means clustering of about 54.27% accuracy was obtained (Tanouz et al., 2021). The authors suggested using other classifiers as a next step for the evaluation purpose.

Raghavan and Gayar (2019), in "Credit Card Fraud Detection using Machine Learning Algorithms," proposed using clustering methods and classification models on the clustered data before and after applying the Synthetic Minority Oversampling TEchnique (Dornadula and Geetha, 2019).

"Fraud Detection Using Machine Learning and Deep Learning Models" by Raghavan and Gayar (2019) compared various machine learning models and deep learning; the authors conclude that SVM with convolutional neural networks (CNNs) is the better approach for larger datasets.

"Credit Card Fraud Detection using Machine Learning and Data Science" by Rani et al. (2022b) used a multiple anomaly detection algorithm and predicted an accuracy of about 99.6%

Harish Paruchuri (2017), in "Credit Card Fraud Detection using Machine Learning: A Systematic Literature Review," identified phishing and Trojan as the methods used to take the user credentials and card details.

Rani et al. (2022a), in "An Analysis of the Most Used Machine Learning Algorithms for Online Fraud Detection," discussed the different methods for identifying fraud (Minastireanu and Mesnita, 2019a).

In "Light GBM Machine Learning Algorithm to Online Click Fraud Detection," Minastireanu and Mesnita (2019b) used a gradient-boosting decision tree type and obtained an accuracy of about 98%.

In "Predictive Modelling For Credit Card Fraud Detection Using Data Analytics", real-time data was used to detect fraud by using machine learning algorithms, and the authors found that the random forest technique was better than the other models that were considered for the analysis purpose (Patil et al., 2018; Rani et al., 2022b).

In "Credit Card Fraud Detection Using Machine Learning Models and Collating Machine Learning Models," Khare and Yunus Sait (2018) have obtained an accuracy of about 97.7% and 98.6%, respectively, for the algorithms logistic_regression and random_ forest methods.

"Detecting and Preventing Fraud with Data Analytics" by Adrian Banarescu (2015) suggested using "proactive data detection techniques" to identify fraud and prevent it.

8.4 Results

The dataset was taken from Kaggle, which contains European cardholders' transaction details from September 2013. MATLAB R2021b was used for the analysis. The results were obtained by applying tree methods with a maximum number of splits as 100, 20, and 4 for fine tree, medium tree, and coarse tree, respectively. The values were observed by using without Principal Component Analysis (PCA) and with PCA option sets as shown in Tables 8.1 and 8.2, respectively. A fivefold validation was applied on the dataset.

From Tables 8.1 and 8.2 we can see that, the coarse tree with a PAC option set gives us training time of 7.092 s.

From Tables 8.3 and 8.4 we can observe that the accuracy value without the PCA option is about 99.9% for logistic regression, SVM, and KNN. The prediction speed of KNN is about 960 obs/s, which is more efficient than other algorithms.

TABLE 8.1

Without PCA Option

Model Type	Accuracy	Total Cost	Prediction Speed	Training Time
Fine Tree	99.9	2	~890,000 obs/s	20.619 s
Medium Tree	99.9	156	~1,100,000 obs/s	11.876 s
Coarse Tree	99.9	213	~1,200,000 obs/s	7.6955 s

TABLE 8.2

With PCA Option

Model Type	Accuracy	Total Cost	Prediction Speed	Training Time
Fine Tree	99.8%	548	~580,000 obs/s	12.401 s
Medium Tree	99.8%	508	~540,000 obs/s	9.4121 s
Coarse Tree	99.8%	493	~540,000 obs/s	7.092 s

TABLE 8.3

Without PCA Option

Model Type	Accuracy	TotalCost	PredictionSpeed	TrainingTime
Gaussian naïve Bayes	97.8%	6310	~910,000 obs/s	8.6793 s
Logistic regression	99.9%	NA	~860,000 obs/s	28.618 s
SVM	99.9%	183	~640,000 obs/s	63.21 s
KNN	99.9%	156	~960 obs/s	1265.3 s

TABLE 8.4

With PCA Option

Model Type	Accuracy	Total Cost	Prediction Speed	Traning Time
Gaussian naïve Bayes	99.8%	492	~550,000 obs/s	8.7978 s
Logistic regression	99.8%	**NA**	~560,000 obs/s	13.851 s
SVM	99.8%	492	~470,000 obs/s	19.915 s
KNN	99.7%	862	~470,000 obs/s	11.771 s

8.5 Positive Predicted Values and False Discovery Rates Results

From Figures 8.1 through 8.8, we can see the results obtained for the positive predicted values (PPVs), which are the percentage of correctly categorized observations per the predicted class, and the false discovery rates (FDRs) proportion of incorrectly categorized observations per predicted class.

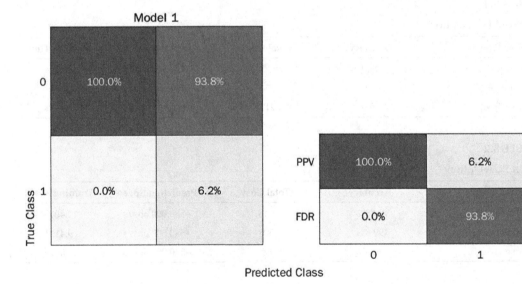

FIGURE 8.1
Naïve Bayes without PCA.

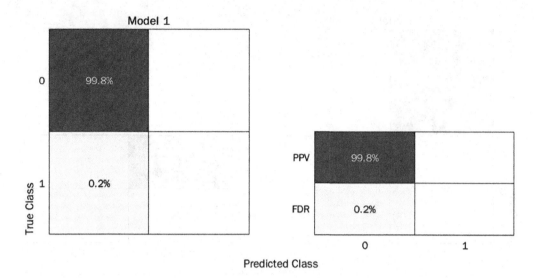

FIGURE 8.2
Naive Bayes with PCA.

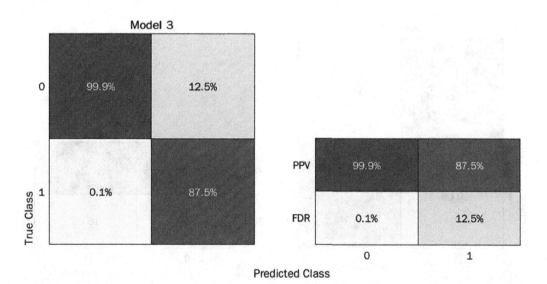

FIGURE 8.3
Logistic regression without PCA.

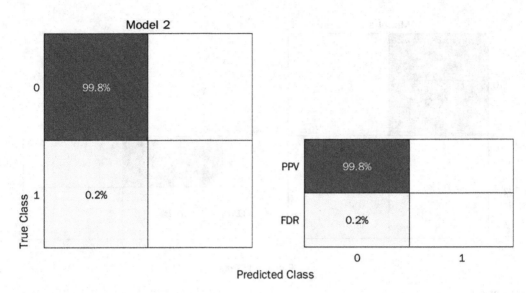

FIGURE 8.4
Logistic regression with PCA.

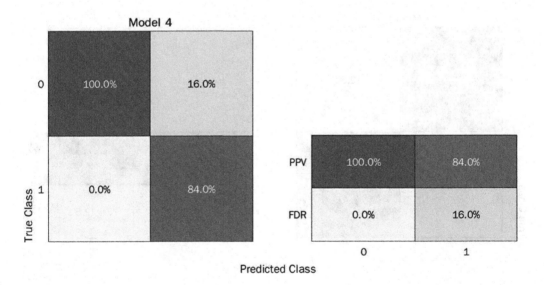

FIGURE 8.5
SVM without PCA.

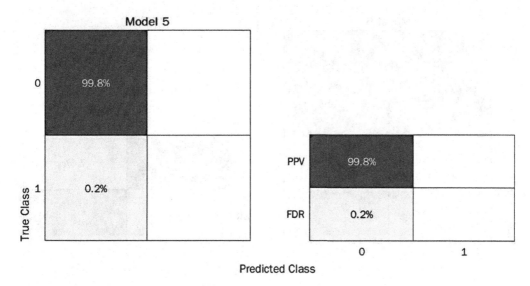

FIGURE 8.6
SVM with PCA.

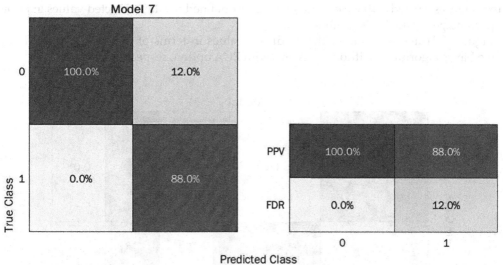

FIGURE 8.7
KNN without PCA.

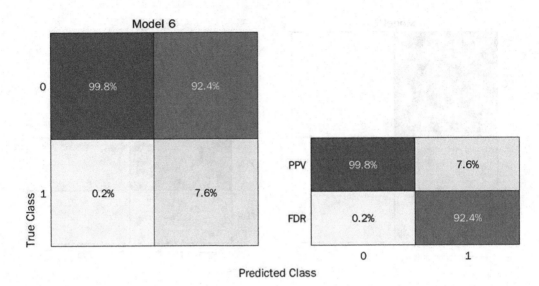

FIGURE 8.8
KNN with PCA.

8.6 Predicted Results

From Figures 8.9 and 8.10 we can see the results obtained for the predicted values in terms of percentage for the KNN method.

Figures 8.11 and 8.12 shows the predicted values in terms of instances, for SVM and naïve Bayes algorithms without PCA and with PCA option, respectively.

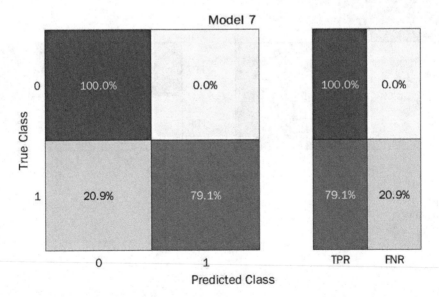

FIGURE 8.9
KNN without PCA.

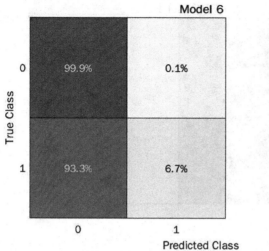
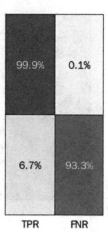

FIGURE 8.10
KNN with PCA.

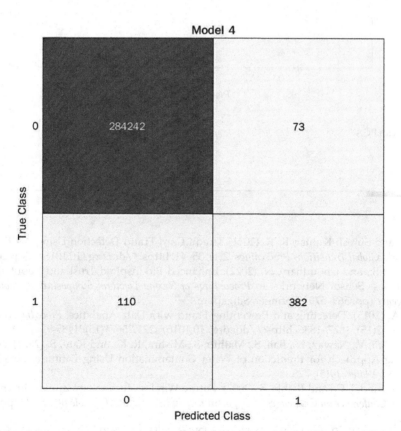

FIGURE 8.11
SVM without PCA.

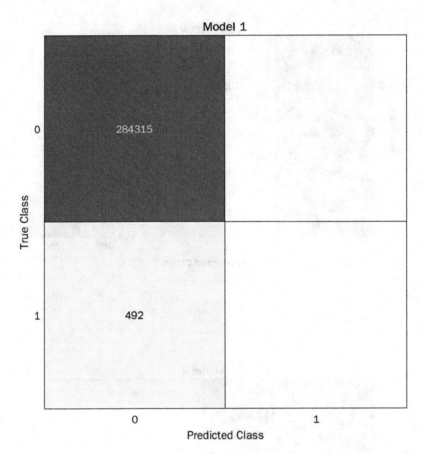

FIGURE 8.12
Naïve Bayes with PCA.

References

Asha, R. B., and Suresh Kumar, K. R. (2021). Credit Card Fraud Detection Using Artificial Neural Network. *Global Transitions Proceedings*, 2(1), 35–41. https://doi.org/10.1016/j.gltp.2021.01.006.

Arya, V., Rani, S., and Choudhary, N. (2022). Enhanced Bio-inspired Trust and Reputation Model for Wireless Sensor Networks. In *Proceedings of Second Doctoral Symposium on Computational Intelligence* (pp. 569–579). Springer, Singapore.

Bănărescu, A. (2015). Detecting and Preventing Fraud with Data Analytics. *Procedia Economics and Finance*, 32(15), 1827–1836. https://doi.org/10.1016/s2212-5671(15)01485-9.

Banerjee, K., Bali, V., Nawaz, N., Bali, S., Mathur, S., Mishra, R. K., and Rani, S. (2022). A Machine-Learning Approach for Prediction of Water Contamination Using Latitude, Longitude, and Elevation. *Water*, 14(5), 728.

Bhambri, L. P., Jindal, C., and Bathla, S. (2007). Future Wireless Technology-ZigBee. In *Proceedings of National Conference on Challenges & Opportunities in Information Technology (COIT)* (pp. 154–156). ACM.

Bhambri, P., Bagga, S., Priya, D., Singh, H., and Dhiman, H. K. (2020). Suspicious Human Activity Detection System. *Journal of IoT in Social, Mobile, Analytics, and Cloud*, 2(4), 216–221.

Bhambri, P., and Gupta, O. P. (2012, December). Development of Phylogenetic Tree Based on Kimura's Method. In *2012 2nd IEEE International Conference on Parallel, Distributed and Grid Computing* (pp. 721–723). IEEE.

Bhambri, P., and Kaur, P. (2014). A Novel Approach of Zero Watermarking for Text Documents. *International Journal of Ethics in Engineering & Management Education (IJEEE)*, 1(1), 34–38.

Chen, J. I.-Z., and Lai, K.-L. (2021). Deep Convolution Neural Network Model for Credit-Card Fraud Detection and Alert. *Journal of Artificial Intelligence and Capsule Networks*, 3(2), 101–112. https://doi.org/10.36548/jaicn.2021.2.003.

Dornadula, V. N., and Geetha, S. (2019). Credit Card Fraud Detection using Machine Learning Algorithms. *Procedia Computer Science*, *165*, 631–641. https://doi.org/10.1016/j.procs.2020.01.057.

Gupta, O., Rani, S., and Pant, D. C. (2011). Impact of Parallel Computing on Bioinformatics Algorithms. In *Proceedings 5th IEEE International Conference on Advanced Computing and Communication Technologies* (pp. 206–209).

Gupta, O. P. (2017). Study and Analysis of Various Bioinformatics Applications Using Protein BLAST: An Overview. *Advances in Computational Sciences and Technology*, 10(8), 2587–2601.

Harleen, B. (2016). A Prediction Technique in Data Mining for Diabetes Mellitus. *Journal of Management Sciences and Technology*, 4(1), 1–12.

Kanchana, M., Chadda, V., and Jain, H. (2020). Credit Card Fraud Detection. *International Journal of Advanced Science and Technology*, 29(6), 2201–2215. https://doi.org/10.46501/ijmtst0705009.

Kaur, J., Bhambri, P., and Gupta, O. P. (2013). Distance based Phylogenetic Trees with Bootstrapping. *International Journal of Computer Applications*, 47, 6–10.

Khare, N., and Yunus Sait, S. (2018). Credit Card Fraud Detection Using Machine Learning Models and Collating Machine Learning Models. *International Journal of Pure and Applied Mathematics*, *118*(20), 825–838.

Kshirsagar, P. R., Jagannadham, D. B. V., Ananth, M. B., Mohan, A., Kumar, G., and Bhambri, P. (2022). Machine Learning Algorithm for Leaf Disease Detection. In *AIP Conference Proceedings* (vol. 2393(1), p. 020087). AIP Publishing LLC.

Kumar, R., Rani, S., and Awadh, M. A. (2022). Exploring the Application Sphere of the Internet of Things in Industry 4.0: A Review, Bibliometric and Content Analysis. *Sensors*, 22(11), 4276.

Minastireanu, E.-A., and Mesnita, G. (2019a). An Analysis of the Most Used Machine Learning Algorithms for Online Fraud Detection. *Informatica Economica*, 23(1/2019), 5–16. https://doi.org/10.12948/issn14531305/23.1.2019.01.

Minastireanu, E.-A., and Mesnita, G. (2019b). Light GBM Machine Learning Algorithm to Online Click Fraud Detection. *Journal of Information Assurance & Cybersecurity*, April, 1–12. https://doi.org/10.5171/2019.263928.

Paruchuri, H. (2017). Credit Card Fraud Detection Using Machine Learning: A Systematic Literature Review. *ABC Journal of Advanced Research*, 6(2), 113–120. https://doi.org/10.18034/abcjar.v6i2.547.

Patil, S., Nemade, V., and Soni, P. K. (2018). Predictive Modelling for Credit Card Fraud Detection Using Data Analytics. *Procedia Computer Science*, 132, 385–395. https://doi.org/10.1016/j.procs.2018.05.199.

Raghavan, P., and Gayar, N. El. (2019). Fraud Detection using Machine Learning and Deep Learning. In *Proceedings of 2019 International Conference on Computational Intelligence and Knowledge Economy, ICCIKE 2019*, December 2019, pp. 334–339. https://doi.org/10.1109/ICCIKE47802.2019.9004231.

Rani, S., Arya, V., and Kataria, A. (2022c). Dynamic Pricing-Based E-commerce Model for the Produce of Organic Farming in India: A Research Roadmap with Main Advertence to Vegetables. In *Proceedings of Data Analytics and Management* (pp. 327–336). Springer, Singapore.

Rani, S., Bhambri, P., and Chauhan, M. (2021a). A Machine Learning Model for Kids' Behavior Analysis from Facial Emotions using Principal Component Analysis. In *2021 5th Asian Conference on Artificial Intelligence Technology (ACAIT)* (pp. 522–525). IEEE.

Rani, S., and Gupta, O. P. (2016). Empirical Analysis and Performance Evaluation of Various GPU Implementations of Protein BLAST. *International Journal of Computer Applications*, 151(7), 22–27.

Rani, S., Kataria, A., and Chauhan, M. (2022b). Cyber Security Techniques, Architectures, and Design. In *Holistic Approach to Quantum Cryptography in Cyber Security* (pp. 41–66). CRC Press, USA.

Rani, S., Kataria, A., Chauhan, M., Rattan, P., Kumar, R., and Sivaraman, A. K. (2022a). Security and Privacy Challenges in the Deployment of Cyber-Physical Systems in Smart City Applications: State-of-Art Work. *Materials Today: Proceedings*, 62(7), 4671–4676.

Rani, S., Mishra, R. K., Usman, M., Kataria, A., Kumar, P., Bhambri, P., and Mishra, A. K. (2021b). Amalgamation of Advanced Technologies for Sustainable Development of Smart City Environment: A Review. *IEEE Access*, 9, 150060–150087.

Sailusha, R., Gnaneswar, V., Ramesh, R., and Ramakoteswara Rao, G. (2020). Credit Card Fraud Detection Using Machine Learning. In *Proceedings of the International Conference on Intelligent Computing and Control Systems, ICICCS 2020*, October 2020, (pp. 1264–1270). https://doi.org/10.1109/ICICCS48265.2020.9121114.

Sharma, M., Sharma, H., Bhutani, P., and Sharma, I. (2021). Credit Card Fraud Detection Using Machine Learning Algorithms. *Lecture Notes in Electrical Engineering*, 788(07), 547–560. https://doi.org/10.1007/978-981-16-4149-7_49.

Tanouz, D., Subramanian, R. R., Eswar, D., Reddy, G. V. P., Kumar, A. R., and Praneeth, C. H. (2021). Credit Card Fraud Detection Using Machine Learning. In *Proceedings - 5th International Conference on Intelligent Computing and Control Systems, ICICCS 2021* (pp. 967–972). https://doi.org/10.1109/ICICCS51141.2021.9432308.

9

Cloud Security Risk Management Quantifications

Gurwinder Singh, Munish Rattan and Gurjot Kaur Walia

CONTENTS

DOI: 10.1201/9781003298335-9

9.1 Introduction

The selection and implementation of the cloud risk management of information systems to an organization are essential activities that can significantly impact the performance and assets of organizations and the well-being of individuals and the Nation (Terroza, 2015). As a result, there are several important questions that organizations need to answer while addressing risk management and security system:

- How is safety control required to meet security recommendations and adequately reduce the risk of using information and information systems to pursue organizational and trade objectives?
- Is security controls started, or is there a system in the field?

The answers to these questions are not provided alone. Therefore, this needs a framework of an adequate risk management corporation that diagnoses, minimizes as crucial, and continuously supervises risks that come from its information and knowledge systems (NIST Publication, 2019). This chapter guides managing security risks in three categories: organizational structure, business structure, and information systems. The risk management described in this chapter suggests that corporations meet their security needs or use it as an accurate risk management system that supports their information security systems.

9.1.1 Risk Management Characteristics

- Promotes real-time risk management authorized through the exercise of robust nonstop monitoring procedures
- Encourages using industrialization to offer executives essential facts; expenditure, hazard primarily selections regarding the organizational records structures supporting their core targets
- Manage safety in the organization structure and develop a system business cycle
- Presents a prominence on draft, exercising, assessing, and management of protection control, authentication of systems
- Links with risk management procedure at the information systems stage to threat

9.1.2 Background

Cloud security risk management was developed as a uniform framework to protect the information of the organizations and their contractors. The framework goal is to unify application security, reinforce risk management processes, and promote uniformity within the public sector. The amend process highlights (1) the structure protection possibilities in the information systems of an organization (Liu, 2019) through highest developed security controls, performance, and technology; (2) the preservation of awareness of the security status of the information systems on an ongoing basis despite improved monitoring systems; and (3) providing important information to executives to make an opinion for recognition of risks to of the organization (Campbell, 2016). The best way to achieve the balance between energy usage and quality of service is workload-aware energy-efficient virtual machine (VM) consolidation (Kaur et al., 2020). In collaboration with machine learning and artificial intelligence, anomaly detection systems are vastly used in behavioral analysis so that you can help identify and predict the prevalence of anomalies (Bhambri et al., 2020; Rani et al., 2022). To produce pulse-width modulation pulses for the generator-side converter, a proportional integral controller is utilized (Banerjee et al., 2022; Mohanta et al., 2022). The development of a strong charging structure network is broadly known as a vital necessity for a huge-scale evolution to electromobility (Bhambri et al., 2022). Kshirsagar et al. (2022) cover research on various methodologies for the use of neural networks to detect plant leaf diseases. Today, every networking field is working only through it due to COVID-19 (Rani et al., 2021; Bhambri et al., 2022).

9.1.2.1 Stationing Models

Cloud risk management is one of the respective stationing models. Distribution models broadly reflect the management and use of accounting resources to deliver services to consumers and the distinction between consumer categories. A universal cloud is an integrated framework and computer resources accessible to the public via the Internet. It is retained and managed by a cloud provider that delivers cloud services to users and, by definition, is external to the user organization. On the other side are private clouds. A private cloud is a computer space, especially used for a single entity. It is operated by an external organization or company and hosted within or outside its data center. The private cloud can give the organization more significant control over infrastructure, accounting services, and cloud clients than the public cloud. Two other use models are available: public clouds and hybrids. The public cloud falls between the public and private clouds concerning the target set of consumers. It is almost like a private cloud, but the architecture and accounting services are designed for several more organizations with the same privacy, security, and regulatory considerations rather than a single entity.

9.1.2.2 Service Model

9.1.2.2.1 Software-Based

A software-based service delivery model provides one or more applications and accounting services when needed as a turnkey service. Its primary purpose is to reduce apparatus, program upgrades, and system maintenance costs. The provision of protection is made primarily by the cloud provider. The cloud user does not manage the basic infrastructure or individual applications, except the preferred options and limited control system settings.

9.1.2.2.2 Platform-Based

A platform-based service delivery model provides a computer platform as a much-needed service where utilization could be upgraded and arranged. Its primary objective is to scale the expenses and complications of purchasing and executing the platform's basic hardware/software mechanisms, including any required programming and website development tools. The progress space is usually a particular purpose, determined by the cloud provider and in line with the design and architecture of its platform. Cloud buyers can control applications and the settings of the app environment. Security conditions are distinguished between a cloud provider and a cloud buyer.

9.1.2.2.3 Infrastructure-Based

The infrastructure-based service delivery model provides basic computer infrastructure for servers, software, and network equipment as a much-needed service, in which a platform can be developed to develop and deploy applications. Its primary purpose is to avoid purchasing, housing, and managing basic computer hardware and software infrastructure, and instead, we have identified those resources as manageable resources through the service interface. The provision of protection beyond basic infrastructure is made primarily by the cloud buyer.

9.1.2.3 Mission and Applications

This chapter focused on a risk management framework in information systems, including security classification functions, selection and implementation, security management testing, information system authorization, and security management monitoring framework as follows:

- Ensuring that the management of security information related to the information system is in line with the objectives of the organization/business and risk strategy established by senior management through a risk officer (employee)
- Ensuring that security requirements into the organizational business structure and life cycle processes of system development: supporting consistent authorization decisions, safety accountability, or information related to risk management and reconciliation
- Acquiring secure information and information systems through appropriate risk-reduction strategies within the organization (Alavi et al., 2014)

9.2 Fundamentals of Cloud Risk Management

Elementary concepts similar to governing security information systems ideas as follows: (1) assembling disaster management principle approaches toward the organization's comprehensive thinking strategies, business objectives, and processes; (2) approaching security needs in developmental cycle processes; (3) ensuring efficient borders for the security systems of the organization; and (4) assigning protection standards to the information systems of the organization as direct, mixed, or general standard (Rani and Gupta, 2016; Saeidi et al., 2019)

9.2.1 Cloud Risk Multilayered Management

With cloud-based services, some subsystems or components fall out of direct control of the client organization. Most organizations are risk-free if they have much control over the processes and tools involved. At the very least, the high level of control offers the option to measure other items, set priorities, and take decisive action in the organization's best interests in the event of an incident. Risk management is the process of identifying and evaluating risks in an organization's operations or individuals due to the operation of the information system and taking the necessary steps to bring them down to an acceptable level. Community-based cloud programs, such as traditional information systems, require that the risk be controlled throughout the system's life cycle. To the fullest extent possible, organizations should ensure that privacy and security controls are appropriately implemented, functioning as intended, and meeting their requirements. Organizations should understand the privacy and security of cloud service security and make adequate applications (NIST, 2011a; NIST 2011b; Arunachalam, 2021).

9.2.2 Cloud Surveillance Architecture

The cloud security risk management architecture has shown in Figure 9.1. It shows an organized and systematic operation that combines information regarding safety with risk calculation functions in the system.

- Examine safety regulations using a suitable testing process to ensure that the level uses the regulation policy correctly, functions as engaged, and produces the associated result in meeting the system's security requirements
- Authorize the information system based on determining the operational exposure to the association assets, individual, and the state due to the information system working process or the determination that these risks are justified
- Continuously monitor of system security information controls includes monitoring the effectiveness of controls, documenting changes to the system or operating environment, conducting security impact assessments of associated changes, and reporting system security status to designated organizational officials

In short, there is a fundamental level of adaptability in the way institutions use risk management outlined earlier. However, all organization positions must have a regular and efficient risk approach used in whole-risk management protocols. Moreover, executives analyze the resources needed to accomplish the risk management activities covered in this chapter and assure that such possessions are available to qualified individuals. Allocating the resources complies with both funding for risk management activities and the allocation of qualified staff required to perform tasks (NIST, 2019; Rani and Kumar, 2022).

9.2.3 Shield Standard

Organizations need to adequately reduce the risks of information systems for further business objectives and functions (Bhambri and Chhabra, 2022). The security goal for corporations is to figure out a cost-efficient and effective safety management system with the safety requirements set out in applicable state laws, executive orders, regulations, policies, guidelines, or standards negligence of security controls addresses all the organizational security issues in all cases. Choosing the appropriate set of regulations for particular

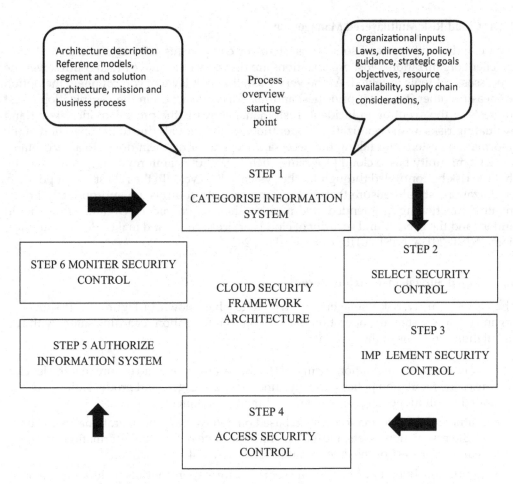

FIGURE 9.1
Cloud security risk management architecture.

circumstances or information systems to reduce risk is an important task that requires a critical understanding of the organization's goal/business priorities, policy, information systems to support, and operating conditions (Rani et al., 2022).

9.3 Matter of Contention

Technological approaches to providing the variety of the promised cloud function are often not publicized to the consumer, thus putting questions consumers can use to ensure the quality of the promised service offered. It may be complicated as the agreement of service does not comply with all specification terms used (Bonazzi et al., 2009). Additionally, effective markets depend on the ability of consumers to corresponding deliver services.

To conclude, cloud security has some open issues into five areas that are discussed in the following subsections: cloud functioning, cloud accuracy, economic policies, compliance, and information security (Gupta et al., 2011; Sen, 2013).

9.3.1 Cloud Functioning

Cloud computing introduces a few operational problems similar to the issues faced by network computer systems that we should be aware of here. Cloud functioning is system performance at different stages with various application requests; for example, mail usually tolerates service disturbance, but industry computerization and the real-time process often need higher efficacy and a higher level of speculation (Rani et al., 2022).

9.3.1.1 Inactivity

Inactivity in time received by the system when processing the request cloud users experience at minimum one round time, for example, buyers request per time. In general, time for the round trip is not the only awaited count but the width and significant variations resulting from clogging, stop miscue, and failure. The supplier or buyer does not usually control the features. However, broadband network development techniques and services accelerate systems used to reduce uncertain performance. The similarity of application requires accurate scrutiny app's sensitivity, tolerance built within the network service provided from variability and system response, and potential adjustments used just behind the fact.

9.3.1.2 Disconnection Status Synchronization

Access to cloud-based documents is a problem if the user has poor connectivity. The capability to sync and process the data whenever the user is offline and storing the information in the software-as-a-service (SaaS) cloud. Achieving translation discipline needs synchronization, team sharing, and other in-cloud skills for synchronization.

9.3.1.3 Expendable Logic

"Extensive" editing using tools like Map Reduce or so online resources require a new evaluation of application development processes. The ability to ask for more computer power carry well-explored computer prototypes, including computing and similar program from laboratories and typical computer applications. Cloud consumers use the information and comply with tasks to utilize the performance of computers and better measure complex computational tasks. Apps will probably be restructured to get all the system features, which are now available on request.

9.3.1.4 Administrating Data Cache

Data available in a cloud context are considered as the operator provides the facility to the user for (1) extra space where needed, (2) perceiving the limit of storage and site of data, (3) ensuring that data are deleted, (4) authorizing the secure disposal process for storage of data, and (5) control data authentication. All these observations are used when an external group hosts data (Rani et al., 2021).

9.3.2 Cloud Accuracy

Accuracy is assigned as the system's non-interruption of service at a particular time within the selected area boundaries. In cloud services, accuracy means a general reliability function of service for each of the four mechanisms: (1) facilities provided by the operator, (2) operational staff, (3) connection to registered users, and (4) customer staff.

This is a challenging task to calculate the accuracy of a particular cloud (operator or user) for two reasons. First, it may be a composite structure, both gaining a degree of reliability when measured independently. The resulting accuracy becomes difficult to predict when these components are combined and may eventually become very course-grained. Second, measuring this is a local task, and it may not be possible to understand the universe in which the cloud operates entirely. As mentioned, the standard definition of fidelity is based on context (environment) and the expected user-free time. Due to the minimum efficiency to check the "genealogy" of these applications inside the cloud service (because of complicated different components that combine), the host for this application level is not a better option. Moreover, it does not mean that cloud technology is not considered in defined areas (e.g., using the cloud to simulate the most crucial security system being developed).

9.3.3 Fiscal Achievements

In both public and external contexts, cloud computing offers consumers the opportunity to use computer services at minimal cost; in addition, the cloud improves business efficiency by cutting its cost for testing efforts and lessening costs through the scale of the economy. However, while the profit can be huge, many economic risks should also be considered.

9.3.3.1 Uncertainty of Business

Consumers can continue to use products in the real estate business, even if retailers terminated their services or quit a business. On the external cloud, users rely on providers' live provision of assistance. However, service closures are expected in the market. This reliance is dangerous for the user as a requirement of the cloud over time. A number of methods are practiced to lower the risk, such as using inactive cloud, suppliers' business life management, and cloud computing (Nocco, 2006; Kaur et al., 2015).

9.3.3.2 Servicing Agreements

Service agreements may define access and security in a direct and limited manner. Additionally, service agreements often place different obligations on consumers to track service agreements' changes and determine when to renew service agreements. Consumers need effective strategies to evaluate and compare service agreements. Currently, service agreements are made by people and used by people. However, the similarities noted in the current terms of the service agreement suggest a basis for the termination of the terms of the agreement of user service. Moreover, the open problem in designing the new service agreement is critical and includes the terms of a standard service agreement. The particular section of such models may grant mechanically testing the agreement of the service. Therefore, confidence between the user and the cloud provider is higher, and it also lessens services cost. A standard descriptive template may support question interactions that allow users to evaluate immediately or analyze critical sections or personally evaluate the term used in the agreement. Before investing, the consumer personally evaluates detailed terms that support the marketplace very efficiently. The agreement of service templates combines with performance and grants users to compare the delivery service with others.

9.3.3.3 Flexibility of Workloads

The first obstacle to cloud capture is moving the local workload to provider infrastructure. This resolution lessens the risk for the consumer if the operator switches to real-time options to deliver service (integrated computer load) to user properties if required. Another issue is that the consumer must move the service from the first supplier to the second. This type of arrangement provides competition to the cloud marketplace. In contrast, cloud service offerings that lease performance-related organizations, which allow user stack (platform as a service) or service-based permissions (service as a service), are not well defined by criteria, so this is why even simple terms are unable to explain how such businesses may be shifted from one supplier to other. While some details such as the apparatus's visible connectors are kept secret by the operator, app descriptions are often specified directly with the vendor.

9.3.3.4 Interoperability Between Cloud Operators

Management is required for functions such as standard data transfer formats, payment and ownership, visual image transfer, and data between providers. Other criteria, such as open real-time operations and interface of cloud data, are being upgraded. Furthermore, improvements and information are required to lessen the cost of collaboration between operators. For an example of safety, the supplier provides relevant information to another supplier before the transfer of the (Gates and Hexter, 2005) buyer's goods is completed after the buyer has requested the transfer. In addition, once the eligibility has been determined, the transfer material formats must be compatible.

9.3.3.5 Adversity Restoration

Adversity restoration includes both physical and electronic malfunctions of consumer property. In emergencies, the duplication of info on terrestrial sites is commendable. Legal involvement may provide the only solution in other physical disasters such as hardware theft. For electronic errors, error tolerance methods such as repetition and variation work, relying on the digital risk secured. Environmental hazard rehabilitation assessment applies to all its resources hosted and should be achieved and implemented as soon as possible. These are complex as the user may not associate with the information where work is held.

9.3.4 Compliance Obligations

Whenever information or process of data is transferred to the remote, the user maintains a high compliance obligation, but the operator may be better positioned to enforce compliance laws. Several problems make it difficult to obey the law and deal with legally binding agreements. The official departments are changing how they provide the solution for problems of users with compliance issues.

9.3.4.1 Deficit Perceptibility

Users may not be familiar with the working of clouds. If so, they will probably not say that their services were performed and delivered securely. Various services of cloud distribution standards sum up the various levels of user command and provide diverse perceptibility levels to the user. Moreover, the alternative for the users to requisition that supplementary examined method used on the user location is acceptable and presently used in offline remote services.

9.3.4.2 Substantial Data Site

Enterprise management decided to install data facilities center by calculating several parameters, including installing expenses, electricity prices, protection issues, skilled employees, exertions expenses, and the variety of public infrastructure. Customers may be required to comply with worldwide, federal, or national legal guidelines that restrict the cache of data without unique restrictions.

9.3.4.3 Sovereignty and Governance

Consumers may be subject to various regulations, such as the Credit Card Industry, Data Security Standard, the Health Information and Accountability Act, the Information Security Act, and the Management Act. Consumers responsible for keeping their data processed in supplier plans need to be assured by providers that they are helping to comply with applicable laws. Consumers also need to guarantee legal capacity in cloud offerings so that if vendors fail to conform, legal remedies are understood in advance. These requirements are convoluted because carriers frequently view the monitoring of their offerings as patent or do not offer customers transparency on the information (Scott, 2007). It is not easy for users to ensure that providers comply with the law unless they receive independent research from a trusted third party. The auditing of companies is limited in assurance provided, as the cloud system may be quietly swept away by noncompliance, and further monitoring of cloud configuration and health may be desirable (NIST, 2013).

9.3.4.4 Forensic Support

To respond to an incident, the purpose of digital forensics is to (1) identify what befell, (2) recognize what components of the machine are affected, (3) discover ways to prevent such incidents from occurring again, and (4) collect information approximately viable prison movements through the years in the future. Forensics in the cloud shows new matters:

- How are event management obligations defined?
- Do clocks sync all data locations to rebuild a series of functions?
- Are notification laws treated in international locations?
- Can the cloud provider look at data when sharing hard drive images?
- What is the user authenticated to see in the test log; for example, are data compared to other cloud users secure?
- What is the consumer's obligation to complain to the private service model?
- Can the provider legally interfere with forestalling the application attack in its cloud if it is far more superficial than an oblique contract courting (e.g., three classes of clients)?

9.3.5 Security Advice

Security recommendation is worried about confidentiality and integrity of facts and making sure facts availability. The organizations that manage its information technology (IT) operations generally take the following types of measures to protect its data:

- Physical control is related to the protection of storage media and storage facilities.
- Ownership and access control, technical controls, data encryption at rest and on the go, and other data test management requirements are needed to comply with regulatory requirements.

Organization registers for the cloud and all the data generated and processed remain in the domain owned and operated by the provider. In this context, the critical issue is whether the consumer can ensure that the supplier uses a similar assessment. Moreover, the problems come when a client tries to verify the availability of these controls:

- For data encryption, the clout of the encoding algorithm, the key-encryption support schemes supported by the operator, and several individual information data holders.

This is because consideration affects data security and processing done in the cloud. For example, the quality of cloud use, the location of the cloud attack, the potential for attackers, the complexity of the system, and the level of technology of cloud controllers are just a few of the factors that affect cloud security.

Unfortunately, none of these assumptions determines cloud security, and there are no apparent answers when compared to the cloud and non-cloud systems about which ones are the most secure to operate. However, one full feature in cloud systems is reliance on "reasonable separation," as opposed to "physical separation" of users' workloads, and the use of sensible methods to protect consumer resources.

9.3.5.1 Data Acknowledgment Liability

In the typical case, the user stores sensitive information in different directions in the system or different mail messages on the email server. Here, confidential data are handled to neglect unintentional networks. Moreover, if a customer uses the cloud to create a computer-resistant computer while maintaining the security benefits of computer architecture.

9.3.5.2 Data Isolation

Data isolation deals with the privacy of the data of certain companies, such as users' or others' information is processed by the system. Its confidentiality holds a legal or binding concern and is considered a technical issue and ethical consideration. Securing confidentially of the system is a technical provocation in a cloud system, thus claiming compounded from the widespread nature of the cloud user consciousness.

9.3.5.3 Service Principle

Clouds need protection against deliberate decay or destruction. Inside the cloud are participants: buyers, suppliers, and various managers. The ability to separate access rights for each group while keeping malicious attacks away is vital in maintaining cloud integrity. In the cloud system, any absence of accountability could make it complicated for clients to test the virtue of remote-based utilities.

9.3.5.4 Diverse Holding

It gains suitable financial efficiency by resource fragment to operator aspect. Because the sharing methods used in the provider center depend on complexity factors to keep consumer responsibility divergent, the hazard of segmentation collapse occurs. However, digital classification errors were recorded in achieving data. It is alleviated by encoding the info before embedding it to the cloud. With cloudy performing statistics, mitigation is possible by lessening the types of information refined in the cloud operator of special operational methods.

9.3.5.5 Gateways

Several applications use the buyer's gateways as a cloud interface with an image. However, the technique grants the user to provide cloud computing software "sounds like space," which works with cloud architecture. Furthermore, sometimes operators distribute client tools here. Gateways are also used to set up customer accounts and resource management, including creating economic data. Unfortunately, gateways contradict the ramification of preexisting applications, and gateways are shown to have safety features and are esteemed to almost all social security issues. Providers work with various gateways and consumers; controlled storage systems and gateways may not be adequately handled to be secure or not up-to-date. If the buyer's gateways are terminated, all consumer services provided by the cloud provider are at risk.

9.3.5.6 Hardware Service Certainty

Hardware service certainty support may allow clients to comprehend the reliability of clouds. Furthermore, hardware service certainty aims to maintain various quality checks started at the beginning of the system and confirm when prompted that the system has started in available parts. As the visual equipment moves, the Trusted Platform Module (TPM) trust network appears to weaken. Different groups have tried to make High Performance Computing (HPC) a reality or create a conflict where a revived HPC (Racz et al., 2020) can restore trust in servicing hardware, but this problem is still the same.

9.3.5.7 Executive Service

Safeguarding user-encoded data keys seems to need collaboration with cloud operators. Moreover, issues are remote computers, creating an egg in a memory buffer may not remove the key if (1) the memory is backed up by a continuous hypervisor, (2) the Executive Service (ES) takes a summary, and (3) information is configured to transfer on the number of systems.

9.4 Administering Prospect in the Cloud

Administrating prospect cloud systems may be evidence from a stunning departure excursion. Consumers should avoid using the cloud for sensitive-time programs.

- The most critical security software. Due to the absence of competence to thoroughly scan the "genealogy" of all subordinate systems that make up the cloud and due to network variability, the use of cloud technology in the most critical security applications at this time is not recommended.

- Working Time Support. Before deciding to submit an altered request in the cloud, the buyer must secure that the respiratory is admitted in the integration stage and the respiratory is concurring the performance stage.
- Configure utilization. Users must confirm that the new request is configured to operate securely and correlate with business to implement business/agency security framework principles (Mather et al., 2009). In addition, users should select cloud-based services and tools when possible.

In the cloud ecosystem, the structure accord between cloud roles, entity character objectives, word processing, and knowledge support systems needed an integrated, comprehensive risk management ecosystem, which directs all the needs of cloud roles. An information system based on a cloud model is authoritative for assessing the perceived risk, based on the limit placed on risk supervise security risks at the ecosystem stage; the briefing features must be rectified:

- Risk management obligations of cloud participating in the cloud ecosystem chart. Each cloud continues to delegate to its senior leaders, managers, and representatives.
- Establishing an ecosystem-wide risk cloud and communicating this risk through service-level agreements (SLAs), which include propaganda on judging risk activities.
- Through management, detection, and perception by each cloud Host, the security information results from the operational and exercise of a system that supports the ecosystem of the cloud and resilience for the remaining ecosystem risk as shown in Figure 9.2.

9.4.1 Risk Managing Policy

Generally, the liability is portrayed for the potential action for a negative result multifolded by magnitude. In information security, opportunities are perceived as a function of system threats' potential risks, and the results of these risks are used. Ideally, securing risk assessment focuses on recognition where harmful drills of the ecosystem occur.

The operations of RMF are primarily in phase III of the disaster management phase and interact with phase I and phase II. Risk-based access to organizing information systems is a complete task committed to being utterly open to all aspects of the association, from preparing to circulation processing of system progress to allocating security controls and continuity. Other exemplary interventions comply with the safety officer's assessment for administration, monitoring, and broadcasting reports to official authorities or owners of the system information.

9.4.2 Cloud Operators' Risk Utilization Process

The risk management framework presented in Figure 9.1 process that government institutions and industry organizations should evaluate as the best alternative to their traditional knowledge systems. Managing surveillance for a group and designing and establishing self-solutions are complex, highly expensive processes to reduce risk effectively. Providers and resellers that best meet the needs of the cloud buyer choose from a user directly or in place of accredited cloud providers. Moreover, remaining security and privacy controls

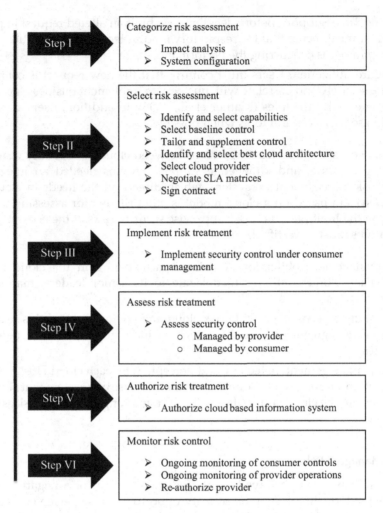

FIGURE 9.2
Cloud risk management framework applied to the cloud ecosystem.

need to be addressed in agreements between cloud consumers and other eligible cloud actors. Finally, review and approve the protection plan risk treatment (design mitigation policies and programs). The cloud consumer needs special attention to SLAs and engages procurement professionals, technicians, and organizational policy to ensure that the SLA principles will allow an organization to achieve its goal and operational requirements. Such evade agreements cannot sufficiently cover consumer cloud requirements and may lag user transparency in service delivery methods.

In short, adopting a cloud system, users need solutions to analyze their security requirements actively, evaluate the security and privacy of each service provider, negotiate an SLA with Service agreements, or confidence-building between service operators and the user just before they authenticate the service. Comprehensive risk calculation associated with the composition of the secure cloud ecosystem presented in this chapter and adequate guidance to negotiate SLAs is intended to assist cloud consumers with risk management and informed decision-making by adopting cloud services.

9.5 Reference Guidelines

In the framework of cloud security risk management, some common referencing guidelines are divided into different categories: management, jurisdiction, safety, authenticity, virtual engines, and software utilities (NIST, 2019).

9.5.1 Administration

- **Transferring Data from the Cloud.** Consumers must identify appropriate resources for moving data in and out of the cloud. Users must build a system to transfer data from the cloud and interact with the data when they reside in the cloud. Utilities can be services such as (1) email, (2) data repositories, or (3) service work in virtual circumstances. Buyers should also arrange for the termination of the supplier service at the end of the contract purchase phase, and they should specify how the goods should be returned to the buyer.

- **Regularity in Activities.** The management strategy is to review system integrity, information transfer, and other qualifications. Users request confirmation that the provider is using the subjective functioning method. However, the user audits the operator's business progress plan or job structure to recognize whether the declared method is sustained. Finally, a consideration of users is that a service agreement generally states that providers reimburse users for service interruptions by reimbursing servicing costs. The cloud service availability, storage capacity, and risk recovery should be based on the emergency and continuous process to safeguard the recovery. If required, the recovery of interrupted cloud service and operations, using other resources, equipment, and resources.

- **Compliance with the Law.** The user (1) ensures whether the ability to define the required controls exists within a selected operator, (2) ensures whether those controls are being used correctly, and (3) determines the controls are reliable. Conventional testing methods are impossible, and these needs work with a cloud operator to obtain the required information and system access or allow third-party testing to obtain an adequate level of validation. Also, the buyer reviews the certificates or research statements available from the cloud operator regarding their vision of integration.

- **Staff List.** Internal security is a significant problem in many organizations and is enhanced for cloud operators. Therefore, the users ensure that cloud providers' policies, procedures, and protection controls for malicious invaders are adequate. Consumers should ensure that there are procedures to separate the responsibilities of supplier managers and consumer management responsibilities.

- **Official.** Users should examine whether the operator can support temporary legal applications: (1) e-discovery, such as suspension, and (2) storage and metadata retention.

- **Operational Policies.** Consumers must verify supplier performance policies: (1) their commitment to audits and security certificates; (2) accidental responses or process of recovery, including forensic investigation skills; (3) internal investigation procedures for illegal or improper use of IT services; and (4) specific application evaluation policies, such as system providers and network authority.

- **Configure User Policies**. A provider must ensure that the consumers read and understand the supplier's approved use policy and negotiate an agreement to resolve certain stages of the policy violation in advance with the supplier. In addition, consumers need to know the process as an essential part of how disputes about potential policy violations are resolved between them and the provider.
- **Licensing**. Consumers must ensure that the provider and the buyer have a valid license to own any software installed on the cloud.
- **Financial Management**. Consumers and providers must agree on procedures that a consumer must perform an offline application test to ensure that the application continues to work instead of the necessary online refund procedures. The service agreement should specify system management team plans (Sum, 2012)

9.5.2 Jurisdiction

- **Data Classification**. When data for different sensitivity levels are processed in the cloud, several different clouds can be used simultaneously to provide different levels of protection against sensitive information and sensitive data. Consumers should take this approach to take precautionary measures to separate confidential data from the operator's location.
- **Data Integrity**. Here, users use checksum or repetition technology to store information. In addition, information must be safeguarded from illegal cloud alteration when tested, verified, and used if test statistics are reserved individually.
- **Data Rules**. Users need the cloud server to meet global or national laws and regulations that must be complied with, for example, preventing data retention without certain restrictions. The user must evaluate the risk of achieving data in the cloud as the defined user is answerable to compliance and legal terms related to the data.
- **Data Storage**. User requirements from the cloud operator to provide a way to remove customer data when requested reliably and prove that the data have been removed.
- **Data Recovery**. Consumers should be able to evaluate providers' competencies concerning (1) a backup copy, (2) an archive, and (3) an acquisition (Von Solms and Van Niekerk, 2013).

9.5.3 Safety and Authenticity

- **Consumer Risk Factors**. Users should reduce the likelihood that gateways or different business resources will be assaulted by using the most appropriate method for the protection and stability of client forums and look toward reducing gateway hazards for potentially harmful websites.
- **Crucifixion**. Consumers should require strong encryption for web times and other network communications whenever a hired application requires the privacy of applications and other applications or data transfers. And consumers should demand that the same diligence be applied to the database.
- **Physical Risk**. Physical attacks require conservation techniques, as do online assaults. Users may prescribe recovery guidelines for these assaults. Additionally,

the user must consider whether an operator provides service efficiency on their websites or select nonbinding suppliers in a natural disaster or other disruption.

- **Verification.** Consumers should consider using authentication tokens or other appropriate enhancement certificates provided by other providers to reduce the assassination from hackers and other forms of exploitation.

- **Ownership and Avenue.** Users must have transparency in the following supplier strengths: (1) assurance and access control systems supported by the provider's infrastructure, (2) tools available to consumers to provide verification information, and (3) input tools and maintain consumer user authorizations and applications without provider intervention.

- **Maintenance Needs.** They should evaluate the real-time maintenance grades of the app that obtain the essential points before applying to the provider's site. Key performance points include interactive application responses and bulk data transfer functionality for applications that must regularly transfer (input or output) large amounts of data.

- **Appearance.** Consumers seek operator access to services that alter certain customer information or work on that information, combining managing services (NIST, 2013).

9.5.4 Virtual Engines

When providers provide computer services in the form of virtual engines (VEs), consumers should ensure that the provider has a way to protect VEs from (1) other VEs in the same virtual host, (2) the host itself, and (3) the network.

9.5.5 Software Utilities

The most crucial software utility applications that require an accurate completion time seem to be unsuitable for the public and specific computer computing systems outsourced due to differences.

9.6 Conclusion and Future Work

Cloud security risk assessment in this chapter, assesses the concerned model, risk, threats and calculates the individual risks related to the asset. The approach also incorporates combined risk values from cloud security services. Furthermore, the risks associated with these assets are modeled using their strengths and usability. Finally, risk factors are attributed to organizations and stakeholders. It should be noted that the risk management factor is essential for a particular cloud organization to determine specific measures (reduction/block/transfer/acceptance) that should be used to protect its security. Moreover, when a cloud corporation ensures to utilize another organization's services, participants' unique risks should be considered in selecting an appropriate service provider.

Future work is focused on validating the proposed approach to organizations and developing a tool based on this. In addition, we aim to include information about cloud security capabilities while calculating risk factors. This may help to assure security measures are taken by your cloud service provider.

The quantitative cloud risk assessment methodology proposed in this chapter, models assets, vulnerabilities, and threats and computes the individual risks associated with an asset. The methodology also computes combined risk values from the perspectives of communication service providers, common service centers, and common type systems. The proposed scheme first lists the various assets of a cloud organization.

Values are assigned to these assets after considering the possible physical and logical dependencies between them. The vulnerabilities associated with these assets are modeled using their severity and exploitability values. Similarly, the modeling of threats is performed using LoC (likelihood of occurrence) values. Then, the breachability value is calculated for threat-vulnerability pairs, and security concern is derived from the breachability and severity values. Finally, risk factors are computed for assets and stakeholders.

It should be noted that the asset-specific risk factor is essential for a particular cloud organization for deciding the specific measures (mitigation/prevention/transfer/acceptance) that should be implemented to protect its assets. However, when a cloud organization needs to utilize the services of another organization, the stakeholder-specific risk should be considered for choosing a suitable service provider. Future work is geared toward the validation of the proposed methodology in actual organizations and the subsequent development of a tool based on this.

Moreover, we intend to include information regarding cloud security capabilities (e.g., data-at-rest encryption, multifactor authentication, trusted cloud computing platform) of the provider during the computation of risk factors. This would help provide assurance about the security measures that are deployed by the cloud service provider.

References

Alavi, R., Islam, S., and Mouratidis, H. (2014). A Conceptual Framework to Analyze Human Factors of Information Security Management System (ISMS) in Organizations. In *Proceedings of the Second International Conference on Human Aspects of Information Security, Privacy, and Trust, 8533* (pp. 297–305). doi:9.907/978-3-319-07620-1_26.

Arunachalam, P., Janakiraman, N., Sivaraman, A. K., Balasundaram, A., Vincent, R., Rani, S., ... Rajesh, M. (2021). Synovial Sarcoma Classification Technique Using Support Vector Machine and Structure Features. *Intelligent Automation & Soft Computing, 32*(2), 1241–1259.

Banerjee, K., Bali, V., Nawaz, N., Bali, S., Mathur, S., Mishra, R. K., and Rani, S. (2022). A Machine-Learning Approach for Prediction of Water Contamination Using Latitude, Longitude, and Elevation. *Water, 14*(5), 728.

Bhambri, P., Aggarwal, M., Singh, H., Singh, A. P., and Rani, S. (2022). Uprising of EVs: Charging the Future with Demystified Analytics and Sustainable Development. In *Decision Analytics for Sustainable Development in Smart Society 5.0* (pp. 37–53). Springer, Singapore.

Bhambri, P., Bagga, S., Priya, D., Singh, H., and Dhiman, H. K. (2020). Suspicious Human Activity Detection System. *Journal of IoT in Social, Mobile, Analytics, and Cloud, 2*(4), 216–221.

Bhambri, P., and Chhabra, Y. (2022). Deployment of Distributed Clustering Approach in WSNs and IoTs. In *Cloud and Fog Computing Platforms for Internet of Things* (pp. 85–98). Chapman and Hall/ CRC, Singapore.

Bonazzi, R., Hussami, L., and Pigneur, Y. (2009). Compliance Management is Becoming a Major Issue in IS Design. In *Information Systems: People, Organizations, Institutions, and Technologies* (pp. 91– 98). Springer, doi:9.907/978-3-7908-2148-2, ISBN 978-3-7908-2147-5, archived from the original (PDF) on 209-03-9, retrieved 2013.

Campbell, T. (2016). Organizational Security. In *Practical Information Security Management: A Complete Guide to Planning and Implementation* (pp. 43–61). Chapter 4, APress. Springer, New York.

Gates, S., and Hexter, E. (2005). *From risk management to Risk Strategy*. The Conference Board, New York.

Gupta, O., Rani, S., and Pant, D. C. (2011). Impact of Parallel Computing on Bioinformatics Algorithms. In *Proceedings 5th IEEE International Conference on Advanced Computing and Communication Technologies* (pp. 206–209). IEEE.

Kaur, G., Kaur, R., and Rani, S. (2015). Cloud Computing-A New Trend in IT Era. *International Journal of Scientific and Technology Management*, 1(3), 1–6.

Kaur, K., Dhanoa, I. S., and Bhambri, P. (2020). Optimized PSO-EFA Algorithm for Energy Efficient Virtual Machine Migrations. In *2020 5th IEEE International Conference on Recent Advances and Innovations in Engineering (ICRAIE)* (pp. 1–5). IEEE.

Kshirsagar, P. R., Jagannadham, D. B. V., Ananth, M. B., Mohan, A., Kumar, G., and Bhambri, P. (2022). Machine Learning Algorithm for Leaf Disease Detection. In *AIP Conference Proceedings* (vol. 2393, no. 1, p. 020087). AIP Publishing LLC.

Liu, X. (2019). The Role of Enterprise Risk Management in Sustainable Decision-Making: A Cross-Cultural Comparison. *Sustainability*, *11*, 299.

Mather, T., Kumaraswamy, S., and Latif, S. (2009). *Cloud Security and Privacy. Printed in the United States of America*, O'Rellly, Beijing.

Mohanta, H. C., Geetha, B. T., Alzaidi, M. S., Dhanoa, I. S., Bhambri, P., Mamodiya, U., and Akwafo, R. (2022). An Optimized PI Controller-Based SEPIC Converter for Microgrid-Interactive Hybrid Renewable Power Sources. *Wireless Communications and Mobile Computing*, 2022, 25–32.

NIST Publication (2019). *Cloud Computing Synopsis and Recommendations*. Department of Commerce, Washington DC, USA.

NIST Special Publication (2011a). *Guidelines on Security and Privacy in Public Cloud Computing*. Department of Commerce, Washington DC, USA. 800-144.

NIST Special Publication (2011b). *The NIST Definition of Cloud Computing*. Department of Commerce, Washington DC, USA.

NIST Special Publication (2013) *Security and Privacy Controls for Federal Information Systems and Organizations*. Department of Commerce, Washington DC, USA.

NIST Special Publication (2019). Guide for Applying the Risk Management Framework to Federal Information Systems. *A Security Life Cycle Approach*, Department of Commerce, Washington DC, USA.

Nocco, B. W., and Stulz, R. (2006). Enterprise Risk Management: Theory and Practice. *Journal of Applied Corporate Finance*, *18*(4), 8–20.

Racz, N., Weippl, E., and Seufert, A. (2020). A Frame of Reference for Research of Integrated GRC. In *Communications and Multimedia Security, 11th IFIP TC 6/TC 11 International Conference, CMS 209 Proceedings*, (pp. 96–117). Springer, Berlin.

Rani, S., Bhambri, P., and Chauhan, M. (2021). A Machine Learning Model for Kids' Behavior Analysis from Facial Emotions using Principal Component Analysis. In *2021 5th Asian Conference on Artificial Intelligence Technology (ACAIT)* (pp. 522–525). IEEE.

Rani, S., Bhambri, P., and Gupta, O. P. (2022). Green Smart Farming Techniques and Sustainable Agriculture: Research Roadmap towards Organic Farming for Imperishable Agricultural Products. In *Handbook of Sustainable Development through Green Engineering and Technology* (pp. 49–67). CRC Press, Florida, USA.

Rani, S., and Gupta, O. P. (2016). Empirical Analysis and Performance Evaluation of Various GPU Implementations of Protein BLAST. *International Journal of Computer Applications*, *151*(7), 22–27.

Rani, S., Kataria, A., and Chauhan, M. (2022). Fog Computing in Industry 4.0: Applications and Challenges—A Research Roadmap. *Energy Conservation Solutions for Fog-Edge Computing Paradigms*, Chapman and Hall/CRC, Florida, USA, (pp. 173–190).

Rani, S., Kataria, A., Chauhan, M., Rattan, P., Kumar, R., and Sivaraman, A. K. (2022). Security and Privacy Challenges in the Deployment of Cyber-Physical Systems in Smart City Applications: State-of-Art Work. *Materials Today: Proceedings*, *62*(7), 4671–4676.

Rani, S., Kataria, A., Sharma, V., Ghosh, S., Karar, V., Lee, K., and Choi, C. (2021). Threats and Corrective Measures for IoT Security with Observance of Cybercrime: A Survey. *Wireless Communications and Mobile Computing*, *2021*, 1–30.

Rani, S., and Kumar, R. (2022). Bibliometric Review of Actuators: Key Automation Technology in a Smart City Framework. *Materials Today: Proceedings*, *60*(3), 1800–1807.

Rani, S., Mishra, R. K., Usman, M., Kataria, A., Kumar, P., Bhambri, P., and Mishra, A. K. (2021). Amalgamation of Advanced Technologies for Sustainable Development of Smart City Environment: A Review. *IEEE Access*, *9*, 150060–150087.

Saeidi, P., Sayyedeh, P.S., Saudah, S., Mehrbakhsh, N., and Mardani, A. (2019). The Impact of Enterprise Risk Management on Competitive Advantage by Moderating Role of Information Technology. *Computer Standards & Interfaces*, *6*, 29–36.

Scott,L. M. (2007). GRC360: A Framework to Help Organizations Drive Principled Performance. *International Journal of Disclosure and Governance*, *4* (4), 279–296, doi:9.957/palgrave.jdg.2050066.

Sen, J. (2013). Security and Privacy Issues in Cloud Computing. In *Innovation Labs, Security and Privacy Handbook*. Tata Consultancy Services Ltd., Kolkata, India.

Sum, R. M. (2012). Risk Management Decision Making: The Analytic Hierarchy Process Approach. In *Expo 2012 Higher Degree Research: Book of Abstracts* (p. 54), Sydney, November 12–13.

Terroza, A.K.S. (2015). Information Security Management System (ISMS) Overview. In *The Institute of Internal Auditors*. Archived from the original (PDF) on 7 August 2016. Retrieved 2018.

Von Solms, R., and Van Niekerk, J. (2013). From Information Security to Cyber Security. *Computers & Security*, *38*, 97–102.

10

Relevance of Multifactor Authentication for Secure Cloud Access

Charanjeet Singh and Ramandeep Kaur

CONTENTS

10.1 Introduction

The cloud computing paradigm has advanced at a rapid pace in the past two and half decades. The reduced operational costs and capital expenditures have been the major motivational factors for organisations to adopt this technology (Bhambri and Chhabra, 2022). In addition, its ability to offer multidimensional values, such as agility, innovation and scalability, have also motivated organisations to embrace this technology to support their businesses. According to a report by Fortune Business Insights, in 2020, the global cloud computing market size was US$219.00 billion. The market is likely to reach from US$250.04 billion in 2021 to US$791.48 billion in 2028 at a compound annual growth rate (CAGR) of 17.9% between 2021 and 2028. This growth is attributed to the deployment of progressive technologies such as artificial intelligence and machine learning in cloud computing (Fortune Business Insights, 2021).

DOI: 10.1201/9781003298335-10

The best way to achieve the balance between energy usage and quality of service is workload-aware energy-efficient virtual machine (VM) consolidation (Kaur et al., 2020). In collaboration with machine learning and artificial intelligence, anomaly detection systems are vastly used in behavioural analysis to help in identifying and predicting the prevalence of anomalies (Bhambri et al., 2020; Gupta and Rani, 2013). To produce pulse-width modulation pulses for the generator-side converter, a proportional and integral (PI) controller is utilized (Mohanta et al., 2022). As more and more organisations are adopting cloud technology, information security is becoming crucially important. About 85% of organisations keep their sensitive data in the cloud, and about 70% of these have serious concerns about security matters (Vormetric, 2016; Rani and Gupta, 2017). In the absence of physical control and dependence on third-party resources, it is sheer important to ensure that the processed end users' data and the credentials are safe from unauthorised access. Thus, security concerns top the list in preventing organisations from moving to infrastructure as a service (IaaS; Brodkin, 2010). The development of a strong charging structure network is broadly known as a vital necessity for a huge-scale evolution to electromobility (Arunachalam et al., 2021; Bhambri et al., 2022). Kshirsagar et al. (2022) cover research on various methodologies for the use of neural networks to detect plant leaf diseases.

Cloud computing has several different security issues such as data leakage (Zuo et al., 2019), insider attacks (Duncan et al., 2012), outsider attacks (Krombholz et al., 2015), Denial-of-service (DoS) attacks (Bonguet and Bellaiche, 2017), attacks related to change over, poor recovery management, data segregation issues and access management issues that cause organisations to refrain from adopting it. These security issues hamper CIA (confidentiality, integrity and availability) aspects of security (Abbas et al., 2017). Today, every networking field is working only through it due to COVID-19 (Bhambri et al., 2022).

In addition to earlier cited issues, the deployment of a poor authentication model is also considered a major threat to users' data in a cloud environment (Jesudoss and Subramaniam, 2014). Thus, employing a strong authentication mechanism is a critical requirement in cloud access so as to ensure end users' transparency and privacy.

10.2 Authentication

Authentication is a process of verifying users' identities with an intent to provide access to a specific resource only to a legitimate user. Therefore, it plays a vital role in information security in insecure cloud environment. Authentication is a three-step process that involves identifying, authenticating and authorising the user (Renaud, 2005).

Due to the speedy digitalization of multiple resources and their on-demand availability in the cloud, authentication is a ubiquitous exercise. It is no longer limited to financial transactions or the workplace; it is integrated into our everyday lives, ranging from making a phone call to visiting our favourite online store. Therefore, a traditional username-password authentication scheme does not provide sufficient security against modern means of attack (Ran et al., 2021, 2022).

In cloud environment, as organisations and users leave their assets open to intrusions by bad actors or other cyberthreats, a strong authentication mechanism is critical for maintaining secure information technology (IT) infrastructure. Hence, developing and employing a robust authentication model is imperative and need of the hour (Singh et al., 2019a;

Rani and Kaur, 2012). There are numerous ways of verifying the identity of users, that is, to authenticate them before providing access to a resource ranging from simple systems such as a username-password scheme to complex systems, such as biometric and/or one-time-usage-based variable tokens/one-time passwords (OTPs). The next section discusses these ways on the basis of these factors.

10.2.1 Authentication Factors

In a cloud environment, identity verification systems evaluate users for specific charac-teristics provided by them during registration in order to verify that they are the same persons that they claim to be. In this way, they are validated before granting them access to a software application or a network (Gupta and Rani, 2010; Lim et al., 2017). These characteristics or the specific pieces of information used to validate the identity of a user are also known as authentication factors. The authentication factors are classified in three categories:

1. **Knowledge-Based**: *Something that a user knows.* It includes the information that a user carries mentally in terms of characters, letters, digits and/or their combina-tion. Graphical images, patterns locks, the order of clicks on specific icons/images and PINs are knowledge-based authentication (KBA) factors.

2. **Possession-Based**: *Something that a user has.* It includes physical objects that a user carries. It may perhaps be in the form of hardware or software tokens/certificates. It also includes hardware devices such as USB devices, cell phones, key cards, badges, smart cards and so on. OTPs generated by smartphone apps and OTPs delivered via text or email also fall under this category. Mobile authentication, in which the user receives a code via a smartphone, variations that include text mes-sages and phone calls sent to a user as an out-of-band method are also possession-based methods.

   Although this factor relieves the user from the burden of memorising and recall-ing the information mentally,it requires the user to produce proof of ownership to the system.

3. **Inherent Qualities-Based**: *Something the user is.* It includes biological features such as fingerprints, retina, iris, facial pattern, hand geometry, earlobe geometry and voice pattern. It also includes certain behavioural characteristics of a user such as handwriting and typing speed. These factors are unique to each and every user.

4. **Location-Based**: *Somewhere the user is.* It includes verifying the location of a user before granting access to an application, network or system. IP addresses, MAC address of the users' device (unique to an individual computing device) or geo-location of the user can be used for location-based authentication (Intelligence, 2022).

The summary of various authentication techniques based on different categories of factors is presented in Table 10.1 (Singh et al., 2019b; Rani and Kumar, 2022).

Authentication factors can also be categorised either as transparent or interactive. Transparent authentication does not involve user interaction such as Bluetooth device proximity and geofencing. On the other hand, interactive authentication requires user to do something (Kaur et al., 2015; Zhang et al., 2018), for example, entering a PIN or a pattern code.

TABLE 10.1

Various Authentication Factors

Category	Technique	Explanation	
Knowledge-Based	Numeric Password	A secret numeric 4/6/8-digitpassword, e.g., ATM PIN	
	Alphanumeric Password	Alphanumeric string of characters	
	Graphical Password	Recall-based: Recalling pictures chosen during registration process	
		Pure recall–based: Recall pictures without any hint	Cued recall–based: Recall pictures with a hint
		Recognition-based: Choose a set of preselected pictures from a set of pictures	
Possession-Based	Tokens	Static token: Device that store secret number, cryptographic keys, digital signature, or biometric data	
		Synchronous dynamic token: OTPs	
		Asynchronous tokens: Enter a challenge number on the token keypad to generate a response to the challenge	
		Challenge-response token: Smart cards	
Inherent Quality–Based	Biological Features	Fingerprints, iris and retina, face, hand and ear geometry	
	Behavioural Characteristics	Voiceprint, keystroke dynamics and signature dynamics	
Location-Based		IP address, MAC address of a device or geographical location of user	

10.3 Authentication Based on Number of Factors

Based on the number of factors involved in an authentication scheme, it is classified into three basic types:

1. **Single Factor (SFA)**: Single-factor authentication uses only one factor that is typically a knowledge-based. It is either a textual username-password scheme requiring the user to recall a password or a graphical password scheme whereby the user gets authenticated by selecting a specific set/sequence of images. It characterizes weakest form of authentication.

2. **Two Factor (2FA)**: Two-factor authentication adds one more factor (token or OTP) in addition to username-password scheme. It enhances security by adding an extra layer above the first factor. The most common example of 2FA is the verification method used for ATM transactions in which a PIN is used as a second factor in addition to the ATM card for withdrawing money.

3. **Multifactor (MFA)**: MFA integrates two or more authentication factors to provide access to a resource. These factors may be the combination of knowledge-, possession-, inherence- or location-based (Figure 10.1). 2FA is a type of MFA. In order to qualify to be MFA scheme, it is imperative that a scheme must have authentication factors at least from two different categories. For example, an ATM transaction

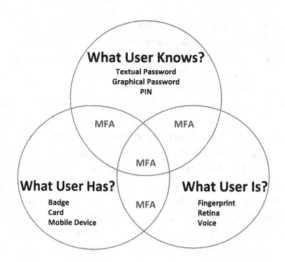

FIGURE 10.1
MFA.

done via smart card and PIN is MFA as two factors involved belong to two distinct categories, that is, possession- and knowledge-based, respectively. However, scheme that authenticates a user by entering a password and a PIN is not an MFA scheme as both the factors involved are knowledge-based only. MFA is a principal constituent of a robust identity and access management policy and is often referred as *strong authentication*.

10.4 Need for MFA

To meet the objective of ensuring adequate data security in the cloud, it is important to deploy an authentication system with an appropriate design that implements proper data access policies (Anakath et al., 2019). Poorly designed authentication model not only compromises an organisation's critical data but also places the entire IT infrastructure at risk.

The traditional username-password system is an SFA scheme that is most popular because of its ease of use. However, it is considered to be the most insecure mode due to its susceptibility to multiple attacks including brute force, password guessing, snooping and dictionary attacks. Graphical passwords, another KBA-SFA scheme, however, provide protection against these attacks but suffer from shoulder surfing and usability issues such as longer registration and login times (Suresh and Prakash, 2015; Gupta, 2017).

The deployment of possession-based SFA scheme also does not guarantee adequate security. It not only incurs additional costs of hardware devices but also makes it difficult on the part of users to carry cards, badges and tokens physically, thereby inviting the fear of their loss and theft. Although inherence-based SFA techniques have gained substantial attention because of their reliability, accuracy and permanency and uniqueness of biological features, they involve a huge expenditure in terms of infrastructure setup and maintenance for capturing, processing and matching biological features (Alsaadi, 2015). Such systems usually include a reader, a database and software to convert the scanned biometric data into a standardized digital format and compare match points of the observed data with stored data. Inherence- and possession-based authentication factors may be the robust means of securing a network or application against unauthorized access but depending solely on them in a cloud environment is a risky affair. Individual authentication factors on their own may present security vulnerabilities, either due to user behaviour patterns and habits or because of the limitations of technology.

In an insecure cloud environment, the only reliable solution for strengthening security by means of strong authentication is to create an MFA model by integrating multiple factors or by creating a multilevel authentication structure (Bhivgade et al., 2014; Rani and Gupta, 2016).The confidence of authenticity increases exponentially when multiple authentication factors are involved in the verification process.

MFA creates a layered or multi-level defence structure that helps in keeping data and systems secure by adding numerous barriers that stop bad actors in their paths, thereby making it difficult for an illegitimate user to access an application, service or resource. In such an environment, if one authentication factor is compromised, the unauthorised user also has a second or third authentication factor to breach before successfully breaking into the system. Furthermore, the time required to break an authentication system with multiple factors costs additional effort.

An MFA scheme is adaptive in nature in the sense that it adjusts per the security risk posed by the intruder. It offers the highest level of security for checking the validity of a user as each factor creates a new barrier that an intruder has to cross independent of the previous factor. Thus, the probability of breaching various factors in an MFA scheme is very less in comparison to SFA and 2FA (Gupta et al., 2011; Singh, 2019).

10.5 Benefits of MFA

The essence of multifactor authentication is to harden security access to systems and applications through varied hardware and software (Shacklett, 2022). The potential benefits of employing MFA include the following (Malik, 2021):

1. MFA enhances security. Illegitimate users fail to breach the security and gain access to resources even if they succeed in stealing passwords, mobile devices or OTPs as chances to access to all or multiple credentials are prevented in MFA. MFA thus not only lowers the incidence of stolen credentials and unauthorized access to data but also adds an additional layer of security for local access, back-end access and other common network entry points.

2. Employing MFA helps in reducing the risk from compromised passwords. The problem posed by reused or shared passwords is decreased manifold. A report by Microsoft security (Maynes, 2020) reveals that the risk of identity compromise can be reduced by as much as 99.9% over the passwords alone if an MFA system is used.

3. With MFA, enterprises can offer customisable security solutions to their users.

4. MFA can be easily integrated with SSO (single-sign-on) applications.

5. MFA is scalable and can be easily set up for multiple users, including employees, customers and vendors.

6. It offers flexibility in log-in options from a variety of devices and locations, thus helping manage change in workplace and complex access requests.

7. It offers suitability for financial transactions as well as for critical data access applications, thereby offering adaptability for different user cases.

10.6 Application Areas of MFA

In the past, MFA was only utilised in environments that demands an extremely high level of security. But these days it is a common practice to use it for multiple purposes, including online transactions, banking and shopping. It is becoming a mandatory feature for cloud-based services, especially for accounts with administrative purposes.

MFA finds its application in three core areas, namely commercial, governmental and forensic (Ometov et al., 2018). Several different organisations use MFA techniques for financial, physical access control and e-commerce purposes. Examples of such organisations include Rackspace, Bank of America, Amazon Web Services (AWS), Microsoft, GitHub, Apple and the US Department of Defense. Numerous MFA software such as Duo Multi-Factor Authentication, Prove MFA, HID Global Identity and Access Management, ESET Secure Authentication, Ping Identity, Typing DNA Verify 2FA, Thales SafeNet Trusted Access, Twilio Authy, OKTA Adaptive Multi-Factor Authentication, RSA SecureID Access and SecureAuth Identity Platform are available in the market that offers commercial use. Various governmental applications of MFA include verifying identity documents, government ID, passport, driver's licence, social security, border control and so on, whereas forensic applications include criminal investigation, missing children, corpse identification and more.

The usage of MFA or 2FA is most common practice for financial transactions. Even in India, the Reserve Bank of India has made it mandatory to use 2FA for all online transactions via a debit or credit card. Many organisations like Google, Facebook and Yahoo are now offering OTP-based 2FA to their users as an optional feature (Fleischhacker et al., 2014; Banerjee et al., 2022).

10.7 Implementation of MFA

Many MFA products require users to deploy client software to make MFA systems work. The process usually involves different stages, namely registration/enrolment and login/authentication (Otemuyiwa, 2016; Rani et al., 2021). A majority of multifactor authentication schemes employ KBA factor usually username-password as the first factor for authentication. For the second factor, there are a number of choices, such as Time-based One Time Password (TOTP), biometric or tokens (hardware/software), that vary from vendor to vendor or depend on clients' requirements. To accomplish authentication using a second factor, the user needs to register a specific set of information, such as phone number/email id or fingerprint/retina/hand/iris/face pattern, during enrolment process. Depending on the type of second factor used for an MFA scheme, the authentication/verification stage delivers TOTP either on a user's registered phone number/email for verification that needs to be reconfirmed via SMS from the registered number or by entering it into an authentication interface (Google Cloud Identity Platform, 2022). A second or third factor may also make use of any of the biometric or behavioural factors stored in the authentication system for verification during enrolment. Thus, there is always a choice between possession-based mobile devices or hardware tokens and inherence-based fingerprints/iris/signature patterns as a second factor. Some vendors have created separate installation packages for network login, web access credentials and VPN connection credentials.

10.7.1 Usage of a Combination of Transparent and Interactive Factors

While implementing MFA usage of transparent and interactive factors offers an effective combination. In such a system, for low-risk activities transparent factor can authenticate a user whereas for higher-risk activities an interactive factor can be employed.

10.7.2 Usage of Client-Side Authentication

The increasing use of smartphone devices for accessing various services has influenced smartphone giants like Apple and Samsung to integrate fingerprint readers in these devices. This development has further propelled the usage of client-side authentication in MFA technology. With this, users have a choice of selecting among various transparent and an interactive authentication factor, thereby offering flexibility and strength. In client-side authentication, as all data and authentication processes are stored safely and processed locally on the user's device, it is inaccessible to both the authentication server as well as the requesting application (Bedell and Thelander, 2018).

10.7.3 Usage of Out-of-Band Authentication

Another important implementation strategy for MFA includes the usage of out-of-band authentication. It further strengthens the authentication process as the users' credentials are submitted and verified via two separate channels, making it difficult for the hacker to steal the login credentials and breach the authentication process (Abdellaoui, 2015). This is more secure in contrast to in-band authentication, whereby credentials are provided and authenticated via the same channel.

10.7.4 Usage of a Decentralised Architecture

Employing decentralised authentication further augments the security as storage and verification of credentials is done via an out-of-band method for each user whereas centralized authentication takes place in-band. Moreover, a centralised system or application stores credentials of all its users at one location, thereby just providing a single layer of authentication that can be easily breached, thereby compromising the entire credential store.

Decentralised authentication architecture is beneficial for both users as well as businesses. It provides protection against massive credential theft as the authentication layer is shifted outside the application. Moreover, the usage of separate out-of-band channel for each user confines the credential breach only to a specific user. Additionally, it protects the central repository of credentials by confining the risk to the application layer itself.

The authentication layer is distributed among multiple user clients, whereby users can themselves manage them, thereby increasing the convenience that results in greater user adoption. Decentralization is also well suited for Internet of Things (IoT) environments that involve diverse devices and networks as it shifts the load of user authentication to mobile devices. These two factors also suit businesses as they need not invest heavily in an authentication infrastructure and IT professionals, thus reducing additional costs.

Another crucial requirement for implementing MFA is dynamic authentication whereby users and companies have the flexibility to change security requirements from application to application, as well as within each application itself. It offers a multi-layered approach that helps in adapting to specific authentication policies in real time. As a result, MFA technologies are able to adapt to varying risk conditions (Athmani, 2019).

10.8 Challenges of MFA

The adoption of MFA may be a challenging task not only for users but for organisations as well as it requires a lot of efforts to configure and deploy it.

Adding varied authentication factor on the top of traditional username-password scheme augments the security, but at the same time, it may adversely affect usability. The low-usability issue is a major area of concern in MFA (Gunson et al., 2011; Bonneau et al., 2012). There is always a trade-off between security and usability. It is crucial that a good MFA should strike a balance between the two. The process of registration and login should not be complicated that users refrain from adopting an MFA technique (Singh, 2019). In addition, the cognitive load of the scheme should be minimal.

The design of an MFA feature may have substantial implications on security, usability, and cost in any context. Employing a higher assurance second factor may increase the hassle for both end users and administrators. This can impact the adoption of MFA technique, thereby decreasing security. The effective solution to this problem is to use adaptive authentication that considers context and behaviour while authenticating the user such as location/time/device/network type of the user while accessing the service or resource.

Users find MFA to be inconvenient as it slows them down when they log into multiple accounts per day. To address this challenge a one-time login application called SSO can be used that automatically logs authorized users into all the connected accounts.

In order to offer robust protection, it is important that the next-generation MFA technologies should address and resolve issues pertaining to centralized credential stores as password-based techniques in centralised architecture present a liability.

Employing MFA does not itself guarantee a complete solution to security. The misconfigurations and improper practices by users and organisations can expose an MFA system to hackers and may also compromise the system's security.

An MFA system that uses hardware equipment to verify biometric- or possession-based factors often incurs additional costs that may not fit in the budget of certain organisations and users. Although many mobile device companies have developed mobile phone with integrated facial, fingerprint and retina scan systems, still such devices are costly and troublesome for a certain set of users.

Apart from the previously cited issues, additional challenges in the adoption of MFA techniques include vendor dependency and biometric-factor dependency. An MFA solution not being an open-source technology is another challenge in its adoption. As a majority of MFA solutions available in the market use a biometric as a second factor, it may pose integration issues as well.

10.9 Future of MFA

The future scope of MFA includes integrating authentication with authorization so as to determine the access right that a user has on a specific resource. This integration will save the time as the user will be granted the specific right at the time of verifying the identity itself.

In 2020, the MFA market was valued at US$10.64 billion, and it is expected to reach US$28.34 billion by 2026 and grow at a CAGR of 17.83% over the forecast period (2021–2026) (Mordor, 2022). Two upcoming trends in MFA are blockchain and decentralized authentication systems. These technologies are likely to replace centralized data and application servers. In order to provide better authentication, user identities will be represented with encryption keypairs that can be tied to a user's inherence factors.

Risk-based authentication is another upcoming field that will enhance security beyond the second factor for specific situations.

10.10 Conclusion

The usage of MFA tops the list of best practices to ensure cybersecurity. During the COVID-19 era, it has gained rapid acceptance in a cloud environment that requires a remote workforce. MFA makes it difficult for an adversary to exploit the login process and prevents them from gaining unauthorised access. It is important that an MFA scheme should strike an adequate balance between enhanced security and usability. The augmented security should neither affect ease/comfort of use nor the cost factor for an organisation or individual.

References

Abbas, H., Maennel, O., and Assar, S. (2017). Security and Privacy Issues in Cloud Computing. *Annals of Telecommunications*, 72(5–6), 233–235. https://doi.org/10.1007/s12243-017-0578-3.

Abdellaoui, A., Khamlichi, Y. I., and Chaoui, H. (2015). Out-of-Band Authentication Using Image-Based One Time Password in the Cloud Environment. *International Journal of Security and Its Applications (IJSIA)*, 9(12), 35–46.

Alsaadi, I. M. (2015). Physiological Biometric Authentication Systems, Advantages, Disadvantages and Future Development: A Review. *International Journal of Scientific and Technology Research*, 4(12), 285–289.

Anakath, A., Rajakumar, S., and Ambika, S. (2019). Privacy Preserving Multi Factor Authentication Using Trust Management. *Cluster Computing*, 22, 10817–10823. https://doi.org/10.1007/s10586-017-1181-0.

Arunachalam, P., Janakiraman, N., Sivaraman, A. K., Balasundaram, A., Vincent, R., Rani, S., ... Rajesh, M. (2021). Synovial Sarcoma Classification Technique Using Support Vector Machine and Structure Features. *Intelligent Automation and Soft Computing*, 32(2), 1241–1259.

Athmani, S., Bilami, A., and Boubiche, D. E. (2019). EDAK: An Efficient Dynamic Authentication and Key Management Mechanism for Heterogeneous WSNs. *Future Generation Computer Systems*, 92, 789–799.

Banerjee, K., Bali, V., Nawaz, N., Bali, S., Mathur, S., Mishra, R. K., and Rani, S. (2022). A Machine-Learning Approach for Prediction of Water Contamination Using Latitude, Longitude, and Elevation. *Water, 14*(5), 728.

Bedell, C. and Thelander, M. (2018). *Multi-Factor Authentication for Dummies* Special Edition, Iovation, USA.

Bhambri, P., Aggarwal, M., Singh, H., Singh, A. P., and Rani, S. (2022). Uprising of EVs: Charging the Future with Demystified Analytics and Sustainable Development. In V. Bali, V. Bhatnagar, J. Lu, and K. Banerjee (Eds.), *Decision Analytics for Sustainable Development in Smart Society 5.0* (pp. 37–53). Springer, Singapore.

Bhambri, P., Bagga, S., Priya, D., Singh, H., and Dhiman, H. K. (2020). Suspicious Human Activity Detection System. *Journal of IoT in Social, Mobile, Analytics, and Cloud, 2*(4), 216–221.

Bhambri, P., and Chhabra, Y. (2022). Deployment of Distributed Clustering Approach in WSNs and IoTs. In P. Bhambri, S. Rani, G. Gupta, and A. Khang (Eds.), *Cloud and Fog Computing Platforms for Internet of Things* (pp. 85–98). Chapman and Hall/CRC.

Bhivgade, T., Bhusari, M., Kuthe, A., Jiddewar, B., and Dubey, P. (2014). Multi-Factor Authentication in Banking Sector. *International Journal of Computer Science and Information Technologies, 5*(2), 1185–1189.

Bonguet, A., and Bellaiche, M. (2017). A Survey of Denial-of-Service and Distributed Denial of Service Attacks and Defenses in Cloud Computing. *Future Internet, 9*(3), 1–19.

Bonneau, J., Herley, C., Van Oorschot, P. C., and Stajano, F. (2012). The Quest to Replace Passwords: A Framework for Comparative Evaluation of Web Authentication Schemes. In *2012 IEEE Symposium on Security and Privacy (SP)* (pp. 553–567). IEEE.

Brodkin, J. (2010). 5 Problems with SaaS Security. *Network World.* [Online]. https://www.networkworld.com/article/2219462/5-problems-with-saas-ecurity.html (Accessed: June 2019).

Duncan, A., Creese, S., and Goldsmith, M. (2012). Insider Attacks in Cloud Computing. In *IEEE 11th International Conference on Trust, Security and Privacy in Computing and Communications* (pp. 857–862). IEEE Computer Society, Washington, DC, USA.

Fleischhacker, N., Manulis, M., and Azodi, A. (2014). A Modular Framework for Multi-Factor Authentication and Key Exchange. In L. Chen and C. Mitchell (Eds.), *Security Standardisation Research. SSR 2014. Lecture Notes in Computer Science* (vol. *8893*). Springer, Cham. https://doi.org/10.1007/978-3-319-14054-4_12.

Fortune Business Insights. (2021). Cloud Computing Market, 2021-2028. *Cloud Computing Market to Reach USD 791.48 Billion by 2028* (globenewswire.com) (Accessed: February 2022).

Google Cloud Identity Platform. (2022). Adding Multi-Factor Authentication to your Web App. *Adding Multi-Factor Authentication to your Web App | Identity Platform Documentation | Google Cloud.* (Accessed: February 2022).

Gunson, N., Marshall, D., Morton, H., and Jack, M. (2011). User Perceptions of Security and Usability of Single-Factor and Two-Factor Authentication in Automated Telephone Banking. *Computers and Security, 30*(4), 208–220.

Gupta, O., Rani, S., and Pant, D. C. (2011). Impact of Parallel Computing on Bioinformatics Algorithms. In *Proceedings 5th IEEE International Conference on Advanced Computing and Communication Technologies* (pp. 206–209). IEEE.

Gupta, O. P. (2017). Study and Analysis of Various Bioinformatics Applications Using Protein BLAST: An Overview. *Advances in Computational Sciences and Technology, 10*(8), 2587–2601.

Gupta, O. P., and Rani, S. (2010). Bioinformatics Applications and Tools: An Overview. *CiiT-International Journal of Biometrics and Bioinformatics, 3*(3), 107–110.

Gupta, O. P., and Rani, S. (2013). Accelerating Molecular Sequence Analysis Using Distributed Computing Environment. *International Journal of Scientific and Engineering Research, 4*(10), 262–266.

Jesudoss, A., and Subramaniam, N. P. (2014). A Survey on Authentication Attacks and Countermeasures in a Distributed Environment. *Indian Journal of Computer Science and Engineering (IJCSE), 5*(2), 71–77.

Kaur, G., Kaur, R., and Rani, S. (2015). Cloud Computing-A New Trend in IT Era. *International Journal of Scientific and Technology Management, 1*(3), 1–6.

Kaur, K., Dhanoa, I. S., and Bhambri, P. (2020). Optimized PSO-EFA Algorithm for Energy Efficient Virtual Machine Migrations. In *2020 5th IEEE International Conference on Recent Advances and Innovations in Engineering (ICRAIE)* (pp. 1–5). IEEE.

Krombholz, K., Hobel, H., Huber, M., and Weippl, E. (2015). Advanced Social Engineering Attacks. *Journal of Information Security and Applications*, 22, 113–122.

Kshirsagar, P. R., Jagannadham, D. B. V., Ananth, M. B., Mohan, A., Kumar, G., and Bhambri, P. (2022). Machine Learning Algorithm for Leaf Disease Detection. In *AIP Conference Proceedings* (vol. 2393, no. 1, p. 020087). AIP Publishing LLC.

Lim, S. Y., Kiah, M. M., and Ang, T. F. (2017). Security Issues and Future Challenges of Cloud Service Authentication. *Acta Polytechnica Hungarica*, 14(2), 69–89.

Malik, Z. (2021). 8 Benefits of Multi-factor Authentication (MFA). *8 Benefits of Multi-Factor Authentication (MFA)* (pingidentity.com). (Accessed: February 2022)

Maynes, M. (2020). IT Executives Prioritize Multi-Factor Authentication in 2020. Microsoft Security. *IT Executives Prioritize Multi-Factor Authentication in 2020* (microsoft.com). (Accessed: February 2022).

Mohanta, H. C., Geetha, B. T., Alzaidi, M. S., Dhanoa, I. S., Bhambri, P., Mamodiya, U., and Akwafo, R. (2022). An Optimized PI Controller-Based SEPIC Converter for Microgrid-Interactive Hybrid Renewable Power Sources. *Wireless Communications and Mobile Computing*, 2022, 25–32.

Mordor Intellegence. (2022). Multi-Factor Authentication Market—Growth, Trends, COVID-19 Impact, and Forecast (2022–2027). https://www.mordorintelligence.com/industry-reports/multifactor-authentication-market (Accessed: March 2022).

Ometov, A., Bezzateev, S., Mäkitalo, N., Andreev, S., Mikkonen, T., and Koucheryavy, Y. (2018). Multi-Factor Authentication: A Survey. *Cryptography*, 2(1). https://doi.org/10.3390/cryptography2010001.

Otemuyiwa, P. (2016). What are the Different Ways to Implement Multifactor Authentication? https://auth0.com/blog/different-ways-to-implement-multifactor/ (Accessed: February 2022).

Rani, S., Bhambri, P., and Chauhan, M. (2021). A Machine Learning Model for Kids' Behavior Analysis from Facial Emotions using Principal Component Analysis. In *2021 5th Asian Conference on Artificial Intelligence Technology (ACAIT)* (pp. 522–525). IEEE.

Rani, S., and Gupta, O. P. (2016). Empirical Analysis and Performance Evaluation of Various GPU Implementations of Protein BLAST. *International Journal of Computer Applications*, 151(7), 22–27.

Rani, S., and Gupta, O. P. (2017). CLUS_GPU-BLASTP: Accelerated Protein Sequence Alignment Using GPU-Enabled Cluster. *The Journal of Supercomputing*, 73(10), 4580–4595.

Rani, S., Kataria, A., and Chauhan, M. (2022). Fog Computing in Industry 4.0: Applications and Challenges—A Research Roadmap. In R. Tiwari, M. Mittal., and L. M. Goyal (Eds.), *Energy Conservation Solutions for Fog-Edge Computing Paradigms* (Vol. 74, pp. 173–190). Springer, Singapore.

Rani, S., and Kaur, S. (2012). Cluster Analysis Method for Multiple Sequence Alignment. *International Journal of Computer Applications*, 43(14), 19–25.

Rani, S., and Kumar, R. (2022). Bibliometric Review of Actuators: Key Automation Technology in a Smart City Framework. *Materials Today: Proceedings*, 60(3), 1800–1807.

Rani, S., Mishra, R. K., Usman, M., Kataria, A., Kumar, P., Bhambri, P., and Mishra, A. K. (2021). Amalgamation of Advanced Technologies for Sustainable Development of Smart City Environment: A Review. *IEEE Access*, 9, 150060–150087.

Renaud, K. (2005). Evaluating authentication mechanisms. In L. Cranor, and S. Garfinkel (Eds.), *Security and Usability: Designing Secure Systems That People Can Use*, Chapter 6 (pp. 103–128). O'Reilly Media, USA.

Shacklett, M. E. (2022). *What is Multifactor Authentication (MFA) and How Does it Work?* (techtarget.com.) (Accessed: Febuary 2022.)

Singh, C. (2019). *An Enhanced Multifactor Authentication Model for Cloud Computing* (Doctoral dissertation, I K Gujral Punjab Technical University, Kapurthala, Punjab).

Singh, C., and Singh, T. D. (2019a). A 3-Level Multifactor Authentication Scheme for Cloud Computing. *International Journalof Computer Engineering Technology (IJCET)*, 10(1), 184–195.

Singh, C., and Singh, T. D. (2019b). Evaluation of 3 Level Multifactor Authentication Model based on Click-GPass Graphical Password Scheme. *International Journal of Innovative Technology and Exploring Engineering (IJITEE)*, 8(7), 1904–1913.

Suresh, S., and Prakash, G. (2015). On Reviewing the Limitations of Graphical Password Scheme. *Journal of Computer Science and Engineering Research*, 2014, 1(1), 31–35.

Vormetric (2016). 85% of Enterprises Store Sensitive Data in the Cloud. 70% are Very Concerned. *PRNewswire*, San Jose. [Online]. https://www.prnewswire.com/news-releases/85-of-enterprises-keeping-sensitive-data-in-the-cloud-70-very-or-extremely-concerned-about-it-according-to-2016-vormetric-data-threat-report--cloud-big-data-and-iot-edition-300225175.html (Accessed: June 2019).

Zhang, J., Tan, X., Wang, X., Yan, A., and Qin, Z. (2018). T2FA: Transparent Two-Factor Authentication. *IEEE Access*, 6, 32677–32686.

Zuo, C., Lin, Z., and Zhang, Y. (2019). Why Does Your Data Leak? Uncovering the Data Leakage in Cloud from Mobile Apps. In *Proceedings of the 2019 IEEE Symposium on Security and Privacy*, San Francisco, CA.

11

LBMMS: Load Balancing with Max-Min of Summation in Cloud Computing

Ranjan Kumar Mondal, Payel Ray, Enakshmi Nandi and Debabrata Sarddar

CONTENTS

11.1 Introduction

Load balancing [1] with task scheduling is an imperative research topic in the cloud computing field. To gain high-quality performance, efficient load balancing of a task is

DOI: 10.1201/9781003298335-11

necessary. Finding an optimal resource allocation algorithm for the effective utilization of resources is a crucial job. The basic motivations of load balancing are finding the resource, collaborating on resource statistics, and carrying out a job.

With growing crime rates and a lack of confidence globally, many countries are adopting precise anomaly detection systems as an approach to make areas more comfortable [2, 3]. Today, every networking field is working only through it due to COVID-19 [4]. The best way to achieve a balance between energy usage and quality of service is a workload-aware energy-efficient virtual machine (VM) consolidation [5, 6]. Cloud users accomplish their applications in a distributed manner. After this process, users submit their tasks to the respective cloud resource broker. The resource broker, at that time, wants to know about the cloud information service and their properties for the availability of resources. In the next stage, cloud resources are registered in more than one information service. After the scheduling process, the resource broker monitors the job execution process and collects the results. In the last stage, the results are sent back to the users [3].

For decreasing the makespan, numerous load-balancing methods are available [7–11]. All these algorithms identify the resources that should be allocated to the tasks in order to lower the overall task completion time. Minimizing the total execution time of all tasks does not imply that the actual execution time of each task is minimized [12, 13].

Min-Min [14–16] and Max-Min [17] are two simple yet well-known load-balancing algorithms. Two algorithms function by taking into account the time it takes for each task to be completed on each cloud computing server. The Min-Min algorithm first finds the task with the shortest execution time. Then, out of all the jobs now running, it picks out the one with the shortest execution time. The system then assigns jobs to the resources that take the least amount of time to complete [18, 19]. Min-Min continues in this manner until all chores have been scheduled. The disadvantage of the Min-Min algorithm is that it prioritizes the smallest tasks, resulting in higher resource utilization and execution power. However, there is a risk that smaller tasks will take precedence over larger ones. As a result, the Min-Min scheduling process's technique is not ideal [20, 21]. The Max-Min algorithm was created to solve this problem, allowing larger tasks to be completed first. However, the Max-Min algorithm has sometimes increased the waiting time for smaller tasks [22].

The algorithm proposed in this chapter performs tasks related to make span and load-balancing factors. Hence, a better load balancing is achieved, and we get an improved reduced execution time across the whole system with our proposed algorithm than other already-existing algorithms [23–25]. Here the proposed algorithm applies the well-known Hungarian method. Then, we discuss a literature review of existing algorithms and their drawbacks in this work. Then, we propose our work.

11.2 Background

Cloud system is a term that refers to a new form of internet-based network-based computing that is a step up from utility computing, which is a group of integrated and networked hardware, software, and web infrastructure [26]. Clients get hardware, software, and networking services when they use the web for communication and the transportation of data [27]. By providing an elementary applications programming interface (API), these platforms hide the complexity and details of the underlying infrastructure from clients and applications [28]. Furthermore, the platform provides on-demand services that may be accessed at any time and from any location [29]. Pay for usage and elastic scaling up and down in capacity and functionalities are needed [30]. Hardware and software services are obtainable by the public, businesses, and markets [31]. The term *cloud system* is used to describe web-based services [32].

Everything in Cloud Computing

FIGURE 11.1
Cloud computing architecture.

Because it is distributed in nature, a cloud system is primarily used. It is made for remote access and storage heterogeneity. It also provides services such as computation capabilities and applications, among other things. The cloud system enters the picture today because it delivers great reliability over a large network. However, because demand is dynamic in nature, it necessitates dynamic resource allocation. Because of the dynamic resource allocation in cloud systems, effective load-balancing mechanisms are required. Load balancing is the process of evenly distributing resources among clients or demands so that no machine is overloaded or inactive [4]. If the load balancing is incorrect, the effectiveness of some overloaded machines can degrade, resulting in a service-level agreement (SLA) violation. Based on their nature, load-balancing algorithms can be classified into three categories: static, dynamic, or mixed scheduling algorithms.

1. A static load-balancing technique is appropriate for small-scale distributed systems with fast web speeds and no communication delays.

2. A dynamic load-balancing algorithm is primarily used to decrease communication delays and time to completion in large distributed systems.

3. A mixed load-balancing algorithm is used to achieve symmetrical distribution of assigned computing tasks while lowering the cost of communication between distributed computing machines. As stated previously, cloud systems are classified as part of the second category. It means that balancing the load in the background of a

cloud system necessitates a focus on dynamic load-balancing algorithms. Process migration is less expensive in conventional dispersed environments because the processing granularity is minimal, but it is more expensive in computing environments because the data granularity is large [33]. As a result, the background of a cloud system requires a load-balancing algorithm that can change client service demands while providing optimized load balancing. In the context of cloud computing, the following parameters exist in the literature for evaluating the effectiveness of a load-balancing algorithm: reliability, adaptability, fault tolerance, throughput, and wait time.

FIGURE 11.2
The benefits of cloud computing.

There are three service models present in cloud systems:

1. **IaaS**: The infrastructure-as-a-service model only provides the hardware and network. It allows clients to develop and install their operating system and software and run any application they want on their cloud hardware [34].

2. **PaaS**: The platform-as-a-service model provides the client with an operating system, hardware, and network. It allows clients to create cloud-based applications using vendor-specific tools and languages.

3. **SaaS**: In the software-as-a-service model, the client receives a prebuilt application along with any required software, hardware, operating system, and network.

11.2.1 Deployment Models

There are three deployment models present in cloud systems:

1. **Public Cloud**—This deployment model is a notable one that can be accessed in the cloud background. Web-based public services are provided based on predefined policies. Dropbox, Gmail, Office 365, Google, Amazon, Yahoo, and Microsoft are examples of private clouds that provide public services.

2. **Private Cloud**—A client or a single business group uses a private cloud model. Because the unique setup is implemented safely within the firewall, the private cloud solves the security issues. The private cloud model is only available to a single client or business group. This company can fully utilize the cloud to meet all of its requirements. IBM's WINDOW AZURE is an example of a sun cloud.

3. **Hybrid Cloud**—A hybrid cloud that associations public and private cloud services. Google Compute Engine is an example.

11.3 Load Balancing

Load is a system performance that is also a unit of computational work. There are various types of loads available: CPU load and network delay load, the amount of memory used. So we can say that load balancing is, therefore, one of the significant results in the era of cloud computing. Load balancing is a method of balancing processing over-the-internetwork so that multiple devices are used. Load balancing is essential for networks as it is challenging to forecast the requests from users' nodes that are issued to a host server. If any server goes, it starts to get interchanged, and then requests are transferred to another server that has more capacity, and the busy server provides two or more web servers for load-balancing purposes. The main issue of load balancing is to reduce the utilization of resources, exploit throughput, reduce response time, and avoid overloading the resources [35].

The goals of load balancing are to

- increase system performance considerably,
- have a backup facility in case the system fails,
- maintain system consistency, and
- provide stability against system changes.

Efficient load-balancing algorithms are needed to ensure balance and even load distribution on nodes or servers.

11.4 Problem Definition

In this case, the suggested algorithms have been settled for an assumption:

- The completed applications are constituted within a collection of inseparable tasks that are independent of each other.
- The tasks having no deadlines or priorities cooperated with them.
- The expected execution time of task foreach machine that is known can be assessed. These evaluations can be provided before a task is implemented or at the time it is submitted.

- The mapping process is to be carried out statically in a batch mode trend.
- The mapper runs on several machines and confines the execution of all jobs on all machines in the suite.
- Each machine executes a single task simultaneously, consorting with the assigned tasks.
- The dimensions of the meta-tasks and the figure of machines in the various computing environment is known.

11.4.1 Virtualization

Virtual workspaces are a simplified version of a complete backdrop that may be made dynamically accessible to authorized clients via well-defined protocols, resource limits, and software setup (e.g., operating system, provide services) and virtual machines.

11.4.2 Implementation

A hypervisor is an abstraction of a physical host computer that intercepts and emulates instructions from virtual machines and allows management of virtual machines, such as Xen, providing the following infrastructure API: hardware/support structure plugins. Virtual machines offer the following benefits: they can execute operating systems even if physical hard drives are unavailable. Constructing new machines, backup machines, and so on is easier. Software testing is carried out on "clean" operating systems and software installations. More machines that are physically present should be emulated on a single host, time-share lightly loaded systems. Troubleshoot issues (suspend and resume the problem machine), and virtual machine migration is simple (shutdown needed or not) to carry on with legacy systems [36].

11.4.3 Scheduling

Threads, processes, and data flows are granted access to system resources (e.g., processing time, communications capacity) through scheduling. This is generally done to properly load balance a system or attain a desired level of service quality. The necessity for most contemporary systems to conduct multitasking (running many processes at the same time) and multiplexing necessitates the use of a scheduling mechanism (transmit multiple flows simultaneously) [37]. The scheduler is mostly concerned with the following:

1. **Throughput**: The total number of completed processes per time unit
2. **Latency in particular**:
   - Turnaround time is the amount of time it takes for a procedure to be completed after it is submitted.
   - Response time is the time it takes for a request to be processed from the moment it is sent to the time it receives its first response.
3. **Waiting Time**: Each process receives equal CPU time (or, more broadly, suitable times based on the importance of each task). It is the amount of time a process stays in the ready queue.

11.5 The Motivation for Load Balancing

There are more thana million servers connected to the internet that deliver various types of web services to cloud customers. A small number of cloud-connected servers must simultaneously perform over a million operations. As a result, completing all jobs at the same time is difficult. Because some nodes do all jobs, all loads must be balanced at the same time. Load balancing reduces completion time and ensures that all activities are completed consistently. Maintaining an equivalent number of servers is impossible to carry out equal duties.

The tasks to be accomplished in cloud computing would be greater than the connected computers could handle at times. A million jobs must be completed on a limited number of servers. We propose an approach in which certain nodes execute jobs in which the number of jobs is more than the nodes, and all nodes are balanced to maximize the quality of cloud computing services [38].

Example 1:

One million servers are available to execute one million or more jobs simultaneously. Suppose an information technology (IT) company has 1,000 servers and has to execute 1,000tasks or subtasks at a time. It wants to execute all tasks at a certain time. There are many procedures to solve this problem to complete all tasks. We propose a new technique to execute all tasks in minimum time with load balancing.

In a cloud computing system, there are multiple different nodes. Specifically, each node has a different capability to do the work, so considering merely the CPU remaining on the node when selecting a node to execute a task is insufficient. As a result, in cloud computing, knowing how to choose a competent node to complete a task is critical. So it is a very difficult job to execute all different tasks on different machines at the same time. When a user wants to execute their value task on a company server, they will want to execute their task in minimum time; otherwise, they go to another company server. If many users have to wait more time, when the waiting time is greater than the expected execution time of a particular task, it is a drawback to that company. All machines' capabilities to execute a task or tasks are not equal, and the completion time or execution time of all tasks, subtasks, or particular tasks may not be equal by a particular machine.

11.5.1 Meta-Task About Machines

Suppose executing a particular task to be executed by different machines takes different times as follows:

Machine	M_1	M_2	M_3	M_4	M_5	....	M_m
Task (ms)	10	12	13	13	11		16

As the different machines have different capabilities for executing the same task, similarly, the same machine executes different tasks indifferent times as follows:

Task	T_1	T_2	T_3	T_4	T_5	....	T_n
Machine (ms)	26	22	18	26	19		21

So some machines execute some tasks in different times as follows:

T_iM_j	M_1	M_2	M_3	M_4	M_5	....	M_m
T_1	17	24	31	29	34	...	27
T_2	25	34	23	28	25	...	32
T_3	19	32	23	27	36	...	29
T_4	23	34	23	34	42	...	29
T_5	25	14	23	25	35	...	19
...	...	...	...	...	...	...	...
T_n	17	23	23	32	27	...	28

11.5.2 System Manager

A cloud is made up of multiple separate machines. Specifically, each machine has a different skill set for completing work; thus, considering merely the machine's remaining CPU is insufficient when selecting a machine to do a task. As a result, choosing the right machine to do a task is a critical challenge in cloud computing. Due to the task's unique characteristics, the user may be required to pay for its performance. As a result, it requires some specific resources. For example, implementing organism sequence assembly is likely to have a high memory need. And in order to achieve the most efficient execution of each task, we will aim for a task property to adopt a distinct condition decision variable in which the decision variable is set according to a resource of task requirement. In this study, a service manager obtains the associated information from each machine in this cloud computing system, such as CPU capabilities, memory, and network bandwidth. After all this information is obtained, it will be given to the manager, who will use it to help maintain the system's load balancing. The following are the definitions of the factors:

V_1, which represents the remaining CPU capabilities;

V_2, which represents the remaining memory; and

V_3, which represents the transmission rate.

To help the manager select appropriate machines, all the machines in the system (including the service manager and service machine) will be evaluated against a threshold generated from the demand for resources required to complete the task. The service manager who passes the "service manager threshold" is regarded as effective and will be the manager's candidate for effective machines. The service machines that pass the "threshold of service machine" are regarded as effective and will be considered by the service manager as candidates for effective machines.

The cloud computing environment is made up of heterogeneous machines, each with its own set of characteristics. In other words, the CPU's computing capability, accessible memory size, and transmission rate are all different. Furthermore, because cloud computing makes use of each system's resources, the available resources of each machine may fluctuate in a complicated situation. The presented CPU capacity, accessible memory size, and transmission rate are the three decisive criteria for the duration of execution in terms of job completion time. As a result, the threshold for estimating service manager values in our study was set at the presented CPU capacity, accessible memory size, and transmission rate. As an example of specific, consider the following:

1. The CPU capability of 510 MB/s
2. The memory of 205438 KB/s
3. Bandwidth rate 8.03 MB/s

J_iM_j	M_1	M_2	M_3	M_4	M_5	....	M_m
J_1	12	24	32	27	24	...	25
J_2	15	34	23	28	25	...	32
J_3	17	32	23	26	36	...	27
J_4	23	33	33	36	42	...	29
J_5	15	14	23	45	55	...	27
...	...	...	...	...	...	...	...
J_n	17	13	23	42	17	...	26

11.5.3 Problem Definitions

The assignment problem is the problem of assigning various types of jobs to different computers in a cloud system in such a way that the assignment cost is kept to a minimum. An unbalanced assignment problem occurs when the number of tasks does not equal the number of machines.

Consider an issue involving a collection of "m" devices. $M_n = M_1, M_2, ..., M_n$. A set of "n" jobs ($J = J_1, J_2, ..., J_n$) is considered, each of which must be assigned to one of the m existing machines for execution. The cost of executing each job on all machines is acknowledged and recorded in an n-dimensional matrix. The goal is to find the cheapest option. This problem is handled using the well-known and widely used Hungarian approach.

11.5.4 Machine Specification

Each machine has a meta-task, which is listed in the following table. The processing speed and bandwidth of M_1 and M_5 are also shown. The processing speed is measured in millions of instructions per second, and the bandwidth is measured in megabits per second.

Machine	Processing Speed (MIPS)	Bandwidth (MBPS)
M_1	180	60
M_2	156	76
M_3	185	68
M_4	210	56
M_5	160	83

11.5.5 Job Specification

J_1 to J_8's instruction and data volumes are represented in the following table. The instruction volume is expressed in million instructions, and the data volume is expressed in megabytes.

Job	Instruction Volume (MI)	Data Volume (MB)
J_1	7845	327
J_2	10564	224
J_3	9285	126
J_4	12010	207
J_5	8960	183
J_6	7596	306
J_7	10245	517
J_8	11472	475

11.5.6 The Execution Time of the Jobs of Each Machine

The following table shows the execution time of each job of their corresponding machine.

Job/Machine	M_1	M_2	M_3	M_4	M_5
J_1	43.58	50.28	42.40	37.35	49.03
J_2	58.69	67.71	57.10	50.30	66.02
J_3	51.58	59.52	50.18	44.21	58.03
J_4	66.72	76.99	64.92	57.19	75.06
J_5	49.78	57.43	48.43	42.67	56.00
J_6	42.20	48.69	41.05	36.17	47.47
J_7	56.91	65.67	55.37	48.78	64.03
J_8	63.73	73.53	62.01	54.62	71.70

11.5.7 Required Algorithms

Suppose one company has one server only and executes one task at a time; there is no need to apply any algorithm. If there is more than one server and only one task, then for the server that is most suitable for that task, the task is to be assigned to that machine. We apply two existing algorithms if there are more servers and equal tasks. But these algorithms are not optimized, so we propose a new algorithm that can give a better result. If there is an equal number of servers to tasks, where the number of tasks is greater than the number of machines, then we apply our proposed algorithm. In this chapter, we work with some machines and some tasks parallel as the number of tasks is greater than the number of machines to get the minimum completion time and optimal value. In this type of algorithm, we follow a procedure like a matrix as follows:

J_n/M_m	M_1	M_2	M_3	M_4	M_5
J_1	151	277	185	276	321
J_2	245	286	256	264	402
J_3	246	245	412	423	257

J_n/M_m	M_1	M_2	M_3	M_4	M_5
J_4	269	175	145	125	156
J_5	421	178	185	425	235
J_6	257	257	125	325	362
J_7	159	268	412	256	286
J_8	365	286	236	314	279

11.6 Flow Chart of the Load-Balancing Algorithm

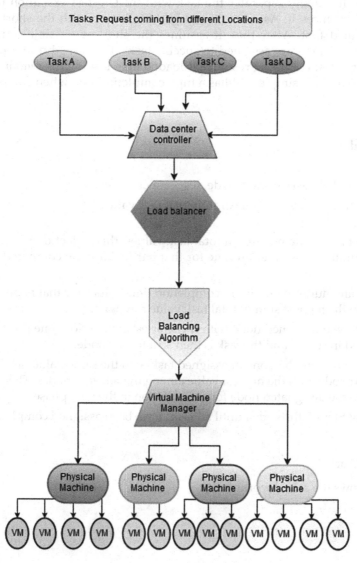

FIGURE 11.3
The procedure of the load-balancing algorithm.

11.7 Proposed Method

We look at a problem with a set of m machines to calculate the matrix cost and a mix of tasks versus machines in an unbalanced matrix problem. $M = M_1, M_2, \ldots, M_n$. The execution cost C_{ij}, as $I = 1, 2, \ldots, m$ and $j = 1, 2, \ldots, n$ are stated in the cost matrix as $m > n$, is regarded to be assigned to a set of n tasks $J = J_1, J_2, \ldots, J_n$ for execution on the m existing machines.

11.7.1 Load Balancing with Max-Min of Summation

Load balancing with Max-Min of summation(LBMMS) is the name of our suggested cloud scheduling method. The method begins by completing the steps in each node's total jobs first. It initially separates the task with the shortest execution time from the resource that produces it. As a result, in LBMMS, the job with the shortest execution time is scheduled first. After that, it assumes the shortest possible completion time because some resources are assigned to specific tasks. Because Min-Min prioritizes the shortest jobs, the fast-executing resource is loaded first, leaving the remaining resources inactive. However, it is simple and has a high completion rate when compared to other algorithms.

11.7.2 Method

Step 1: First, add all tasks of each node, respectively.

Step 2: Find the node with the maximum total task value.

2.1.　　If we get two same maximum total task values, then select that task value that has a minimum completion time for that particular node compared to another node.

2.1.1.　If there are multiple minimum completion time values for that node, choose the one with the highest sum of total task value row-wise.

Step 3: Select the unassigned node with the shortest completion time for the task designated in step 2, and the task is then sent to that node.

Step 4: If we find more than one unassigned task with the same value, select the unassigned node with the highest value among the relevant nodes. This task is then sent to the designated node for computation in the next phase.

Step 5: Repeat Steps 2 through 4 until all tasks have been assigned completely.

11.7.3 Flow Chart

Figure 11.4 shows the actual work.

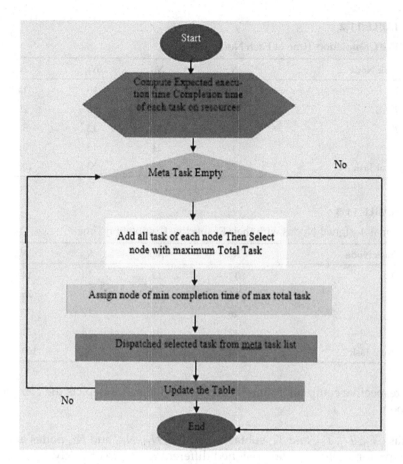

FIGURE 11.4
The flowchart showing the adopted process used in the algorithm.

11.8 Illustration of an Example

Let us a set that has four machines $M = \{N_{11}, N_{12}, N_{13}, N_{14}\}$ and eight jobs $T = \{T_{11}, T_{12}, T_{13}, T_{14}\}$. The set contains the execution costs of every job to each machine.

An example of four tasks that need to be processed is given in Table 11.1. Table 11.2 shows the completion time of each node. Table 11.3 demonstrates the final assigned nodes

TABLE 11.1

An Example of Four Tasks at Different Computing Nodes

Task Node	N_{11}	N_{12}	N_{13}	N_{14}
T_{11}	12	13	10	14
T_{12}	16	24	13	25
T_{12}	26	31	12	33
T_{14}	17	24	18	31

TABLE 11.2

The Completion Time of Each Node

Task Node	N_{11}	N_{12}	N_{13}	N_{14}
T_{11}	12	13	10	14
T_{12}	16	24	13	25
T_{13}	26	31	12	33
T_{14}	17	24	18	31
Total Task	71	92	53	103

TABLE 11.3

Final Assigned Nodes with their Respective Completion Time

Task Node	N_{11}	N_{12}	N_{13}	N_{14}
T_{11}	12	13	10	**14**
T_{12}	16	24	13	25
T_{13}	26	31	12	33
T_{14}	17	24	18	31
Total Task	71	**92**	53	**103**

with their respective completion time, whereas the Table 11.4 depicts the completion time for each node.

Step 1: Task T_{11}, T_{12}, T_{13}, and T_{14} subtasks and N_{11}, N_{12}, N_{13}, and N_{14} nodes are needed to perform all tasks with assigned different nodes accordingly.

Step 2: Then add all subtasks of individual nodes and find the maximum summation result of individual nodes. Here we see that N_{14} is that node whose total subtask result is high, that is, 103.

Step 3: Then, choose the subtask of node N_{14} with the shortest completion time, which is 14 seconds. Then this node was given the number N_{14}, and its minimum completion time was set at 14. Then, from the meta-task list, dispatch the job with the matching node N_{14}. Select the second-higher subtask summation value of the rest of the unassigned nodes, 92, and then the node's minimum subtask completion value. The value is 13; however, it will not be taken into account

TABLE 11.4

The Completion Time for Each Node Assigned Accordingly

Task\Node	N_{11}	N_{12}	N_{13}	N_{14}
T_{11}	12	13	10	**14**
T_{12}	**16**	24	13	25
T_{13}	26	31	12	33
T_{14}	17	**24**	18	31
Total Task	**71**	92	53	**103**

TABLE 11.5

Final Assigned Nodes with their Respective Completion Time

Task Node	N_{11}	N_{12}	N_{13}	N_{14}
T_{11}	12	13	10	14
T_{12}	16	24	13	25
T_{13}	26	31	12	33
T_{14}	17	24	18	31
Total Task	71	92	53	103

because the matching value of row and column of value 14 of N_{14} should not be taken into account in this situation since node N_{14} has already been assigned. Then we go to value 24, but the node N_{12} completion time remains the same. First, we look at the next-highest summation value, which is 71, and then we look at the next comparable subtask value in that column of both T_{12} and T_{14} task values. T_{14} has a corresponding value of 16 in the next-higher summation unassigned node N_{11}, and T_{14} has a comparable value of 17 in N_{11}. As a result, T_4 has a larger value than T_{12}. As a result, choose the 24 value for task T_4 and assign it to node N_{12}.

Step 4: Select the next-greater summation value, which is 71, and then the minimum task completion time value, which is 12, but that row has already been deleted, and the next minimum completion time value is 16. As a result, task T_{12} with subtask value 16 was assigned to node N_{11}.

Step 5: Finally, choose the highest value, which is 53. Here, the minimum completion time is 10, which has already been taken into account in the previous row. Then choose the next task T_3's minimum completion time value of 12. Assign node N_{14} of subtask T_{13} value 12 as a result. As a result, the final finished meta-task list of various sub-task values with various assigned nodes is listed in Table 11.5.

11.9 Comparison Among Other Load-Balancing Algorithms

Figure 11.5 shows each task's execution time (in ms) across all nodes. Experiments were carried out. The system runs on a Windows 7 platform and is powered by an Intel Core i3 4th Generation processor with a 3.4 GHz CPU and 4GB RAM. We have thought about makespan. The simulation scenarios that we ran are shown in Figure 11.5, which depicts the task execution time (ms) at various computing nodes.

The implementation time for each task at various computer nodes is depicted in Figure 11.5. The figure shows a process for calculating the presentation of our suggested work. In our technique, the figure depicts the evaluation of all nodes' execution times. The makespan is 33, 35, and 24 ms, respectively, for finishing each task using the proposed algorithm, Load Balancing with Max-Min (LBMM), Max-Min (MM), and Load Balancing with Max-Min of Summations (LBMMS). In comparison to previous algorithms, our technique achieved the quickest completion time and better load balancing.

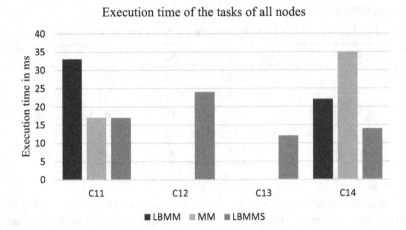

FIGURE 11.5
Execution time (in ms) of each task ofrespected computing nodes.

11.10 Conclusion

This research presents LBMMS, a proficient scheduling algorithm for cloud computing networks that allot jobs to compute nodes based on their resource capabilities. Our goal is to build an optimized scheduling technique that achieves the shortest completion and execution times while maintaining optimal load balancing. Similarly, our approach may optimizethe load-balancing technique and provide higher performance than other algorithms in the case study, such as LB3M, MM, and LBMM. We want to use our innovative technology in cloud computing applications in the future.

References

[1] Padhy, R. P. (2011). Load balancing in cloud computing systems. Diss., National Institute of Technology, Rourkela.

[2] Bhambri, P., Bagga, S., Priya, D., Singh, H., and Dhiman, H. K. (2020). Suspicious human activity detection system. *Journal of IoT in Social, Mobile, Analytics, and Cloud, 2*(4), 216–221.

[3] Rani, S., Kataria, A., Sharma, V., Ghosh, S., Karar, V., Lee, K., and Choi, C. (2021). Threats and corrective measures for IoT security with observance of cybercrime: A survey. *Wireless Communications and Mobile Computing, 2021*, 1–30.

[4] Nzanywayingoma, F., and Yang, Y. (2019). Efficient resource management techniques in cloud computing environment: A review and discussion. *International Journal of Computers and Applications, 41*(3), 165–182.

[5] Kaur, K., Dhanoa, I. S., and Bhambri, P. (2020). Optimized PSO-EFA algorithm for energy efficient virtual machine migrations. In *2020 5th IEEE International Conference on Recent Advances and Innovations in Engineering (ICRAIE)* (pp. 1–5). IEEE.

[6] Singh, P., Gupta, O. P., and Saini, S. (2017). A brief research study of wireless sensor network. *Advances in Computational Sciences and Technology, 10*(5), 733–739.

[7] Behal, V., and Kumar, A. (2014). Cloud computing: Performance analysis of load balancing algorithms in cloud heterogeneous environment. In *2014 5th International Conference-Confluence The Next Generation Information Technology Summit (Confluence)* (pp. 200–205). IEEE.

[8] Kokilavani, T., and Amalarethinam, D. G. (2011). Load balanced min-min algorithm for static meta-task scheduling in grid computing. *International Journal of Computer Applications, 20*(2), 43–49.

[9] Mao, Y., Chen, X., and Li, X. (2014). Max–min task scheduling algorithm for load balance in cloud computing. In *Proceedings of International Conference on Computer Science and Information Technology* (pp. 457–465). Springer, India.

[10] Mohanraj, M. (2013). Reduction of sags and swells in a distributed generation system based on environmental characteristics. *International Journal of Emerging Technology and Advanced Engineering, 3*(12), 382–385.

[11] Samal, P., and Mishra, P. (2013). Analysis of variants in Round Robin algorithms for load balancing in cloud computing. *International Journal of Computer Science and Information Technologies, 4*(3), 416–419.

[12] Gupta, O. P., and Rani, S. (2013). Accelerating molecular sequence analysis using distributed computing environment. *International Journal of Scientific and Engineering Research, 4*(10), 262–266.

[13] Kshirsagar, P. R., Jagannadham, D. B. V., Ananth, M. B., Mohan, A., Kumar, G., and Bhambri, P. (2022). Machine learning algorithm for leaf disease detection. In *AIP Conference Proceedings* (vol. 2393, no. 1, p. 020087). AIP Publishing LLC.

[14] Amis, A. D., and Prakash, R. (2000). Load-balancing clusters in wireless ad hoc networks. In *Proceedings 3rd IEEE Symposium on Application-Specific Systems and Software Engineering Technology, 2000*. IEEE.

[15] Bhambri, P., and Chhabra, Y. (2022). Deployment of distributed clustering approach in WSNs and IoTs. In *Cloud and Fog Computing Platforms for Internet of Things* (pp. 85–98). Chapman and Hall/CRC, Florida, USA.

[16] Braun, T. D., Siegel, H. J., Beck, N., Boloni, L. L., Maheswaran, M., Reuther, A. I., Robertson, J. P., et al. (2001). A comparison of eleven static heuristics for mapping a class of independent tasks onto heterogeneous distributed computing systems. *Journal of Parallel and Distributed Computing, 61*(6), 810–837.

[17] Chapman, C., Musolesi, M., Emmerich, W., and Mascolo, C. (2007). Predictive resource scheduling in computational grids. *IEEE International Parallel and Distributed Processing Symposium, 26*, 1–10.

[18] Mohanta, H. C., Geetha, B. T., Alzaidi, M. S., Dhanoa, I. S., Bhambri, P., Mamodiya, U., and Akwafo, R. (2022). An optimized PI controller-based SEPIC converter for microgrid-interactive hybrid renewable power sources. *Wireless Communications and Mobile Computing, 2022*(12), 1–10.

[19] Rani, S., and Gupta, O. P. (2017). CLUS_GPU-BLASTP: Accelerated protein sequence alignment using GPU-enabled cluster. *The Journal of Supercomputing, 73*(10), 4580–4595.

[20] Arunachalam, P., Janakiraman, N., Sivaraman, A. K., Balasundaram, A., Vincent, R., Rani, S., … Rajesh, M. (2021). Synovial sarcoma classification technique using support vector machine and structure features. *Intelligent Automation and Soft Computing, 32*(2), 1241–1259.

[21] Bhambri, P., Aggarwal, M., Singh, H., Singh, A. P., and Rani, S. (2022). Uprising of EVs: Charging the future with demystified analytics and sustainable development. In *Decision Analytics for Sustainable Development in Smart Society 5.0* (pp. 37–53). Springer, Singapore.

[22] Dhanalakshmi, R., Anand, J., Sivaraman, A. K., and Rani, S. (2022). IoT-based water quality monitoring system using cloud for agriculture use. In *Cloud and Fog Computing Platforms for Internet of Things* (pp. 183–196). Chapman and Hall/CRC, Florida, USA.

[23] Rani, S., Arya, V., and Kataria, A. (2022). Dynamic pricing-based e-commerce model for the produce of organic farming in India: A research roadmap with main advertence to vegetables. In *Proceedings of Data Analytics and Management* (pp. 327–336). Springer, Singapore.

[24] Rani, S., Bhambri, P., and Gupta, O. P. (2022). Green smart farming techniques and sustainable agriculture: Research roadmap towards organic farming for imperishable agricultural products. In *Handbook of Sustainable Development through Green Engineering and Technology* (pp. 49–67). CRC Press, Florida, USA.

[25] Vidyarthi, D. P., Sarker, B. K., Tripathi, A. K., and Yang, L. T. (2009). *Scheduling in Distributed Computing Systems: Analysis, Design and Models*. Springer Science & Business Media, USA.

[26] Yuvaraj, M. (2015). Cloud computing software and solutions for libraries: A comparative study. *Journal of Electronic Resources in Medical Libraries*, 12(1), 25–41.

[27] Lee, A. R., and Kim, K. K. (2018). Customer benefits and value co-creation activities incorporate social networking services. *Behaviour and Information Technology*, 37(7), 675–692.

[28] Sarna, D. E. (2010). *Implementing and Developing Cloud Computing Applications*. CRC Press, Florida, USA.

[29] Schoenberger, E. (1990). US manufacturing investments in Western Europe: Markets, corporate strategy, and the competitive environment. *Annals of the Association of American Geographers*, 80(3), 379–393.

[30] Smith, R. (2009). Computing in the cloud. *Research-Technology Management*, 52(5), 65–68.

[31] Malerba, F. (2005). Sectoral systems of innovation: A framework for linking innovation to the knowledge base, structure and dynamics of sectors. *Economics of innovation and New Technology*, 14(1–2), 63–82.

[32] Bushhousen, E. (2011). Cloud computing. *Journal of Hospital Librarianship*, 11(4), 388–392.

[33] Yang, C., Goodchild, M., Huang, Q., Nebert, D., Raskin, R., Xu, Y., Bambacus, M., and Fay, D. (2011). Spatial cloud computing: How can the geospatial sciences use and help shape cloud computing? *International Journal of Digital Earth*, 4(4), 305–329.

[34] Rani, S., Bhambri, P., and Chauhan, M. (2021). A machine learning model for kids' behavior analysis from facial emotions using principal component analysis. In *2021 5th Asian Conference on Artificial Intelligence Technology (ACAIT)* (pp. 522–525). IEEE.

[35] Sidana, S., Tiwari, N., Gupta, A., and Kushwaha, I. S. (2016). NBST algorithm: A load balancing algorithm in cloud computing. In *International Conference on Computing, Communication and Automation (ICCCA)* (pp. 1178–1181). IEEE.

[36] Purba, S., ed. (2001). *New Directions in Internet Management*. CRC Press, Florida, USA.

[37] Bradley, D. A., Burd, N. C., Dawson, D., and Loader, A. J. (1991). *Mechatronics: Electronics in Products and Processes*. CRC Press, Florida, USA.

[38] Bitam, S., Zeadally, S., and Mellouk, A. (2018). Fog computing job scheduling optimization based on bees swarm. *Enterprise Information Systems*, 12(4), 373–397.

12

Convergence Time Aware Network Comprehensive Switch Migration Algorithm Using Machine Learning for SDN Cloud Datacenter

S. R. Deepu, B. S. Shylaja and R. Bhaskar

CONTENTS

12.1 Introduction

Software-defined networking (SDN) is a revolutionary telecommunications and computer network paradigm. SDN's major purpose is to address issues that arise in Internet Protocol (IP)based networks, such as complex management. In SDN, the control and the data plane are separated from each other, which implies control logic is relocated from network devices to a central controller. Today, every networking field is working only through it due to COVID-19 (Bhambri et al., 2022; Kaur et al., 2022). A centralized controller guides dataflow using a southbound application programming interface.

Visualizing the Indian crime index, which stands at 42.38, the adoption of anomaly detection structures is an alarming want of time (Bhambri et al., 2020). The data plane oversees packet forwarding and routing in accordance with the flow table's regulations. When the initial packet of a flow comes and the switch does not find an entry for it in its flow table, it passes a packet-in message to the controller, which gives metadata. Then the controller uses the packet-in message and network domain knowledge to compute the packet's route and sends a packet-out message to switch with forwarding rules. It becomes very urgent to curtail the increase in the energy requirement for cloud service providers, with the provision of sufficient quality of service to end users (Kaur et al., 2020; Rani et al., 2022).

To avoid packet-forwarding delays and packet loss, traditional network failures, such as device or connection faults, demand specialized solutions for a speedy recovery

DOI: 10.1201/9781003298335-12

(Casas-Velasco et al., 2021). As a result, fault-resilient approaches are becoming increasingly important in traffic engineering for operator networks, providing speedy failure recovery, and, ultimately, meeting end-user expectations. An SDN link failure recovery was mentioned in Fonseca and Mota (2017) and Rani et al. (2022). We investigate the ways for detecting and recovering from connection failures in SDN in this survey.

One of the advantages of machine learning (ML) is its ability to deal with difficult challenges. Based on vast data inputs, ML can actively predict and accurately schedule network resources. Network policies and regulations are centralized with SDN applications. They also have several capabilities that allow administrators to use ML to fix network problems. In the SDN architecture, network traffic control and management are handled using ML approaches at the same time (Rani et al., 2021a; Kothandaraman et al., 2022)

We use the advantages of SDN in network monitoring in this chapter to continuously record traffic attributes in both normal and failure scenarios. Different traffic parameters, such as round-trip delay, packet loss, and packet rate, are considered by the SDN controller to predict backup paths in various failure scenarios. The switches are updated a priori with the computed backup pathways, allowing for quick failure recovery (Arya et al., 2022; Mohanta et al., 2022).

To train our learning model, we use several ML algorithms, including decision trees, support vector machines, neural networks, and random forests, among others. The demonstration of SDN-based failure recovery employing many ML techniques such as decision trees, support vector machines, and others. A graph is used to demonstrate ML techniques.

The rest of the chapter is organized as follows: Section 2 describes the literature survey, Section 3 describes the system architecture, Section 4 describes the implementation, Section 5 describes the results and discussion, and Section 6 describes the conclusion.

12.2 Literature Survey

Using the switch migration protocol, an improved and advanced distributed control plane was designed to tackle the challenge of elevated reaction time of overloaded controllers. This approach minimizes reaction time when the number of messages exceeds a predetermined threshold (Dixit et al., 2013).

In Liang et al. (2014) and Kumar et al. (2022), the coordinator was added, which is a centralized controller that receives statistics of load from controllers on a regular basis and chooses whether to undertake switch migration. However, due to the frequent exchange of messages across controllers, this affects performance. If the centralized coordinator fails, entire balancing process will be failed, which is incompatible with availability and scalability aspects of SDN distributed controllers.

We designed a safe migration mechanism in Aly and Al-anazi (2018) by selecting a nearby controller as the destination controller. Consider the distance between the migrated switch and the target controller when calculating migration expenses. The entire system's loss of packet and time of response are reduced because of this.

Using a nearby controller as the target controller for switch migration without considering the workload of the target controller, however, will result in a new controller load imbalance.

In Zhou et al. (2014) proposes dynamic and adoptive load balancing (DALB), which the controller that is closest to the underloaded controller is picked to receive load shifting during switch migration. This results in a faster execution time and lower migration costs, but it causes traffic congestion during load balancing.

Controller adaption and migration decision (CAMD) picks the least-loaded controller selector from underloaded controllers for switch migration during load shifting. When compared to DALB, this provides higher performance in respect of migration cost and throughput. This, however, may result in a low load-balancing rate (Sahoo and Sahoo, 2019, p. 264).

Traditional network restrictions are broken by SDN. Its basic concept is the separation of the forward and control layers. The controller offers critical information for flow scheduling decisions by centralizing network resource management and monitoring network status in real time (Ren et al., 2016).

The probability of network connection congestion is increased by the uneven distribution of network flows. A continuous study investigates a multipath routing algorithm in an SDN, which can fairly distribute flow across multipath to improve network performance and utilization of link bandwidth. The dynamic load-balancing routing method, which redefines the key link and key degree of link and optimizes link weight, is explained in Maksic (2021).

In a paper, Huangwu et al. (2016) presented a load-balancing multipath routing method based on SDN, in which the controller collects global link load information and calculates all forward-able paths between source and destination nodes, selects path with fastest link load, and provides flow table to the switch. However, in a real-world network, the network state is so complicated that this approach would take too long to calculate (Kshirsagar et al., 2022).

Various strategies dedicated to addressing routing difficulties in a computer network through machine learning algorithms have emerged because of the development of machine learning algorithms (Bhambri et al., 2022).

A prediction-based SDN load-balancing dual-weight switch migration strategy is suggested for multiple distributed controllers (Zhong et al., 2022). To estimate future traffic loads, the method uses historical data from previous traffic loads. We can estimate when the controller will be overwhelmed using predictive technology, allowing us to do the switch migration procedure ahead of time. The control plane increased processing and communication overhead required for periodic active load information across distributed controllers is solved using a triggered load information algorithm. The suggested approach advises that the management of individual switches be moved across controllers based on historical data. This approach balances the load between controllers quickly and reduces the frequency of switch migrations.

Wang et al. (2016b) suggested an ant colony algorithm–based traffic-scheduling method. To improve the performance of an SDN, Xue et al. (2019) used the advantage of a quick global Genetic Algorithm (GA) search and efficient tracking of an ideal solution. Traditional network load-balancing method optimization effects and robustness are not perfect due to the network-restricted perception. Traditional algorithms are incapable of obtaining information about network resources in various dimensions like time and space. As a result, after distributing the flow table, local network congestion is common.

In the form of experience, methods based on deep learning (DL) or reinforcement learning (RL) will optimize load balancing of network in several ways. The Reinforcement Learning and Software-Defined Networking Intelligent Routing (RSIR) algorithm based on Q-learning is proposed by authors in [7] and it optimizes network in three dimensions:

throughput, latency, and packet loss rate. However, after gathering connection information, its Q-learning method necessitates a large amount of time to train the Q-table between the individual pair of hosts. It has no ability to learn from prior network data and has high expectations for the performance of the controller.

Madapuzi Srinivasan et al. (2018) advised analyzing traffic attributes with machine learning techniques to discover link breakdowns in complex networks. None of these studies, however, considers rapid and adaptive failure recovery, which comprises rerouting failed traffic to a different destination based on traffic dynamics.

Failure recovery entails redirecting failed traffic to a new destination based on traffic dynamics. There is even a scarcity of related research on effect of controller-to-switch transmission latency on network load balancing. Because of the network load-balancing mechanism, which is based on real-time network status, this delay in a real network cannot be ignored.

The classification algorithms used to train the ML model include support vector machines (SVMs), neural networks (NNs), random forests (RFs), linear regression (LR), and decision trees (DTs). The number of backup paths grows in lockstep with the number of nodes, resulting in a large increase in flow-matching overhead.

The goal of this research is to find a solution to the challenges caused by CAMD and DALB. The proposed Comprehensive Switch Migration Algorithm using Machine Learning (CTSML) analyses controller behavior by learning link failure and traffic situations using an ML-based method. This technique takes traffic conditions into account to improve response time, migration time, throughput, and convergence time.

12.3 System Architecture

The SDN platform enables networking devices to include intelligence. The diversity of network devices makes it difficult to organize, optimize, maintain, and manage network resources as shared in Figure 12.1. For simplicity of organization, optimization, maintenance, and management, intelligence must be built into networking equipment. ML for device control is problematic due to the distributed topology of the networking architecture.

When ML algorithms can learn, they are the most effective. This skill improves over time because of practice and progress. For each network traffic class, the statistical features of network trace, such as duration, the length of the packets, and inter-arrival time of the packets, are unique. Using specified training data set, the system picks up this uniqueness in the pattern of the network. The pattern in the network data is determined using a machine learning technique. For optimal network use, an important network management solution is necessary to meet the exponential network traffic growth.

Rather than establishing conclusions based on predefined parameters in the algorithm, data are an important part of ML (Rani et al., 2021b). Labeled data are used for classification and regression in supervised learning. Unsupervised learning is concerned with the classification of unlabeled data into separate classes (Banerjee et al., 2022). The agent communicates with the environment and learns actions that maximize reward in reinforcement learning. To classify traffic based on customers' QoS parameter requirements, a semi-supervised learning approach is used (Wang et al., 2016a; Letswamotse et al., 2019, p. 2397).

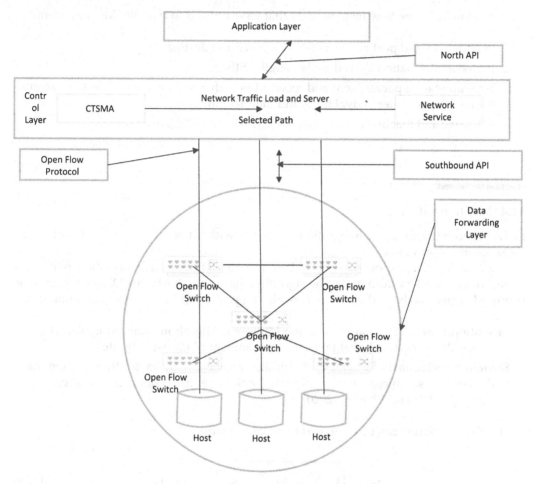

FIGURE 12.1
System architecture.

The supervised learning method builds knowledge that may be used to classify incoming flow circumstances into previously specified categories. The relationship between output and input is modeled in supervised learning. Training and testing are the two steps of supervised learning.

Training: The classification model is constructed by considering a training dataset throughout the learning phase, that is, the training process.

Testing: A new instance is classified using the model generated throughout the training phase. The mapping of active to output network traffic class is determined using a supervised learning approach. Obtaining a tagged data collection is the first hurdle in network traffic classification. One option is to utilize some of the data (say, 80%) as a training set and use the remaining (say, 20%) as the testing set. The second issue is that new network traffic may not fit into any of the already-defined traffic types. The final problem is classifying traffic as it is processed in real-time online.

The following is the flow instance data that were utilized to train the ML algorithm:

1. IP addresses and port numbers for the source and destination
2. Protocol information as well as the length of the header
3. Total number of packets sent and received in both directions, as well as the size of the packets, the inter-arrival time, and their length
4. All active and inactive users, as well as PUSH and URG, are counted.

12.4 Implementation

In the proposed method, the integration of an SDN with ML techniques for network traffic classification is provided.

The fundamental purpose of machine learning–based SDN switch migration methods is to improve network performance. The algorithm detects the use of an SDN switch, and the overused switch can be addressed by considering past usage history and migration time.

Migration time: This strategy uses the Minimum Migration Time principle, which selects the SDN switch that takes the least amount of time to migrate.

Standard deviation: If the SDN switch utilization changes dramatically, the standard deviation is significant, indicating that the SDN switch is not being used consistently (Shylaja and Bhaskar, 2020).

Standard deviation can be estimated by using Equation 12.1:

$$st_{dev} = \sqrt{\frac{1}{n}\sum_{i=1}^{n}\left(util\left(sw_i\right) - Avg\_util\left(sw\right)\right)^2}. \tag{12.1}$$

The problem of traffic classification is formulated as follows. The flow collected is $M = M1, M2,\dots,Mn$. Mi, for example, has k characteristics. The jth characteristic in kth instance of flow is referred to by M_{ik}. The inter-arrival time, duration, bytes transferred, and packets are the attributes used to classify network traffic.

Data acquired using certain data collection protocols are frequently used in ML algorithms for classifying traffic. The switches' forwarding rules (Flow Entries) match packets into flows at various degrees of granularity, and Open Flow maintains flow statistics. These data can be collected by access switches with a minimum traffic flow, core switches, or gateway switches with a large number of traffic flows. Data may be gathered in a variety of ways. Choose multiple flow granularities for various traffic types and evaluate the configurable number of packets in the controller before implementing the flow rule in the switch to collect data.

This chapter discusses an SDN application that collects Open Flow information from switches under control. The application produces a Flow Entry instructing the controlled switches to divert all traffic to controller using Open Flow. The transport protocol of a packet is determined when it arrives at the controller (as part of an Open Flow Packet In message). Transmission Control Protocol (TCP) flags are inspected for TCP packets to determine which packets are involved in the initial TCP handshake. The size and the arrival time-stamp of each one are preserved.

Algorithm: Switch Migration Scheduling algorithm
Inputs:

$$\forall ck \in C, \forall si \in S, \forall \alpha k \in \alpha$$

Outputs:
Migration Schedule
Initialization: Boolean low

$$C_l \leftarrow \text{Get Total No Of Controllers}(); \{C_l \leftarrow C_1, C_2, \ldots, C_n\}$$

$$SW_l \leftarrow \text{Get Total No of Switch}(); \{SW_l \leftarrow S_1, S_2, \ldots \ldots, S_m\}$$

for each switch S in SW compute load

$$L_t^m = \sum_{i=1}^{k} L_t^i * x_i^m \tag{12.2}$$

Compute standard deviation

$$st_{\text{dev}} = \sqrt{\frac{1}{n} \sum_{i=1}^{n} \left(util(sw_i) - Avg\_util(sw)\right)^2} \tag{12.3}$$

if ($K_t^m \geq 90$ && $St_{de} ==$ low)
   add S_i to mig$_{\text{list}}$
   flag = 1
   if flag == 0
   choose the switch with the smallest load and add it to mig$_{\text{list}}$.
   while mig$_{\text{list}}$ = null
   choose the switch si with the smallest load.
   delete si from mig$_{\text{list}}$

12.5 Results and Discussion

In this section, the study's experimentation is detailed. For the performance valuation, this research work considers a simulation approach and assessed convergence, migration time, number of migrations, and response time.

The experiment is conducted in computer with an Intel i7-6800HQ processor running at 3.0GHz, 32GB of 1800MHz memory, Windows 11 operating system. The Simulation is carried out using Jupyter notebook compiler, which is an open-source (FOSS) software that permits the users to write code.

The results of this experiment are compared to two other similar studies (Li et al., 2018; Sahoo and Sahoo, 2019, p. 264). To compare the three methods in the simulation analysis, this research employed average response time. The average response time of the three methods increases as the incoming load grows. The suggested CTSML outperforms CAMD and DALB in terms of response time, with roughly 5.4% and 1% less, respectively, as shown in Figure 12.2.

In this study, the response time was calculated using Equation 12.4 developed by Net forecast.

The formula that has been employed is

$$T_R = R_{\text{delay}} + R_t,\tag{12.4}$$

where

$$R_{\text{delay}} = 2\left[D + C_p + C_{tcp}\right] + \left[D + \frac{\left[C_p + C_{\text{server}}\right]}{2}\right]\frac{AT - 2}{mf} + Dl_n r\left[\frac{AT - 2}{mf} + 1\right] + GT\left(\frac{L1}{1 - L1}\right)\tag{12.5}$$

$$R_t = \frac{MAX\left[8p\dfrac{1 + \text{OHR}}{\text{BW}} \times D\dfrac{\text{PL}}{\text{WS}}\right]}{1 - \sqrt{\text{L}}}.\tag{12.6}$$

In Equation 12.4, T_R represents response time, R_{delay} represents delay time of propagation, and R_t represents the delay time of transmission.

In Equation 12.5, D represents the delay in the round trip; C_p represents present the processing time; C_{tcp} represents the processing of server TCP; C_{server} represents the processing time of server; AT represents the application turns; mf represents the multiplex factor; $Dl_n r$

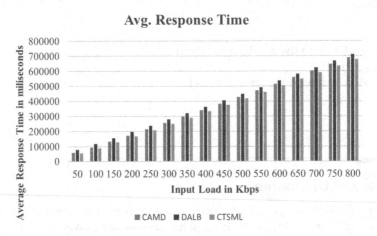

FIGURE 12.2
Average response time.

represents the ratio of packet loss, and *G* represents tTCP timeout. Similarly, in Equation 12.6, PL represents the length of the payload; OHR represents the ratio of the overhead; BW represents the minimum path bandwidth, and WS represents the effective window size. CTSML performs better than CAMD and DALB.

Figure 12.3 indicates how many times each approach must undertake migration on average. It shows that when the incoming load grows, the average number of migrations for the three techniques grows as well. The proposed CTSML carried out was superior to DALB and CAMD, with 0.9% and 5.9% less, respectively. As a result, when noted to DALB and CAMD, the suggested method will reduce the number of times it migrates a switch under controller load imbalance. This leads to a remarkable reduction in number of times migration takes place. As a result, the number of times migration occurred decreased significantly.

Figure 12.4 indicates the average migration time based on the number of migrations. The proposed CTSML shows less migration time compared to the other two methods

Figure 12.5 shows a comparison of convergence time for three methods. The system is composed of one or more cloud-based routers, and when a connection failure occurs inside a system, the break is detected, and traffic is rerouted. The convergence time is measured based on the time taken to reroute the packet in case of failures. The convergence time is calculated using Equation 12.7:

$$Cv_{time} = N_{rp} * h_c * \alpha. \tag{12.7}$$

where

Nrp represents the number of routing packets,

h_c represents the hop counts from the router to the target, and

α represents the ratio of the number of sent packets to the number of received packets.

The convergence time of CTSML is less compared to CAMD and DALB as shown in Figure 12.5.

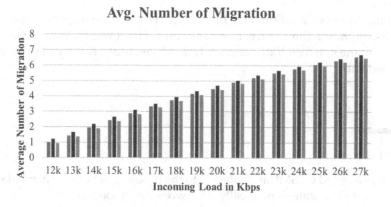

Avg. Number of Migration

Incoming Load in Kbps

■ CAMD ■ DALB ■ CTSML

FIGURE 12.3
Average number of migration.

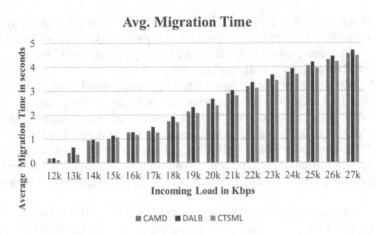

FIGURE 12.4
Average migration time.

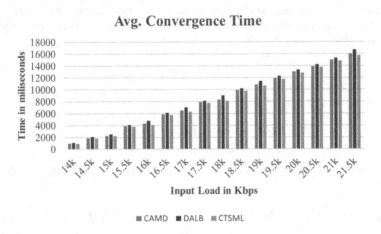

FIGURE 12.5
Comparison of convergence time.

CTSML outperforms CAMD and DALB in respect of average response time, the number of migrations, migration time, and convergence time. However, the performance efficiency is dependent on the network traffic and analysis of past usage history of switches and current traffic behavior.

12.6 Conclusion

This research presented CTSML as a solution to the problem of SDN load imbalance caused by changes in network scale dynamically. This work developed a convergence time–aware network comprehensive switch migration algorithm using machine learning approach for balancing multi-controller loads and seeks to optimize the migration time and response time. The simulation results show CTSML achieves low controller response time, a lower number of migrations, and less migration time when the network scale changes. However, performance depends on the switch usage history and the reappearance of the same traffic load pattern.

References

Aly, W. H. F., and Al-anazi, A. M. A. (2018). Enhanced controller fault tolerant (ECFT) model for software defined networking. In *2018 Fifth International Conference on Software Defined Systems (SDS)*. IEEE. https://doi.org/10.1109/sds.2018.8370446.

Arya, V., Rani, S., and Choudhary, N. (2022). Enhanced bio-inspired trust and reputation model for wireless sensor networks. In *Proceedings of Second Doctoral Symposium on Computational Intelligence* (pp. 569–579). Springer, Singapore.

Banerjee, K., Bali, V., Nawaz, N., Bali, S., Mathur, S., Mishra, R. K., and Rani, S. (2022). A machine-learning approach for prediction of water contamination using latitude, longitude, and elevation. *Water*, 14(5), 728.

Bhambri, P., Aggarwal, M., Singh, H., Singh, A. P., and Rani, S. (2022). Uprising of EVs: Charging the future with demystified analytics and sustainable development. In *Decision Analytics for Sustainable Development in Smart Society 5.0* (pp. 37–53). Springer, Singapore.

Bhambri, P., Bagga, S., Priya, D., Singh, H., and Dhiman, H. K. (2020). Suspicious human activity detection system. *Journal of IoT in Social, Mobile, Analytics, and Cloud*, 2(4), 216–221.

Bhambri, P., and Chhabra, Y. (2022). Deployment of distributed clustering approach in WSNs and IoTs. In *Cloud and Fog Computing Platforms for Internet of Things* (pp. 85–98). Chapman and Hall/CRC, Florida, USA.

Casas-Velasco, D. M., Rendon, O. M. C., and Da Fonseca, N. L. S. (2021). Intelligent routing based on reinforcement learning for software-defined networking. *IEEE Transactions on Network and Service Management*, 18(1), 870–881. https://doi.org/10.1109/tnsm.2020.3036911.

Dixit, A., Hao, F., Mukherjee, S., Lakshman, T., and Kompella, R. (2013). Towards an elastic distributed SDN controller. In *Proceedings of the Second ACM SIGCOMM Workshop on Hot Topics in Software Defined Networking – HotSDN* (pp. 7–12). ACM. https://doi.org/10.1145/2491185.2491193.

Fonseca, P. C. da R., and Mota, E. S. (2017). A survey on fault management in software-defined networks. *IEEE Communications Surveys and Tutorials*, 19(4), 2284–2321. https://doi.org/10.1109/comst.2017.2719862.

Huangwu, N., Huang, C., and Huang, X. (2016). Multipath routing algorithm for SDN-based fat tree data center network. *Computer Science*, 43, 32–34.

Kaur, K., Dhanoa, I. S., and Bhambri, P. (2020). Optimized PSO-EFA algorithm for energy efficient virtual machine migrations. In *2020 5th IEEE International Conference on Recent Advances and Innovations in Engineering (ICRAIE)* (pp. 1–5). IEEE.

Kaur, S., Kumar, R., Kaur, R., Singh, S., Rani, S., and Kaur, A. (2022). Piezoelectric materials in sensors: Bibliometric and visualization analysis. *Materials Today: Proceedings*, 65(8), 3780–3786.

Kothandaraman, D., Manickam, M., Balasundaram, A., Pradeep, D., Arulmurugan, A., Sivaraman, A. K., and Balakrishna, R. (2022). Decentralized link failure prevention routing (DLFPR) algorithm for efficient internet of things. *Intelligent Automation and Soft Computing*, 34(1), 655–666.

Kshirsagar, P. R., Jagannadham, D. B. V., Ananth, M. B., Mohan, A., Kumar, G., and Bhambri, P. (2022). Machine learning algorithm for leaf disease detection. In *AIP Conference Proceedings* (vol. 2393, no. 1, p. 020087). AIP Publishing LLC.

Kumar, R., Rani, S., and Awadh, M. A. (2022). Exploring the application sphere of the internet of things in Industry 4.0: A review, bibliometric and content analysis. *Sensors*, 22(11), 4276.

Letswamotse, B. B., Malekian, R., and Modieginyane, K. M. (2019). Adaptable QoS provisioning for efficient traffic-to-resource control in software defined wireless sensor networks. *Journal* of *Ambient Intelligence and Humanized Computing*, 11(6), 2397–2405. https://doi.org/10.1007/s12652-019-01263-9.

Li, J., Sun, E., and Zhang, Y. (2018). Multi-threshold SDN controllers load balancing algorithm based on controller load. *DEStech Transactions on Computer Science and Engineering*. https://doi.org/10.12783/dtcse/ccnt2018/24732.

Liang, C., Kawashima, R., and Matsuo, H. (2014). Scalable and crash-tolerant load balancing based on switch migration for multiple open flow controllers. In *2014 Second International Symposium on Computing and Networking*. https://doi.org/10.1109/candar.2014.108.

Madapuzi Srinivasan, S., Truong-Huu, T., and Gurusamy, M. (2018). TE-based machine learning techniques for link fault localization in complex networks. In *2018 IEEE 6th International Conference on Future Internet of Things and Cloud (FiCloud)*. https://doi.org/10.1109/ficloud.2018.00012.

Maksic, N. (2021). Topology independent multipath routing for data center networks. *IEEE Access*, 9, 128590–128600. https://doi.org/10.1109/access.2021.3107236.

Mohanta, H. C., Geetha, B. T., Alzaidi, M. S., Dhanoa, I. S., Bhambri, P., Mamodiya, U., and Akwafo, R. (2022). An optimized PI controller-based SEPIC converter for microgrid-interactive hybrid renewable power sources. *Wireless Communications and Mobile Computing*, 2022, 25–32.

Rani, S., Arya, V., and Kataria, A. (2022). Dynamic pricing-based e-commerce model for the produce of organic farming in India: A research roadmap with main advertence to vegetables. In *Proceedings of Data Analytics and Management* (pp. 327–336). Springer, Singapore.

Rani, S., Bhambri, P., and Chauhan, M. (2021a). A machine learning model for kids' behavior analysis from facial emotions using principal component analysis. In *2021 5th Asian Conference on Artificial Intelligence Technology (ACAIT)* (pp. 522–525). IEEE.

Rani, S., Kataria, A., Chauhan, M., Rattan, P., Kumar, R., and Sivaraman, A. K. (2022b). Security and privacy challenges in the deployment of cyber-physical systems in smart city applications: State-of-art work. *Materials Today: Proceedings*, 62(7), 4671–4676.

Rani, S., Mishra, R. K., Usman, M., Kataria, A., Kumar, P., Bhambri, P., and Mishra, A. K. (2021b). Amalgamation of advanced technologies for sustainable development of smart city environment: A review. *IEEE Access*, 9, 150060–150087.

Ren, H., Li, X., Geng, J., and Yan, J. (2016). A SDN-based dynamic traffic scheduling algorithm. In *2016 International Conference on Cyber-Enabled Distributed Computing and Knowledge Discovery (CyberC)* (pp. 514–518). IEEE. https://doi.org/10.1109/cyberc.2016.103.

Sahoo, K. S., and Sahoo, B. (2019). CAMD: A switch migration based load balancing framework for software defined networks. *IET Networks*, 8(4), 264–271. https://doi.org/10.1049/iet-net.2018.5166.

Shylaja, B. S., and Bhaskar, R. (2020). Rough-set and machine learning-based approach for optimised virtual machine utilisation in cloud computing. *IET Networks*, 9(6), 279–283.

Wang, P., Lin, S.-C., and Lu, M. (2016a). A framework for QoS-aware traffic classification using semi-supervised machine learning in SDNs. In *IEEE International Conference on Services Computing (SCC)* (pp. 760–765). IEEE. http://dx.doi.org/10.1109/SCC.2016.133.

Wang, Y., Yuan, K., Fang, W., Liu, Y., and Jun, M. (2016b). Research of a SDN traffic scheduling technology based on ant colony algorithm. *DEStech Transactions on Engineering and Technology Research*. https://doi.org/10.12783/dtetr/iect2016/3754.

Xue, H., Kim, K., and Youn, H. (2019). Dynamic load balancing of software-defined networking based on genetic-ant colony optimization. *Sensors*, 19(2), 311. https://doi.org/10.3390/s19020311.

Zhong, H., Xu, J., Cui, J., Sun, X., Gu, C., and Liu, L. (2022). Prediction-based dual-weight switch migration scheme for SDN load balancing. *Computer Networks*, 205, 108749. https://doi.org/10.1016/j.comnet.2021.108749.

Zhou, Y., Zhu, M., Xiao, L., Ruan, L., Duan, W., Li, D., Liu, R., and Zhu, M. (2014). A load balancing strategy of SDN controller based on distributed decision. In *2014 IEEE 13th International Conference on Trust, Security and Privacy in Computing and Communications*. IEEE. https://doi.org/10.1109/trustcom.2014.112.

13

IoT Network Used in Fog and Cloud Computing

Bhavesh Borisaniya and Saurabh Kumar

CONTENTS

13.1 Introduction

In recent years, the number of devices is increasing exponentially all around the world. These devices are responsible for performing operations in different application areas such as consumer products with smartwatches, kitchen appliances, home assistants, IoT-enabled

DOI: 10.1201/9781003298335-13

electric appliances, and trash bins; industrial machinery with pumps and industrial washing machines; intelligent infrastructures with sensors and actuators; fleet and logistics using unmanned aerial vehicles (UAVs); connected markets; and more (Rani et al., 2021, 2022). According to a survey conducted by Statista (2021), there are approximately 22 billion interconnected devices in the world. Today, every networking field is working only through it due to COVID-19 (Bhambri and Chhabra, 2022). The increase in the number of devices is due to the use of digital technologies for communication worldwide. In such a case, there is a need for networking across the globe, irrespective of real-time constraints such as line-of-sight (LoS), non-line-of-sight (NLoS) conditions, multipath propagations, computing and communication power restrictions, and remote and inaccessible regions (Kumar and Zaveri, 2018). Although wireless sensor networks (WSNs) provide services effectively even for remote and inaccessible areas, they suffer because the devices are short-ranged. It becomes a critical issue when the computation needs to be performed among the huge number of heterogeneous devices because mapping these devices with the real world poses a challenge. As a result, long-range communication gets affected on a large scale. In this context, the Internet of Things (IoT) provides an environment for the different types of devices to co-exist and perform operations, irrespective of the locations and characteristics of the deployed devices and the terrain limitations. With the fast-growing IoT, regular connectivity through a range of heterogeneous intelligent devices across the social online networks (SONs) is feasible and effective to analyze sociological principles (Wentao et al., 2021).

In collaboration with machine learning and artificial intelligence, anomaly detection systems are vastly used in behavioral analysis to help identify and predict the prevalence of anomalies (Bhambri et al., 2020). The devices in the IoT environment can be categorized as either the sensor device or the IoT device (Pandey and Zaveri, 2018). They can be considered one of the primary building blocks of the IoT environment through their services at the physical layer (Rani and Kaur, 2012). Also, using Internet Protocol (IP)–based communication under the Internet helps realize long-range communication, even across the world. However, since these devices are distributed and accessed from anywhere and at any time, there is a need for infrastructure that helps these deployed devices carry out the processing of data in a distributed manner, irrespective of the kind of application, location, and characteristics of devices. Moreover, the advent of IoT has helped in its implementation in the industrial environment. In Industry 4.0, the Fourth Industrial Revolution backs up the technologies in the IoT for increasing productivity standards with optimized use of resources (Frank et al., 2019). The use of the Internet has changed the usual working environment in industries. The Industrial Internet of Things (IIoT; Zhou et al., 2017) uses the Internet and IoT technologies to improve industrial processes and predictive analysis of data. It can be observed that a massive amount of data results from such an extensive usage of devices (Harleen, 2016). The data, thus generated, need to be processed for cleaning and analysis to extract useful information for intelligent decision-making. The data analytics must be performed as and when required to provide real-time service delivery (Kaur et al., 2013). Since the IoT devices at the physical layer have a minimal memory footprint, it becomes complicated for them to perform heavy computations locally. It becomes more challenging when the devices are distributed spatially, and data are required from one or more of them. In this context, the cloud provides a solution to support the network of multiple devices, computers, servers, and data analytics, irrespective of their locations. It has become a high need for specialist co-ops, endeavors, IP apparatuses producers, application designers, and governments to start their organizations of IPv6 (Jain et al., 2021).

The cloud provides a platform to share different resources. These resources can be anything related to the storage of data, energy dissipation parameters, networking tools, and components for creating, launching, and testing the applications (Modi et al., 2013). It even provides ready-made software to meet the demands of different businesses. The integration of the IoT with the cloud can be considered a cost-effective solution for enterprises as well. Moreover, the specialized platforms of the cloud help create IoT applications with optimized investments in hardware and software (Gardašević et al., 2017). The cloud for IoT has advantages such as improved performance (both locally and globally), storage capacities, processing capabilities, and reduced costs. However, it suffers from some limitations, such as high latency, network downtime due to technical issues and frequent interruptions, and security and privacy. It can be considerably observed that the limitations of implementing the cloud for the IoT environment can be nullified if the gap between the cloud and physical-layer devices can be reduced (Arunachalam et al., 2021).

Fog computing plays a significant role to achieve this goal (Naha et al., 2018). The fog consists of edge devices that are further connected to the physical devices. In a way, the fog can be thought of as being closer to the physical layer and tries to bring cloud capabilities closer to the end users. The fog provides a distributed decentralized infrastructure and regulates which of the information must be sent to the server and needs to be processed locally at the device end. As a result, the fog acts as an intelligent gateway that provides offline cloud features with more efficient data storage, processing, and analysis.

This chapter discusses the promising role of the IoT environment to fulfill the needs of real-time communication and computation in the current era, wherein connectivity is the most critical challenge. Additionally, the chapter discusses the idea behind cloud and fog computing utilization, their amalgamation with the IoT environment, architectural frameworks, design and implementation potentials, and applications in the current era (Kothandaraman et al., 2022). Finally, some critical applications are explored through case studies to determine the significance of research and development in these fields, a few prospective solutions, and gaps in the study.

13.2 IoT

An increased emphasis on the use of automation in various fields is observed in the last few years. Some of these areas are agriculture, sales, marketing, industrial operations, defense, education, social welfare, mining, medicine, disaster management, research and development, and more (Balaji et al., 2019; Dian et al., 2020). The Internet has played a vital role in bringing about a profound change in these areas. It provides continuous connectivity among different entities involved in operational activities. In the current generation, the aim is to minimize the use of human beings and maximize the use of machines in different processes. The key advantage is to nullify the loss of human lives by using devices in their place. Also, human beings can be employed in other management activities, rather than being busy in the shop floor activities. Thus, the entities involved in the operation must also be automated, and they must communicate effectively among themselves to pass the information related to the progressive work. The evolution of the emergent technology, called the IoT, provides a platform through which these different entities can get connected among themselves and communicate, as and when needed, using a highly reliable and cheaper communication medium known as the Internet (Balaji et al., 2019).

The IoT can be considered as an environment in which various heterogeneous devices coexist, communicate, compute, and transmit the relevant information among themselves using the Internet. These devices may be either *sensors*, *actuators*, or IoT devices (Pandey and Zaveri, 2016a). The sensor devices are used for sensing the different parameters from the environment. Based on the actions required, the actuator device is accountable for performing those actions on the environment. Additionally, with time, it is observed that specific devices can perform operations not supported by the sensor devices since they have low communication and computation potential. In this regard, the IoT environment consists of IoT devices that provide more communication and computation potentials with better lifetime and reliability than sensor devices. Essentially, IoT devices communicate using IP-based protocols that are interoperable, irrespective of the types of applications worldwide. As defined in Pandey and Zaveri (2018), to create an IoT device, pick any device besides a computer, add computational intelligence and communication capability using IP-based protocol to connect to the Internet (Rani et al., 2021, 2021, 2022).

Moreover, from the preceding discussion, it can be concluded that connectivity and communication are two key aspects with which the effective utilization of the IoT environment can be made possible. In turn, it will help implement an efficient network among the entities involved in the operational activities. It is required to understand the standard IoT protocols for communication, as discussed in the following section.

13.2.1 Communication Protocols of IoT

In the implementation process, communication among the entities operating in the IoT environment must be made so effective that there must not be any lag, breakdown, interoperability, and reliability issues when transmitting information (Rani and Gupta, 2017). Some standard communication protocols must be understood, which will help build a concrete IoT environment with better communication mechanisms. It must be understood here that the implementation must be done by keeping in mind that the different scenarios require different ways of implementing the protocols (Kumar et al., 2022). These scenarios may be related to the communication medium such as LoS, NLoS, obstructed LoS, or distance among the devices in the network. Some of the essential protocols are discussed in the following sections.

13.2.1.1 IEEE 802.15.4

The IEEE 802.15.4 provides a standard used at the lower layers (Lin et al., 2017). Effectively, the physical and MAC constitute the definition of the lower layers in this protocol. The protocol is well suited to be implemented for wireless personal area network (WPAN; Pandey and Zaveri, 2016b). The protocol performs better up to the maximum range of approximately 75 m and works best under LoS conditions. There are different variants of the IEEE 802.15.4 protocol (Lin et al., 2017). The basic version is 802.15.4-2003, which has fixed modulation schemes and data rates for three frequency bands—868MHz, 915MHz, and 2.4GHz. The 802.15.4-2006 variant is called as 802.15.4b. The version 802.15.4a increases the range capability of the protocol. The versions 802.15.4c and 802.15.4d support 780MHz in China and 950MHz in Japan, respectively. The version 802.15.4e defines the development for industrial applications. Similarly, 802.15.4f and 802.15.4g are the versions defined for radiofrequency identification (RFID) and energy industry applications, respectively (Molisch et al., 2004).

13.2.1.2 Zigbee

The Zigbee protocol provides a framework for medium-range communication in the IoT environment (Hui and Culler, 2008). It supports the interoperability among multiple devices at a significantly low data rate. It operates at three different frequencies: 868MHz, with one channel using a data transmission rate of up to 20kbps; 902–928MHz, with ten channels using a data transmission rate of up to 40kbps; and 2.4GHz, with 16 channels using a data transmission rate of up to 250kbps. Zigbee supports the relaying of packets by the nodes in the network. Thus, greater distances are covered with lower power consumption and better efficiency due to adaptable duty cycles, low data rates, and low-coverage radios (Ramya et al., 2011). The network topologies supported by Zigbee are star, peer-to-peer, cluster tree–based, and mesh. The protocol defines three types of nodes in the network: *coordinator*, *router*, and *end device*. The Zigbee comes in two variants: *Zigbee* and *Zigbee pro* (Franceschinis et al., 2013). The Zigbee pro supports a scalable, secure, and improved performance with a many-to-one routing scheme being followed in the network.

13.2.1.3 6LoWPAN

The Internet Protocol Version 6 (IPv6) over Low Power Wireless Personal Area Network (6LoWPAN) is responsible for optimizing the IPv6 packet transmission using low power and lossy network. One example of such a network is IEEE 802.15.4, as discussed in Section 2.1.1. It operates at two frequencies: 2400MHz–2483.5MHz worldwide and 902MHz–929MHz in North America (Mulligan, 2007). It utilizes the 802.15.4 at the physical layer in unslotted CSMA/CA mode. This protocol converts the data format to be fitted with IEEE 802.15.4 for the lower layer system. It is needed because IPv6 supports the maximum transmission unit of 1280 bytes, while IEEE 802.15.4 supports only 127 bytes. Thus, an adaptation layer is included between the MAC and the network layer. It is responsible for the fragmentation and reassembly of packets, compression of packet headers, and routing at the data-link layer. The routing at the data-link layer is categorized into two schemes: *mesh-under* and *route-over routing*. The *mesh-under* routing uses the link-layer address to forward the packets, while the *route-over* routing uses the network-layer IP address to perform this activity (Chowdhury et al., 2009).

13.2.1.4 WirelessHART

HART expands to Highway Addressable Remote Transducer protocol (Guochen et al., 2010). This protocol was developed by Rosemount Inc. and was made an open protocol in 1986. It operates in two modes: *point-to-point mode* supporting analog and digital signals and *multi-drop mode* supporting only the digital signals. It is considered an early implementation of Fieldbus (Patzke, 1998), the digital industrial automation protocol. WirelessHART (Song et al., 2008) is a WSN technology that is based on the implementation of HART. Being the first open wireless communication standard, it was released with applications that control industrial processes. There are three main elements of WirelessHART: *wireless field device*, *gateway*, and *network manager*. The protocol supports both the mesh and star network topologies. It is developed for process automation, asset management, location determination, and control applications.

13.2.1.5 Z-Wave

Z-wave is a low-power radio communication technology primarily used for home auto-mation and security systems (Knight, 2006). This protocol is designed as a more straight-forward and cheaper alternative to Zigbee for a small to medium range of connectivity. It operates on three unlicensed bands of 908.42MHz, 868.42MHz, and 2.4GHz and uses mesh network topology to communicate among the devices in the network. The protocol sup-ports 232 devices in a network, irrespective of the type of device. The devices are of two categories: *controller* and *slave*. The controller device acts as a central entity responsible for setting up the network and managing slave devices in the network. The slave devices listen to the commands of the controller device and communicate using the connection hierarchy involving the controller device. The protocol has applications in the home or office automa-tion, intelligent energy management, smart security and surveillance, voice control–enabled applications, and automation and control of different appliances (Knight, 2006).

13.2.1.6 Other Protocols

Various other protocols are directly or indirectly supporting the IoT environment with the aid of different protocols. Some of them include, but are not limited to, ISA 100.11a (Florencio et al., 2020), Bluetooth (Haartsen, 2000), RFID (Weinstein, 2005), near-field com-munication (NFC; Coskun et al., 2011), and others. These are the standards for wireless network technology and is designed specifically for the implementation of automation in the industrial environment; data transfer in text, image, audio, and video; product track-ing in stores; asset and baggage tracking; supply chain management; automobile tracking; authentication; access control in home and office; banking and payments using smart-phones; goods tracking; communication between smartphones; and a low-power home automation system, among other applications.

13.2.2 Networking in IoT

Although the communication protocols discussed in the previous section are essential for transmitting and receiving signals among the devices in a network, networking issues and challenges are crucial to building an efficient IoT environment. IoT devices have three main characteristics: low processing power, small devices, and energy constraints. Similarly, the networks of IoT devices must overcome low throughput and high packet loss, especially in current-generation networking. The reason corresponds to the increased network con-gestion, small payload size, and frequently changing network topology due to mobility observed among the devices operating in the IoT environment (Rani et al., 2021, 2022). Due to these reasons, the classical Internet is not meant for constrained IoT devices.

Moreover, it must be noted that the proprietary non-IP-based solutions provide vendor-specific gateways and APIs, which are difficult to maintain and manage once customized. Thus, to enable the classical Internet for IoT devices, Internet Engineering Task Force (IETF) proposed an IP-based solution with three workgroups. First is 6LoWPAN (Mulligan, 2007), followed by Routing Over Low power and Lossy network (ROLL; Balaji et al., 2019), and Constrained RESTful Environment (CoRE; Balaji et al., 2019). The 6LoWPAN focuses on header compression and encapsulation to transmit and receive IPv6 packets over IEEE 802.15.4 supported networks. ROLL is a new routing protocol responsible for optimizing storage and energy saving in the network. Finally, CoRE extends the integration of IoT devices from the network to the service level (Rani and Gupta, 2016).

Furthermore, there are various quality of services (QoSs) concerning the IoT network that must be maintained throughout the operation phase. The QoSs aims to provide the guarantee of service delivery in the IoT environment by controlling the traffic in the network. It must be noted that since the device configuration and characteristics and heterogeneous, the traffic generated may also be heterogeneous (Rani and Kumar, 2022). IoT network policies include four key QoS policies: *resource utilization, data timeliness, data availability*, and *data delivery*. For resource utilization needs, there must be a level of control on the storage and bandwidth utilization in data transmission and reception. Data timeliness measures the freshness of certain information. This measurement is always performed at the receiver end. However, data availability measures the amount of valid data provided by the sender to the receiver. Finally, data delivery measures the successful delivery of reliable data sent from the source to the destination.

Although communication and networking are vital aspects of the IoT environment, real-time service delivery can only be achieved when the data and information can be made available to the applications promptly. It will further help in real-time computation and analysis of data for further processing. In the last few years, the research and development in cloud computing have provided a unique opportunity to process the real-time data obtained from the physical layer, as discussed in the following section.

13.3 Cloud Computing

With the profound emphasis on realizing the vision of Industry 4.0, the use of the Internet has considerably increased in different fields. In industries, the implementation of IoT under the umbrella of the Industrial Internet of Things (IIoT) provides a platform where the various hardware and software components work together to support efficient productivity (Gupta et al., 2011). There are four pillars concerning IIoT support for Industry 4.0: *sensing, communication, computing*, and *networking*. Altogether, they help achieve digitization in manufacturing and production processes. The digitization process involves data acquisition, asset management, resource management, and knowledge management. Thus, there is a massive amount of data produced from the deployed end devices. It must be noted that the data generated may be unorganized and of varying quality and are heterogeneous due to the heterogeneity in the source of data. Thus, there is a need for the cloud that amalgamates with the IoT environment to provide huge data storage, high computational speed for data monitoring, visualization and analytics, effective data acquisition, and scalable and secure service from anywhere and anytime (Moghe et al., 2012).

Cloud computing has evolved over a while due to its suitability in scientific and business adaptability. It addresses the need for *what, when*, and *where* solutions (Moghe et al., 2012). Also, it supports the mobility of devices with a coherent, expandable, and coordinated business model. According to the National Institute of Standards and Technology (NIST) definition, cloud computing can be understood in infrastructure, platform, and application (Gilchrist, 2016). The infrastructure deals with the network, communication, computation in the network, and bulk data storage. The platform acts as the middleware and provides database services in real time. Finally, the applications support the analytics for decision-making in monitoring and predicting specific attributes depending on the type of application. The following sections describe cloud computing using three crucial parameters: *services, deployment model*, and *end-users*.

13.3.1 Services

There are three different services offered in cloud computing: *software as a service* (Saas; Cusumano, 2010), *platform as a service* (Paas; Pahl, 2015), and *infrastructure as a service* (IaaS; Iosup et al., 2014). In *SaaS*, the applications are embedded with web or software program support and utilize the subscribe–use feature for clients. The service provider manages all the activities. For example, Industrial Machinery Catalyst developed by Siemens is a SaaS that is used in the industries. However, *PaaS* allows the industries to self-develop applications, in which the clients have complete control of the applications and configuration environment. For example, some industrial PaaS providers are Predix by GE, Sentience by Honeywell, and MindSphere by Siemens.

Similarly, some software firms such as Cumulocity, Bosch IoT, and Carriots offer PaaS to be utilized in the IIoT. Finally, *IaaS* provides access to servers, networks, and storage and provisioning on a large scale. The clients use the cloud to access and operate on the virtual data center. The IaaS is also used to implement and deploy SaaS and PaaS. Some of the examples of IaaS are Microsoft Azure, IBM SmartCloud Enterprise, Amazon Web Services (AWS), and Rackspace open cloud, among many others.

13.3.2 Deployment Model

The deployment model provides guidelines on the deployment, maintenance, and management of cloud platforms. It discusses the standards to offer effective cloud services to the clients. According to the cloud computing reference architecture proposed by the NIST (Liu et al., 2011), there are three ways of deployment of a cloud: *public*, *private*, and *hybrid*. In the public deployment model, the cloud is set up to be used by any person or organization worldwide. The different services, which are virtualized, are shared publicly with all the clients accessing the cloud platform. Some examples of the public deployment model are Google compute engine, AWS, and Microsoft Azure, among others. The second deployment model, that is, private deployment, works for a single organization only, for which the cloud is customized to be used. All the virtualized services are shared with only the clients of that particular organization. Cloud management in private deployment is done by the clients only. This type of cloud implementation is considered highly secure. Eucalyptus, OpenStack, OpenNebula, and VMware vCloud are well-known cloud frameworks deployed as a private cloud delivering an IaaS service. Finally, the hybrid model of deployment considers cloud setup by two or more unique cloud setups, which may be public or private. The design is based on both the private and public models; it provides the advantages of both. One of the key advantages of the hybrid model is that it offers the flexibility to move data and applications between the private and public cloud platforms.

13.3.3 End Users

The third component of cloud computing is the end users. The end users are considered one of the most critical components of the cloud, and deployment scalability depends on them. The end users may be either a person, a group of persons, or an organization and industry that want to avail cloud services. These services vary as per the requirements of different users. One of the most crucial reasons for the difference in services is the variation in the products and services of clients. These end users may be from different fields and application areas such as healthcare, transportation, manufacturing plants, refineries, mining, and marine science.

13.3.4 Architecture

Cloud is meant to deliver different types of services such as IaaS, PaaS, and SaaS, as discussed in Section 13.3.1. The general architecture of the cloud consists of a pool of computing resources. Access to these resources is given to the end users on demand through Application Program Interfaces (APIs) over the Internet with a pay-per-use structure. The architecture of the Eucalyptus cloud (Eucalyptus, 2021) is discussed to understand the general architecture and components of the cloud.

Eucalyptus is an open-source cloud framework for building AWS-compatible private and hybrid clouds. This framework ensures the delivery of infrastructure and storage services to the end users. Figure 13.1 shows the general architecture of the Eucalyptus cloud (Eucalyptus, 2021). The core component of the cloud is physical resources that are shared among users through virtualization. Here, node controllers (NCs) are physical machines hosting virtual machines (VMs). The cluster controller (CC) creates a cluster of multiple node controllers placed at different sites. The CC is responsible for scheduling the user-requested VM on eligible NCs. The storage controller (SC) component allows the users to store their data as block storage. With block storage, users can create the storage volumes as per the requirement, attach them to the cloud VM instance, store their data, and detach like an external pen drive. The data stored in block storage remains permanent even if the cloud instance is turned off. Another type of storage is involved with cloud architecture, known as Object Storage Provider (OSP). Eucalyptus provides an AWS S3 (Simple Storage Service)

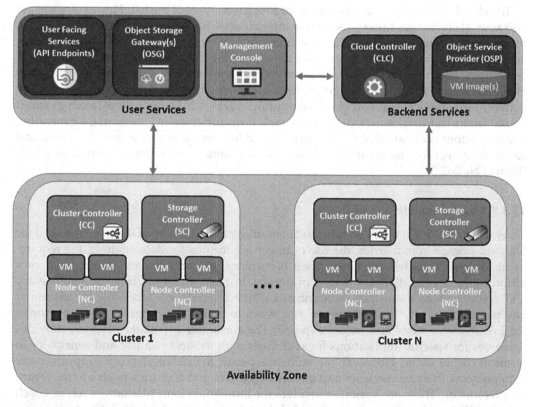

FIGURE 13.1
Eucalyptus cloud architecture.

compatible storage provided through OSP, utilized to store the VM images. S3 service allows users to import/export customized VM images to the cloud. The cloud controller (CLC) is the management component of the cloud dealing with the user requests for scheduling VM over multiple clusters managed by CC(s). It takes the high-level scheduling decision based on the availability of physical resources. Users can make requests and can access the cloud resources through APIs and cloud management consoles. An object storage gateway (OSG) allows users to access the services provided by OSP. There are complex design architectures for the cloud that are provided by various organizations and researchers for versatile requirements of services. Even though many components are proposed in the cloud design, its core functionality remains the same. From an abstract view, in the cloud, users access VMs running on remote machines owned and managed by cloud providers.

In an IoT network, the cloud services mainly opted for are either for storage or computation purposes. IoT sensors generate lots of data that are sent over cloud nodes for storage and processing. Cloud nodes with scalable computing power process these data efficiently and make them available all the time, accessible from anywhere. M. Aazem et al. (2016) have given the basic data communication model for the IoT with the cloud and named it the Cloud of Things (CoT). The data are generated at by heterogeneous IoT devices using different channels and then sent to the cloud. At the cloud layer, these data are stored, processed, and analyzed for high-level user applications. Users are accessing these processed data through various applications running on a variety of end devices. Any of the cloud deployment models, that is, public, private, or hybrid, can be utilized here based on user application requirements.

The cloud solves computation- and storage-related issues of the IoT. However, there are also several challenges raised due to this integration. Challenges such as standardization of communication protocol, identity management, quality of service provisioning, resource allocation, data storage location over the cloud, security and privacy issues of individual technology, and ongoing research in cloud forensics are the primary concerns (Aazam et al., 2016). Figure 13.2 shows the generalized architecture for connection between the IoT network/IoT applications and cloud computing. Various IoT applications, such as smart home, smart industry, smart city, and others, form different IoT network(s) generating massive amounts of data that are sent to the cloud for storage or processing. Processed and stored data over the cloud can be accessed by end users over the Internet from anywhere (Rani et al., 2022).

13.3.5 Cloud Computing in IIoT

Several factors govern the need for cloud computing in IIoT. Some of them are the need for big data storage in industries, the use of heavy algorithms for data analysis, the requirement to predict the failures before their occurrence, the remote configuration and provisioning of devices, the monitoring of devices in real-time, and ensuring data privacy and security in such an open environment where the data are accessible by anyone at any place and at any time. There are two ways to define the usage of cloud platforms for IoT: *consumer-based* and *industry-specific*. The consumer IoT cloud platform provides resources for specific applications for end users with modest security and sensitivity in terms of cost of usage. However, the industry-specific IoT cloud platform supports many data points with robust security and quality of services and is more sensitive to the return on investment. There are various providers for industrial cloud platforms such as Bosch IoT, IBM Watson IoT, Cumulocity, Intel IoT, Uptake, Carriots, Amazon AWS, AirVantage, Honeywell Sentience, XMPRO, SAP Hana Cloud, GE Predix, Siemens MindSphere, C3IoT,

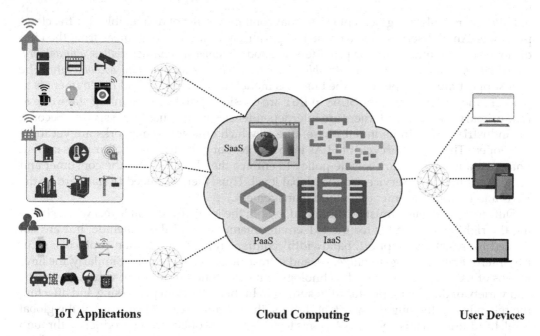

| IoT Applications | Cloud Computing | User Devices |

FIGURE 13.2
IoT and cloud computing connection.

Amplia IoT, Bitstew Systems, Losant IoT, AT&T M2X, Cisco Jasper, TempoIQ, Meshify, and Thingworx (Ganguly, 2016).

13.3.6 Cloud Computing for Device Management

Device management consists of activities such as the initial deployment, configuration, maintenance, management, and redeployment as and when required for different services of the applications. It must be noted that the devices discussed here are both physical and network layer devices. The need for device management revolves around four fundamental reasons. First, there is a significant increase in the number of devices that make IoT more complex. Second, there is a dynamic change in standards and services offered by the devices periodically, especially with speedily changing technologies. Third, there is a need to replace or redeploy the devices, possibly due to the observed faults during operation. Finally, the security requirements of these devices are changing at a rapid rate with time, which must be mapped efficiently and promptly. The current generation of application processing requires data from devices that are located anywhere in the world. Thus, it is considered the best way to perform device management services in the cloud. The cloud platform provides provisioning and authentication, fault monitoring and diagnosis, configuration and control, device decommissions whenever needed, and operations such as updates, security patches, and maintenance. Some examples of cloud platforms with device management functionality are Bosch IoT remote manager, ICP DAS's IoTstar, software AG's Cumulocity, Verismic's cloud management suite, and AWS's IoT device management.

Furthermore, the processing of data in different applications of IIoT requires safety measures because the processing is needed to be performed in real-time. Thus, there is a need to build a service-level agreement (SLA) that contains the list of deliverables for the cloud providers. An SLA serves as one of the key performance indicators in measuring the kind of cloud services offered by the providers. A good SLA has six characteristics: *affordability, achievability, meaningfulness, quantifiability, controllability,* and *mutually acceptability.* The SLA support must comply with the business model for which the cloud deployment is in place. In the current stage, the SLAs in IIoT are considered to be in the infant stage due to four primary reasons. First, there are interdependencies in the quality of services. Second, the industrial IoT is in its initial phase, due to which efficient frameworks are yet to be developed. Third, the life cycle of SLAs in the context of industries is unclear in its current phase. Finally, there is no concrete policy to enforce the SLAs for both the consumer and provider of the cloud services on the global level. Thus, there is a need to standardize the SLAs and their management for cloud management.

Different parameters must be discussed at both the local and global levels when choosing the right cloud vendor for the IoT environment. Some of them include, but are not limited to, scalability support, bandwidth requirement, communication protocols, security, interoperability, edge intelligence, and infrastructure management. Similarly, the limitations of using the cloud-based technology can be outlined in terms of volume, velocity, and variety of data being produced, resulting in higher latency in processing and affecting the reliability of the huge network and, thus, the need for scalable security at the global level. In addition to this, Industry 4.0 aims to achieve more outstanding production through intelligent and optimized decisions to improve the efficiency and availability for analysis and prediction of information based on the collected data. One of the solutions to the problems mentioned earlier is to offer a decentralized or distributed approach along with the cloud to handle the time-sensitive data and immediate actions and quick responses. Thus, fog computing provides an effective tool to achieve the same, as discussed in the following section.

13.4 Fog Computing

Due to the significantly higher number of devices and machines in the IoT environment, there is a consistent release of data from these sensors and other devices operating in the network. The data that are generated may be either time-sensitive or critical to specific applications. In this regard, there is a need for immediate action and quick response for real-time service delivery requirements of current-generation applications. Data processing must be performed timely because the delay in proper actions within the stipulated time may result in hazardous situations. For example, consider the case of the weather monitoring system for cyclones (Yang et al., 2014). During cyclonic disasters, the wind speed and its direction must be judged timely. A lot of times, the initial monitoring data provide a different speed of wind compared to the actual speed on the day of the cyclone. If the actual speed is higher than that of the initial data collection, the disaster may negatively strike the nearby residents and result in more damage. Thus, there is a need to collect and process the data timely and promptly to formulate action strategies. However, the major challenge is to handle the diversity in terms of protocols, data syntax, and data sources. The reduction in the gap between the physical layer and application layer using the concept of fog may help to address the issue of timely processing of data, irrespective of the level of heterogeneity in the network. A decentralized computing infrastructure is utilized in fog computing (Bonomi et al., 2012). It is often called edge computing, which is also a distributed computing paradigm that brings the data computation and storage of data closer to the source of data. Fog computing utilizes an architecture consisting of edge devices that carry out the computation, storage, and communication of data, either locally or with the help of routing using the Internet. An edge device exists at the end of two or more networks and provides local information to the external network. In the presence of two or more different protocols, the edge device is responsible for translating this information to connect the networks.

The term *fog* is used metaphorically in the IIoT. It is derived from the meteorological concept of the cloud being close to the ground. Historically, the OpenFog Consortium was formed in 2015 by Cisco and its partners to promote and standardize the concept of fog computing. In 2019, the OpenFog consortium merged with Industrial Internet Consortium (IIC) to encourage fog computing in IIoT systems. The IIC and OpenFog aim to address the weaknesses of industrial automation by enabling new enriching functionalities along with additional features in process control and its analytics. The architecture of fog computing is discussed in the subsequent section.

13.4.1 Architecture of Fog Computing

Fog computing architecture can be understood in two ways: hierarchical architecture and layered architecture (IIC, 2018; Rahman et al., 2018). There are three layers of hierarchical architecture of fog computing: cloud layer, fog layer, and edge layer. The cloud layer provides storage and access to data and programs over the Internet. The software layer allows organizations to collect data from multiple sites and devices accessible from anywhere and anytime (Banerjee et al., 2022). As discussed in Section 13.3, the utilization of the cloud reduces the latency cost and improves the user experience. The second layer, that is, the fog layer, is responsible for extending cloud computing functionality toward the edge of the network. It moves the data analytics closer to the sensors in the edge layer. It consists of devices such as routers, gateways, access points, and base stations that may or may not be static depending on the application. The nodes in the fog layer provide services to the edge layer. The edge layer consists of all the physical devices such as sensors, actuators, routers, mobiles, and other handheld and non-handheld devices operating the network. Thus, it is also called the things layer. These devices are distributed across different locations, either in the same network or far from each other. This layer performs data sensing and capturing operations. The environment in the edge layer may or may not be heterogeneous, based on the applications. The devices may have different technologies and modes of communication. The hierarchical fog computing architecture is depicted in Figure 13.3.

Similarly, there are six layers in layered architecture of fog computing. In the *physical and virtualization layer*, the nodes are of two types: physical and virtual. These nodes are usually responsible for performing sensing of the environment in which they are deployed. In the *monitoring layer*, the node monitoring operation is carried out depending on the task hierarchy. In the *preprocessing layer*, analytical operations are carried out, such as data cleaning, reliable versus unreliable data, unnecessary data, extraction of meaningful information, and so on. The *temporary storage layer* serves the nonpermanent distribution and replication of data. The fifth layer is the *security layer*, which is involved in preserving the security and privacy of data using different methods. Finally, the *transport layer* uploads the partially processed and secure data to the cloud layer, where these data are permanently stored.

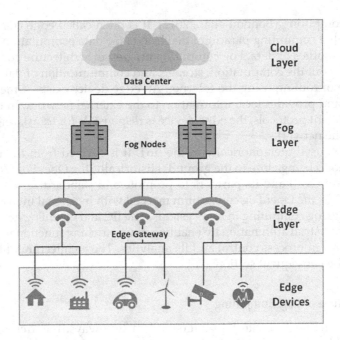

FIGURE 13.3
Hierarchical architecture of fog computing.

13.4.2 Fog-Enabled IoT

The industrial Internet system has improved the efficiency of industrial operations, especially with the profound implementation of IoT technology in industrial processes. In industrial processes, fog computing offers various applications due to its support to the IoT environment. There are three critical entities in the industries that need to be efficiently handled: machine, process, and data analysis. It further helps in optimized decision-making and intelligent operations for increased productivity. Since social ethics are crucial for industrial operations, fog computing provides a bridge between the new level of functioning by smart devices and the production of the system. Fog computing provides support for advanced algorithms at the edge to perform real-time control of the processes. In addition to this, the noisy big data crowd at the cloud is filtered at the edge. It results in the analysis of streaming data in the cloud using the high bandwidth of communication and big data computations offered by the different layers of fog computing.

There are five key features of a fog-enabled IIoT: real-time monitoring and visualization, end-to-end security, scalability and flexibility, reduced overall cost, and innovation of novel trading ideas. These features and their performance depend on each other. For instance, consider the example of the transportation industry. With the implementation of radiofrequency identification and GPS technologies in vehicles, it has become easier to track the location of the vehicles and visualize their actual movement on software-based applications. It has helped with maintaining the secure transportation of the goods and services from source to destination. The cost of damage of goods and services and noncompliance during transport are reduced, resulting in reduced transportation costs. Finally, the use of technologies has helped the transportation industry focus more on devising newer initiatives and techniques to manage and monitor the processes involved in transportation so that they can be utilized irrespective of transportation location. Some of the critical advantages of fog computing are minimization of latency, network bandwidth conservation, reduced operating costs, enhanced security, improved reliability, in-depth analysis with improved security, and improved business agility. There are different fog platform providers in the market, such as FogHorn, Nebbiolo Technologies, Crosser, and Sonm (Hu et al., 2017; Matt, 2018). A few of the current solutions are in blockchain infrastructure, video streaming, machine learning, and video rendering.

13.5 Case Studies

In this section, the various case studies depicting the use of IoT, cloud computing, and fog computing in different fields are presented. The purpose of these case studies is to understand the different domains, their functioning and operational environment, and the significant changes that may result with the implementation of these technologies. This will help in finding the research gaps in these fields to devise solutions to provide easier operations.

13.5.1 Factories and Assembly Lines

In recent years, the traditional manufacturing process is moving towards intelligent manufacturing due to specific challenges associated with conventional manufacturing, such as the unavailability of real-time data, unbalanced workload, longer change over time, and extended production time. An intelligent factory environment consists of all the machines fitted with self-optimization and automation. Some of the broad advantages of smart factories are processing real-time data, online analysis and quality control, reduced production time, and flexibility and ease of management. The features of the smart factories can be summarized with five essential benefits: continuous connectivity that helps in real-time data analysis; optimized productivity, which is made possible with less human intervention in the industrial processes; transparency, which has resulted in the performance parameters being measured with quick decision-making capability; proactiveness in predicting the future outcomes to take preventive actions with the injection of machine learning algorithms; and agility in the form of flexibility and adaptability of the management in terms of newer technologies. A small overview of the smart factory environment is depicted in Figure 13.4.

Consider an example of Airbus, a European aircraft manufacturer that applied IoT technologies in its production. It collects data during flights to improve the in-flight experience. It has launched the digital manufacturing initiative known as the factory of the future. In this initiative, the company has included digital tracking and monitoring, tools with integrated sensors such as smart wearables, and a three-dimensional realization of production process visuals in the assembly lines to produce A330 and A350 aircraft in Toulouse. Also, it has deployed the A400M model's wing assembly operations in the UK.

Similarly, Kuka is an IoT-enabled factory of German robotics where hundreds of robots are connected to the private cloud and 800 cars are produced per day. DeWalt is a tool manufacturing company that has launched the construction IoT initiative. This initiative uses an IoT platform and a Wi-Fi mesh network to track workers and equipment and successfully monitors construction sites the size of a football stadium. Amazon's Robotic Shelves is an e-commerce firm that uses robots to carry and arrange the shelves, and product search is performed in an automated way. It has successfully cut 20% of the operating cost by using robots in its operation. Caterpillar uses augmented reality (AR) technology

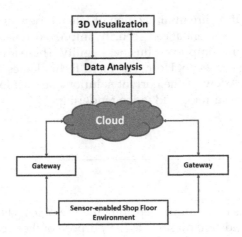

FIGURE 13.4
An overview of the critical components in a smart factory.

to generate the end-to-end view of the factory floor. Hitachi has successfully developed an IoT platform called Lumada that supports five layers in its production process: edge, core, analytics, studio, and foundry. Some of the similar IoT-based smart factories are setup by Fanuc for zero downtime, Gehring for connected manufacturing, Maersk for intelligent shopping, Magna Steyr for smart packaging and driverless transport system, Rio Tinto for mining, and Bosch for tracking and tracing the working tools to save labor and reduce errors in the process.

13.5.2 Other Areas

There are other vital areas where the implementation of IoT, fog, and cloud provide an environment for their efficient growth. However, a lot of research is still needed in these areas. Some of these areas include power plants, which demand innovation in such a way that productivity gets increased with reduced cost and increase efficiency; inventory management and quality control, wherein there is a need to meet the anticipated demands while smoothening the flow of operations; plant security and safety to prevent the hazards and catastrophic events to reduce the loss of human lives; and facility management to support the services for organizations by integrating people, place, and process to improve the quality of the working environment and, hence, the productivity. Furthermore, there is a need to provide extensive values by integrating IoT strategies in the oil, chemical, and pharmaceutical industries. In addition to this, there is a need to perform extensive research in the development of UAVs, which have wide applications in the food industry, agriculture, construction, mining, energy management, telecommunication, delivery and healthcare, oil and gas, warehousing and inventory, forestry, and entertainment.

13.6 Conclusion

Real-time communication and computation are two of the most crucial operations in the current generation applications, irrespective of whether these applications are for personal or industrial usage. The advent of the IoT environment provides a promising opportunity to support real-time service delivery. Moreover, the use of many IoT devices results in a significantly large amount of data getting generated. These data need prompt analysis to create valuable information from them. Thus, the concept of the cloud provides a platform where resource utilization can be provided. Furthermore, there is a need to reduce the gap between the application layer and the physical layer, and thus, fog computing plays a pivotal role in achieving the same. In this context, this chapter discusses the communication protocols and connectivity techniques in the field of IoT. Cloud computing and its significant role in industrial IoT is further addressed with its architecture, services, deployment model, and benefits to the end users. Finally, fog computing and its significance in bridging the gap between cloud and physical layer devices are explained with a few case studies to demonstrate the research and development requirements in the different areas are discussed. As a promising field in research, these concepts serve as the basis for further innovation in various application areas.

References

Aazam, M., Huh, E.-N., St-Hilaire, M., Lung, C.-H., and Lambadaris, I. (2016). Cloud of things: Integration of IoT with cloud computing. In *Robots and Sensor Clouds* (pp. 77–94). Springer, Singapore.

Arunachalam, P., Janakiraman, N., Sivaraman, A. K., Balasundaram, A., Vincent, R., Rani, S., ... Rajesh, M. (2021). Synovial sarcoma classification technique using support vector machine and structure features. *Intelligent Automation and Soft Computing*, 32(2), 1241–1259.

Balaji, S., Nathani, K., and Santhakumar, R. (2019). IoT technology, applications and challenges: A contemporary survey. *Wireless Personal Communications*, 108(1), 363–388.

Banerjee, K., Bali, V., Nawaz, N., Bali, S., Mathur, S., Mishra, R. K., and Rani, S. (2022). A machine-learning approach for prediction of water contamination using latitude, longitude, and elevation. *Water*, 14(5), 728.

Bhambri, P., Bagga, S., Priya, D., Singh, H., and Dhiman, H. K. (2020). Suspicious human activity detection system. *Journal of IoT in Social, Mobile, Analytics, and Cloud*, 2(4), 216–221.

Bhambri, P., and Chhabra, Y. (2022). Deployment of distributed clustering approach in WSNs and IoTs. In *Cloud and Fog Computing Platforms for Internet of Things* (pp. 85–98). Chapman and Hall/CRC, Florida, USA.

Bonomi, F., Milito, R., Zhu, J., and Addepalli, S. (2012). Fog computing and its role in the internet of things. In *Proceedings of the First Edition of the MCC Workshop on Mobile Cloud Computing* (pp. 13–16). ACM.

Chowdhury, A. H., Ikram, M., Cha, H.-S., Redwan, H., Shams, S. M. S., Kim, K.-H., and Yoo, S.-W. (2009). Route-over vs Mesh-under routing in 6LoWPAN. In *Proceedings of the International Conference on Wireless Communications and Mobile Computing: Connecting the World Wirelessly* (pp. 1208–1212). ACM.

Coskun, V., Ok, K., and Ozdenizci, B. (2011). *Near Field Communication (NFC): From Theory to Practice*. John Wiley & Sons, USA.

Cusumano, M. (2010). Cloud computing and SaaS as new computing platforms. *Communications of the ACM*, 53(4), 27–29.

Dian, F. J., Vahidnia, R., and Rahmati, A. (2020). Wearables and the Internet of Things (IoT), applications, opportunities, and challenges: A survey. *IEEE Access*, 8, 69200–69211.

Eucalyptus (2021). *Official Documentation for Eucalyptus Cloud*. https://docs.eucalyptus.cloud/eucalyptus/4.4.5/index.html.

Florencio, H., Dória Neto, A., and Martins, D. (2020). ISA 100.11 a networked control system based on link stability. *Sensors, 20*(18), 5417.

Franceschinis, M., Pastrone, C., Spirito, M. A., and Borean, C. (2013). On the performance of ZigBee Pro and ZigBee IP in IEEE 802.15. 4 networks. In *Proceedings of the 9th International Conference on Wireless and Mobile Computing, Networking and Communications (WiMob)* (pp. 83–88). IEEE.

Frank, A. G., Dalenogare, L. S., and Ayala, N. F. (2019). Industry 4.0 technologies: Implementation patterns in manufacturing companies. *International Journal of Production Economics, 210*, 15–26.

Ganguly, P. (2016). Selecting the right IoT cloud platform. In *Proceedings of the International Conference on Internet of Things and Applications (IOTA)* (pp. 316–320). IEEE.

Gardašević, G., Veletić, M., Maletić, N., Vasiljević, D., Radusinović, I., Tomović, S., and Radonjić, M. (2017). The IoT architectural framework, design issues and application domains. *Wireless Personal Communications, 92*(1), 127–148.

Gilchrist, A. (2016). *Industry 4.0: The Industrial Internet of Things.* Springer, Singapore.

Guochen, A., Zhiyong, M., Hongtao, M., and Bingdong, S. (2010). Design of intelligent transmitter based on HART protocol. In *Proceedings of the International Conference on Intelligent Computation Technology and Automation* (vol. 2, pp. 40–43). IEEE.

Gupta, O., Rani, S., and Pant, D. C. (2011). Impact of parallel computing on bioinformatics algorithms. In *Proceedings 5th IEEE International Conference on Advanced Computing and Communication Technologies* (pp. 206–209). IEEE.

Haartsen, J. C. (2000). The Bluetooth radio system. *IEEE Personal Communications, 7*(1), 28–36.

Harleen, B. (2016). A prediction technique in data mining for diabetes mellitus. *Journal of Management Sciences And Technology, 4*(1).

Hu, P., Dhelim, S., Ning, H., and Qiu, T. (2017). Survey on fog computing: Architecture, key technologies, applications and open issues. *Journal of Network and Computer Applications, 98*, 27–42.

Hui, J. W., and Culler, D. E. (2008). Extending IP to low-power, wireless personal area networks. *IEEE Internet Computing, 12*(4), 37–45.

Industrial Internet Consortium. (2018). Introduction to edge computing in IIoT (White paper). Industrial Internet Consortium.

Iosup, A., Prodan, R., and Epema, D. (2014). IAAS cloud benchmarking: Approaches, challenges, and experience. In *Cloud Computing for Data-Intensive Applications* (pp. 83–104). Springer, Singapore.

Jain, A., Singh, M., and Bhambri, P. (2021). Performance evaluation of IPv4-IPv6 tunneling procedure using IoT. *Journal of Physics: Conference Series, 1950*(1), 012010.

Kaur, J., Bhambri, P., and Gupta, O. P. (2013). Distance based phylogenetic trees with bootstrapping. *International Journal of Computer Applications, 47*, 6–10.

Knight, M. (2006). How safe is Z-Wave? [Wireless standards]. *Computing and Control Engineering, 17*(6), 18–23.

Kothandaraman, D., Manickam, M., Balasundaram, A., Pradeep, D., Arulmurugan, A., Sivaraman, A. K., ... Balakrishna, R. (2022). Decentralized link failure prevention routing (DLFPR) algorithm for efficient internet of things. *Intelligent Automation and Soft Computing, 34*(1), 655–666.

Kumar, R., Rani, S., and Awadh, M. A. (2022). Exploring the application sphere of the internet of things in Industry 4.0: A review, bibliometric and content analysis. *Sensors, 22*(11), 4276.

Kumar, S., and Zaveri, M. (2018). Event localization based on direction of arrival using quasi random deployment in internet of things. In *Proceedings of SAI Intelligent Systems Conference* (pp. 170–188). Springer.

Lin, J., Yu, W., Zhang, N., Yang, X., Zhang, H., and Zhao, W. (2017). A survey on internet of things: Architecture, enabling technologies, security and privacy, and applications. *IEEE Internet of Things Journal, 4*(5), 1125–1142.

Liu, F., Tong, J., Mao, J., Bohn, R., Messina, J., Badger, L., Leaf, D., and others. (2011). NIST cloud computing reference architecture. *NIST Special Publication, 500*(2011), 1–28.

Matt, C. (2018). Fog computing. *Business and Information Systems Engineering, 60*(4), 351–355.

Modi, C., Patel, D., Borisaniya, B., Patel, A., and Rajarajan, M. (2013). A survey on security issues and solutions at different layers of cloud computing. *The Journal of Supercomputing, 63*(2), 561–592.

Moghe, U., Lakkadwala, P., and Mishra, D. K. (2012). Cloud computing: Survey of different utilization techniques. In *Proceedings of the CSI Sixth International Conference on Software Engineering (CONSEG)* (pp. 1–4). IEEE.

Molisch, A. F., Balakrishnan, K., Chong, C.-C., Emami, S., Fort, A., Karedal, J., Kunisch, J., Schantz, H., Schuster, U., and Siwiak, K.(2004). IEEE 802.15. 4a channel model-final report. *IEEE P802, 15*(04), 662.

Mulligan, G. (2007). The 6LoWPAN architecture. In *Proceedings of the 4th Workshop on Embedded Networked Sensors* (pp. 78–82). ACM.

Naha, R. K., Garg, S., Georgakopoulos, D., Jayaraman, P. P., Gao, L., Xiang, Y., and Ranjan, R. (2018). Fog computing: Survey of trends, architectures, requirements, and research directions. *IEEE Access, 6*, 47980–48009.

Pahl, C. (2015). Containerization and the paas cloud. *IEEE Cloud Computing, 2*(3), 24–31.

Pandey, S. K., and Zaveri, M. A. (2016a). Localization for collaborative processing in the internet of things framework. In *Proceedings of the Second International Conference on IoT in Urban Space* (pp. 108–110). ACM.

Pandey, S. K., and Zaveri, M. A. (2016b). Optimized deployment strategy for efficient utilization of the internet of things. In *2016 IEEE International Conference on Advances in Electronics, Communication and Computer Technology (ICAECCT)* (pp. 192–197). IEEE.

Pandey, S. K., and Zaveri, M. A. (2018). Quasi random deployment and localization in layered framework for the internet of things. *The Computer Journal, 61*(2), 159–179.

Patzke, R. (1998). Fieldbus basics. *Computer Standards and Interfaces, 19*(5–6), 275–293.

Rahman, M. A., Hossain, M. S., Hassanain, E., and Muhammad, G. (2018). Semantic multimedia fog computing and IoT environment: Sustainability perspective. *IEEE Communications Magazine, 56*(5), 80–87.

Ramya, C. M., Shanmugaraj, M., and Prabakaran, R. (2011). Study on ZigBee technology. In *Proceedings of the 3rd International Conference on Electronics Computer Technology* (vol. 6, pp. 297–301). Springer.

Rani, S., Arya, V., and Kataria, A. (2022). Dynamic pricing-based e-commerce model for the produce of organic farming in India: A research roadmap with main advertence to vegetables. In *Proceedings of Data Analytics and Management* (pp. 327–336). Springer, Singapore.

Rani, S., Chauhan, M., Kataria, A., and Khang, A. (2021). IoT equipped intelligent distributed framework for smart healthcare systems. *arXiv preprint arXiv:2110.04997.*

Rani, S., and Gupta, O. P. (2016). Empirical analysis and performance evaluation of various GPU implementations of protein BLAST. *International Journal of Computer Applications, 151*(7), 22–27.

Rani, S., and Gupta, O. P. (2017). CLUS_GPU-BLASTP: Accelerated protein sequence alignment using GPU-enabled cluster. *The Journal of Supercomputing, 73*(10), 4580–4595.

Rani, S., Kataria, A., Chauhan, M., Rattan, P., Kumar, R., and Sivaraman, A. K. (2022). Security and privacy challenges in the deployment of cyber-physical systems in smart city applications: State-of-art work. *Materials Today: Proceedings, 62*(7), 4671–4676.

Rani, S., and Kaur, S. (2012). Cluster analysis method for multiple sequence alignment. *International Journal of Computer Applications, 43*(14), 19–25.

Rani, S., and Kumar, R. (2022). Bibliometric review of actuators: Key automation technology in a smart city framework. *Materials Today: Proceedings, 60*(3), 1800–1807.

Rani, S., Mishra, R. K., Usman, M., Kataria, A., Kumar, P., Bhambri, P., and Mishra, A. K. (2021). Amalgamation of advanced technologies for sustainable development of smart city environment: A review. *IEEE Access, 9*, 150060–150087.

Song, J., Han, S., Mok, A., Chen, D., Lucas, M., Nixon, M., and Pratt, W. (2008). WirelessHART: Applying wireless technology in real-time industrial process control. In *Proceedings of the Real-Time and Embedded Technology and Applications Symposium* (pp. 377–386). IEEE. doi:10.1109/RTAS.2008.15.

Statista. (2021). Internet of Things (IoT) and non-IoT active device connections worldwide from 2010 to 2025. https://www.statista.com/statistics/1101442/iot-number-of-connected-devices-worldwide/.

Weinstein, R. (2005). RFID: A technical overview and its application to the enterprise. *IT Professional*, 7(3), 27–33.

Wentao, C. H. U., Kuok-Tiung, L. E. E., Wei, L. U. O., Bhambri, P., and Kautish, S. (2021). Predicting the security threats of internet rumors and spread of false information based on sociological principle. *Computer Standards and Interfaces*, 73, 103454.

Yang, S., Hawkins, J., and Richardson, K. (2014). The improved NRL tropical cyclone monitoring system with a unified microwave brightness temperature calibration scheme. *Remote Sensing*, 6(5), 4563–4581.

Zhou, L., Wu, D., Chen, J., and Dong, Z. (2017). When computation hugs intelligence: Content-aware data processing for industrial IoT. *IEEE Internet of Things Journal*, 5(3), 1657–1666.

14

Smart Waste Management System Using a Convolutional Neural Network Model

Neelam Sharma, Surbhi Gupta, Shefali Kanwar and Vanieka

CONTENTS

14.1 Introduction

We all are familiar with garbage and waste material, which is very harmful to our society. If we talk about the amount of waste, then the world generates at least 5 million tons of waste per day, and this number is still increasing day by day, which is why we need to be aware of waste. To put it another way, trash disposal is unsustainable and will have long-term consequences for future generations (Harleen, 2016). There are a variety of solid waste materials in these landfilled and burned waste items that may or may not be beneficial. However, it is vital to separate the usable elements from the nonessential waste materials to recycle and reuse them. Waste materials must be separated and then recycled for a civilization to be sustainable. Currently, facilities must sort waste manually as part of their segregation and recycling procedures, they use a series of large filters to sort out more specified items.

DOI: 10.1201/9781003298335-14

Manual procedures are now used to distinguish biodegradable (wet waste) from nonbio-degradable (solid waste; separating solid and liquid garbage into two containers; Wentao et al., 2021). With downward economic trends for wireless devices and services, users are finding it more affordable to consider wireless units (Bhambri et al., 2007).

With widespread use of the Internet and other communication technologies, it has become extremely easy to reproduce, communicate, and distribute digital content (Bhambri and Kaur, 2014). The research in bioinformatics has accumulated a large amount of data (Bhambri and Gupta, 2012). Wet waste can be utilized to make manures, fertilizers, biogas, and other products using these processes. However, for dry waste, this is not possible. Dry rubbish may carry recyclable materials, including metal, cardboard, glass, and paper, that may be recycled and reused. Incineration, or the burning of waste, is a conventional method of dry waste segregation. Solid waste separation by hand is a time-consuming and inefficient process. As a result, segregating dry waste at the source is critical to minimize the need for more complex segregation processes at trash disposal locations.

The majority of modern waste disposal technologies, such as landfilling and burning, are growing more expensive and ineffective (Rani et al., 2022b, 2022c). The financial expenses of controlling the long-term environmental consequences of trash disposal are frequently unaffordable. In this chapter, we classify waste into seven different waste materials and show the details of that particular waste material. This will help raise awareness for people to reduce and recycle waste. The goal of this chapter is to develop a model for an automated waste sorting system. Because people do not always sort every-thing with 100% precision, this has the potential to improve processing plant efficiency while also helping reduce waste. Not only will this be good for the environment, but it will also be good for the economy. To prepare this model, we have also considered the cost to the environment, such as negative impacts on the environment, animals, and biodiver-sity (Rani et al., 2021, 2022d).

14.2 Literature Review

This section summarizes previous research on the subject of our suggested model. Many outstanding contributors have left an ineffaceable mark on the subject of waste manage-ment through machine learning and IoT (Rani et al., 2021, 2022a). Cities face several dif-ficulties, including trash reduction, since the population of people living in cities expands at a rapid rate over time. According to the World Bank, about 2.01 billion metric tonnes of trash were generated in 2016 as a result of population and economic growth in urban areas. By 2050, it is predicted to reach 3.40 billion tonnes (Gouin, 2021). According to Robinson (2007) the European Union, 423 million tonnes of garbage were recycled in 2016, accounting for 56% of waste generated locally. Bobulski and Kubanek (2021) utilized image processing and a convolutional neural network (CNN) to create a waste classification system. In their investigation, the authors concentrated on the detection of polyethylene. Sreelakshmi et al. (2019) employed a capsule neural network to remove solid waste; using this model, plastic and non-plastic items can be detected. The author suggested a novel model identify the categories of garbage using deep learning methods in a publication (Huiyu et al., 2019). In addition, the technology was used to recycle waste. A smart solid waste monitoring and collecting system has been proposed and built by Mamun et al. (2014). Sheng et al. (2020) prepared a model that was trained with discarded photos to produce a graph of inference frozen. Hassan et al. (2017) used smart bins with a radiofrequency transmitter with an ultrasonic sensor. Zheng et al. (2020) provided expert advice on many forms of economic, technological, and administrative issues in the collection and treatment of solid waste in developing nations. Hassan et al. (2017) and Arunachalam et al. (2021) proposed an ultrawideband planar antenna in this study. Azim et al. (2021) presented a check password (CPW)–fed antenna for wireless sensor networks, which is the most common service utilized in several applications. White and Clarke (2020) used transfer learning that can be used to update the last layers of pre-trained models at the network's edge. Hong et al. (2014) proposed a smart trash system to reduce food waste. Zavare et al. (2013) developed a smart bin using the Global System for Mobile communication (GSM) to notify the authorized person when the garbage bin is about to be full and relay the bin's location (Pardini et al., 2020; Kumar et al., 2022). The system uses an Internet of Things (IoT) technique in which the discarded garbage collected from the smart bin is monitored by sensors that provide information on the filling level of each compartment. Karadimas et al. (2016) explained the concept and methods of an integrated node for smart-city applications, as well as the architecture and physical implementation. Jajoo et al. (2018) suggested a smart waste bin built around an ultrasonic-level sensor and a variety of gas sensors that detect hazardous gases and the garbage's maximum limit automatically. For Shahidul Islam et al. (2019), the goal was to use a wireless system with Long Range Radio (LoRa) to communicate the collected data from the application my Signals to a personal computer. Yusof et al. (2017) and Rani and Kumar (2022) demonstrated the innovation of a smart garbage monitoring system that measures waste levels in garbage bins and alerts the municipality (Bobulski and Kubanek, 2021). For decades, researchers and academics have worked to efficiently classify photos into their respective groupings. Due to a lack of processing capability and insufficient image datasets. However, thanks to ever-increasing GPU processing power and the availability of large datasets, computer vision methods may now be used efficiently. To classify the type of e-waste, a deep learning CNN was utilized by Nowakowski and Pamuła (2020) and a quicker region-based convolutional neural network (R-CNN) was used to detect the category and size of the waste equipment in the photos. Mao et al. (2021) developed a 40-layer residual net pre-train (ResNet-40) CNN, which was used to classify the waste into different groups that will be used to develop an intelligent waste material classification system. Huang et al. (n.d.) offered a detector that can detect objects in real time. The plant, which uses waste instead of fossil fuels to generate energy, can turn 440,000 tonnes of rubbish into electricity and heat for 30,000 households each year. Taiwan aims to create a mechanism to catch the carbon emitted by the incineration process, store it, or find a commercial purpose for it, even though it still produces CO_2 emissions from burning. It will also assist the city in moving outside its reliance on fossil fuels by tapping an otherwise underused resource. Typically, towns/cities dispatch several trucks to collect different sorts of waste, such as one for recyclable plastic and another for food waste. This, however, entails the use of a huge number of trucks, resulting in higher pricing and traffic congestion. Trash identification is a critical stage in the separation process, and it is possible to do quickly with the use of a variety of machine learning and image-processing techniques. CNNs are the best solution for picture categorization. CNNs may be used to take out distinctive features from photos and then categorize them into groups. As a result of the development of graphics processing units (GPUs), computers' processing capacity has increased tremendously. CNNs have become increasingly popular in recent decades as picture collections can now be analyzed in a relatively short amount of time (Kaur et al., 2013). In addition to CNNs, other machine learning techniques for categorizing pictures include artificial neural networks (ANNs), recurrent neural networks (RNNs), and support vector machines (SVMs). In picture classification, CNN beats most machine learning algorithms when there are a high number of photos in the dataset.

14.3 Hardware and Software Requirements

These hardware and software requirements include the Anaconda Navigator, Tensor flow, Keras, Flask, and Python Packages.

14.3.1 Anaconda Navigator

Anaconda Navigator is a free and open-source data science and machine learning distribution that is based on the Python and R programming languages. It is compatible with Windows, Linux, and Mac OS X. Conda is a cross-platform, open-source package management system. Anaconda includes Jupyter Lab, Jupyter Notebook, Qt Console, Spyder, Glue visual, Orange, RStudio, and Visual Studio Code. Jupiter notebook and spyder are used for this project.

14.3.2 Tensor Flow

This is an open-source machine learning framework that automates the whole process. It has a broad tool ecosystem, libraries, and community resources that allow academics to push machine learning's bounds and developers to easily construct and deploy machine learning–powered solutions.

14.3.3 Keras

This makes high-level neural network application program interface (API) easier and more performant by utilizing multiple optimization approaches. It has the following capabilities:

- An API that is consistent, easy to use, and expandable.
- Simple construction—no frills required to obtain the desired result.
- It works with a variety of platforms and backends.
- It is a user-friendly framework that works on both the CPU and the GPU.
- it is an extremely scalable computation.

14.3.4 Flask

Flask is a web framework used for building web applications.

14.3.5 Python Packages

- *Open anaconda prompt as administrator.*
- *Type "pip install NumPy" and click enter.*
- *Type "pip install pandas" and click enter.*

- *Type "pip install sci-kit-learn" and click enter.*
- *Type "pip install TensorFlow==2.3.2" and click enter.*
- *Type "pip install keras==2.3.1" and click enter.*
- *Type "pip install Flask" and click enter.*

14.4 Experimental Investigations

Image preprocessing includes the following main tasks:

- Import Image Data Generator Library.
- Configure Image Data Generator Class.
- Applying Image Data Generator functionality to the trainset and test set.

Note: The Image Data Generator takes the original data, transforms it randomly, and only returns the new, modified data. As the input image contains three channels, we are specifying the input shape as (128,128,3).

- After a max-pooling layer, we added a convolution layer with the activation function "relu" and the size of the filter (3,3), and the total number of filters is 32.
- The input is downsampled using the max pool layer. (Max pooling is the selection of the maximum element from the region of the feature map covered by the filter.)
- The flatten layer's job is to flatten the input without affecting the batch size.
- A dense layer is a layer of a neural network that is densely coupled. It's the most popular and often utilized layer.

The final stage in the model generation process is a compilation. After the compilation is finished, we may go on to the training step. The loss function is used to identify learning faults or deviations. During the model compilation phase, Keras requires a loss function.

Optimization is a method that compares the prediction and the loss function to optimize the input weights. In this chapter, we are using an Adam Optimizer for optimization.

Metrics are used to assess our model's performance. It is comparable to the loss function, but it is not utilized in training.

14.5 Proposed Methodology

Our main focus in this study is on dealing with organic garbage, which needed careful consideration due to the wide range of recycled values. In this chapter, we have taken organic waste. The organic waste input is combined with a weight sensor. The price of that particular waste material is automatically calculated based on the weight. We have divided this methodology into four sections:

- Classifier Module
- Algorithm Module

- Convolutional Module
- Website Module

14.5.1 Classifier Module

The CNN machine learning technique is used to determine which category to the entering waste material belongs. The model divides the input image into four categories: metal, plastic, paper, and glass. Each class received around 600–1000 photos. Cardboard boxes, plastic bottles, drink cans, paper bags, plastic glasses, papers, glass bottles, and other domestic trash items are prevalent in the photographs. We are regularly adding new photographs to the dataset so that the algorithm can properly categorize a varied range of waste products into their proper categories.

Because CNN is a deep learning method, the amount of data acquired was insufficient to provide the model with a reasonable level of accuracy. Using picture augmentation techniques, we were able to fix this problem. During the training phase, we employed rotation, shifting of width, height, rescaling, normalization, shear transformation, zoom transformation, and horizontal flipping for image augmentation. We applied these changes at random to ensure that our model never saw the same picture twice. This made it easier for us to generalize our model as shown in Figure 14.1.

14.5.2 Algorithm Module

In many aspects, the CNN algorithm differs from other ANN algorithms. Training, testing, backpropagation, and error reduction are all principles that haven't changed. The CNN algorithm is designed to be used for image classification alone. As input, the algorithm takes an image from the dataset. CNNs operate with data that has spatial dimensions, or volumes. This algorithm accepts input in the form of activation volumes and returns activation volumes as output. As a result, the intermediates in CNN are not normal vectors like in a traditional ANN; they do, however, have height, breadth, and depth as spatial dimensions. The method is made up of three layers: the first layer is the convolutional layer, the second layer is a max-pooling layer, and the third layer is the fully connected layer (Banerjee et al., 2022; Hans et al., 2022).

FIGURE 14.1
Image of cardboard (training set).

14.5.3 Convolution Module

The convolutional layer works as follows: it gets some input volume, in this case, an image, that has a defined depth, height, and width. Filters are represented by matrices whose elements are random integers. The size of the masks is small, but they have the same depth as the channels in the input picture. The depth of the RGB filters will be 3, the depth of the Greyscale filters will be 1, and so on. The input volume is convolved with the filtering. It goes across the picture spatially, computing the dot product along the way. Finally, the filters generate activation maps for the input picture as depicted in Figure 14.2.

Using equation $W^T x + b$, we have calculated the dot product, where W represents the filter,

x is the output image, and bias is denoted by b. In CNN, we have taken a hidden layer as Relu (rectified linear units). Relu is the activation function.

It is defined as max $F(x)$ = max $(0, x)$. where x is an integer.

CNNs extract an activation map of the filters after each convolutional layer. If the values are less than zero, then this value is discarded by the activation function. The next layer is a max-pooling layer.

In the max-pooling layer, we just downsampled the activation maps. In this chapter, we have utilized max-pooling layers that contain a 2 × 2 filter and stride 2, which reduces the input activation maps in half the spatial maps. Average pooling is another type of pooling. For the next layer, the average of the submatrix is preserved rather than the maximum.

Fully Connected CNN Layer—At the end, the fully connected CNN layer takes input in the form of volume. It has neurons that compute class scores and are fully connected to the entire input volume, similar to a standard neural network. The output is computed by this layer, which is a score indicating how likely the picture is to belong to each class, using the final matrix multiplier.

The forward-pass and backpropagation phases of the method work in tandem. The image is sent to each of the aforementioned layers during the forward pass, and the output is determined. The error is computed by comparing the predicted and actual outputs. After computing the error, the approach updates the weights. The filters' weights or spatial values are modified during the backpropagation phase. To reduce the error as much as feasible, this backpropagation stage is augmented with optimization techniques, such as

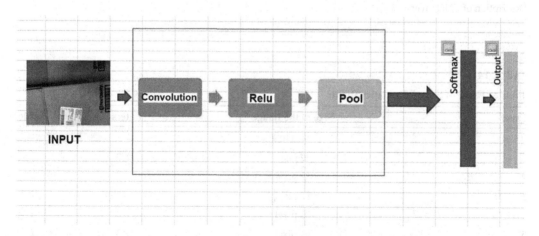

FIGURE 14.2
Model of CNN architecture.

gradient descent. In this chapter, Google's TensorFlow, Keras, a high-level abstraction layer built on top of the Tensor Flow, was utilized to create the CNN. Before being fed as input to the network, all the photos in the dataset were scaled to 140 × 140 pixels. Figure 14.3 shows how the network was created.

The details of hidden layers are given in Table 14.1.

Layer 7 and layer 8 with 64 and 8 neurons, respectively, are fully linked. Software function returns six classes (cardboard, paper, plastic, glass, rubber, metal). The train/test sets split per class was 800–1000/300–400, with 40 epochs used. Because augmented samples were used as input, they were strongly correlated, even though they increased the dataset size. Overfitting of the data could have resulted because of this. The overfitting problem was handled by adjusting the network's entropic capacity, or the quantity of data kept in

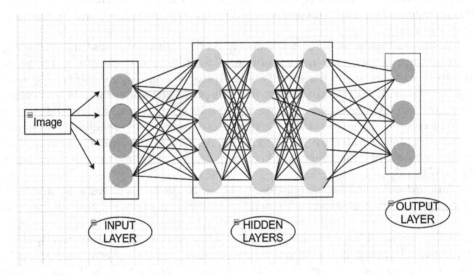

FIGURE 14.3
Description of CNN layers.

TABLE 14.1

Tabular Form of Size, Filter, and Stride

Layer	Size of the Image	Filters	Stride
0	140 × 140 × 3	–	–
1	32 pixel	3 × 3	2
2	32 pixel	2 × 2	2
3	32 pixel	3 × 3	2
4	32 pixel	2 × 2	2
5	64 pixel	3 × 3	2
6	64 pixel	2 × 2	2

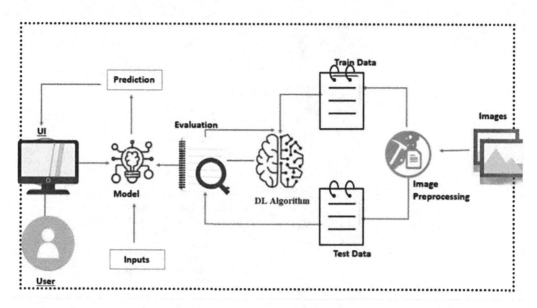

FIGURE 14.4
Block diagram describing the workflow of the garbage classification system.

the machine learning model. This model can store a lot of data and may be more precise, but it also stores features that are not relevant. We utilized a simple CNN with only a few layers and filters per layer, data augmentation, and a dropout of 0.5 in our case. Dropout also prevents a layer from seeing the same pattern many times, which helps to decrease overfitting. As a consequence, the model with fewer data keeps just the most essential qualities extracted from the data, making it more relevant and generalizable.

The flow chart of the garbage classification system is defined in Figure 14.5.

This is a block diagram that describes the internal working of our model. Our deep learning model can detect and classify types of garbage. A web application is integrated with the model, from where the user can upload a garbage image like paper waste, plastic waste, etc., and see the analysed results on User Interface.

14.5.4 Website Module

The website module includes HTML, CSS, JavaScript, and flask code. The website module's primary function is to provide information and a quick overview of the bin's total waste processing. This module uses data that are updated by the Jupiter notebook module to provide a graphic annual detailed survey on the proportion of garbage separated by each bin in the data analysis section, enabling the user to see how much garbage from each category has been handled by each bin. The block diagram describing the workflow of the garbage system is defined in Figure 14.4.

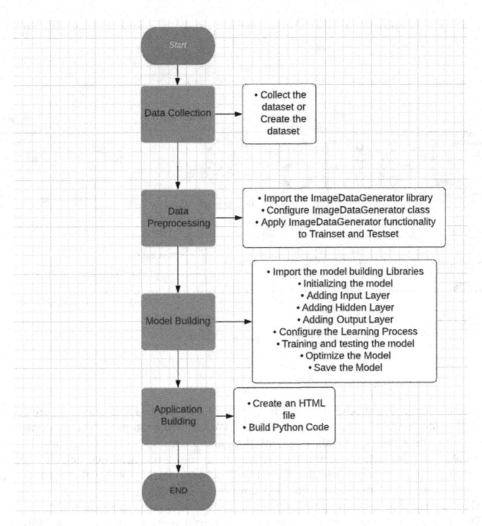

FIGURE 14.5
Flow chart of garbage classification system procedure.

14.6 Results and Discussion

In our data set, recyclable garbage has been divided into seven kinds of our databases. cardboard, paper, plastic, glass, rubber, and metal are among them. Each class receives 600–1000 photos. We are adding new photos to the dataset regularly so that the algorithm can correctly categorize a wide range of waste goods into their appropriate categories. The web application of the garbage classification system has been depicted in Figure 14.6.

Using entirely different CNN models in the machine learning module, initially, we were not able to achieve a high enough level of accuracy to accurately sort the majority of the waste components. Using the mentioned parameters of the model for the CNN, on training data, we were able to attain 91.2% accuracy and 84.6% accuracy on validation data. As a result, for better trash recycling, communities that are becoming more urbanized require

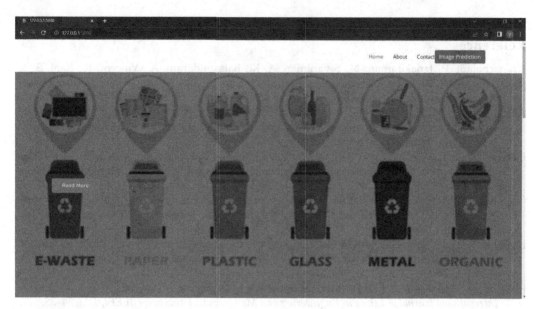

FIGURE 14.6
Web application of garbage classification system.

automatic garbage classification and management. Finally, an intelligent waste categorization model with all its structures and the operating environment required to deploy the model in a meaningful situation is shown.

14.7 Conclusion and Future Work

In this chapter, we have presented the design of a model in which we have used the CNN algorithm for object recognizer. We were able to get 91.2% accuracy on training data and 84.6% accuracy on validation data so that system can easily recognize and classify garbage into plastic, metal, paper, cardboard, and paper. The CNN algorithm can classify a larger range of garbage materials by adding additional photographs to the dataset. The input photo dataset for this system can be tweaked to make it more application-specific. For example, the model can be used in fast-food restaurants such as McDonald's and Subway to classify waste products such as beverage cans, tissue papers, plastic cups, wrappers, and so on. The system can be improved further to improve its accuracy and efficacy. It is anticipated that public support for rubbish classification would grow as the practice is promoted and advanced. Later, garbage classification studies should be done on optimizing each link, such as garbage transportation route construction, various forms of garbage recycling frequency, waste screening with detailed analysis, and so on. It is possible to use occlusion detection to locate hidden things. In addition, sensors in trash cans can be utilized to monitor waste levels. The advantage of this model is that we can minimize the quantity of waste disposal and treatment equipment required. We can also reduce treatment costs, reduce land resource consumption, and provide social, economic, and environmental benefits.

References

Arunachalam, P., Janakiraman, N., Sivaraman, A. K., Balasundaram, A., Vincent, R., Rani, S., … Rajesh, M. (2021). Synovial sarcoma classification technique using support vector machine and structure features. *Intelligent Automation and Soft Computing*, 32(2), 1241–1259.

Azim, R., Islam, M. T., Arshad, H., Alam, Md. M., Sobahi, N., and Khan, A. I. (2021). CPW-Fed superwideband antenna with modified vertical bow-tie-shaped patch for wireless sensor networks. *IEEE Access*, 9, 5343–5353. https://doi.org/10.1109/ACCESS.2020.3048052.

Banerjee, K., Bali, V., Nawaz, N., Bali, S., Mathur, S., Mishra, R. K., and Rani, S. (2022). A machine-learning approach for prediction of water contamination using latitude, longitude, and elevation. *Water*, 14(5), 728.

Bhambri, L. P., Jindal, C., and Bathla, S. (2007). Future wireless technology-ZigBee. In *Proceedings of National Conference on Challenges and Opportunities in Information Technology (COIT)* (pp. 154–156).

Bhambri, P., and Gupta, O. P. (2012). Development of phylogenetic tree based on Kimura's method. In *2012 2nd IEEE International Conference on Parallel, Distributed and Grid Computing* (pp. 721–723). IEEE.

Bhambri, P., and Kaur, P. (2014). A novel approach of zero watermarking for text documents. *International Journal of Ethics in Engineering and Management Education (IJEEE)*, 1(1), 34–38.

Bobulski, J., and Kubanek, M. (2021). Deep learning for plastic waste classification system. *Applied Computational Intelligence and Soft Computing*, 2021, 6626948. https://doi.org/10.1155/2021/6626948.

Gouin, T. (2021). Addressing the importance of microplastic particles as vectors for long-range transport of chemical contaminants: Perspective in relation to prioritizing research and regulatory actions. *Microplastics and Nanoplastics*, 1(1), 14. https://doi.org/10.1186/s43591-021-00016-w.

Hans, S., Ghosh, S., Bhullar, S., Kataria, A., Karar, V., and Agrawal, D. (2022). Hybrid energy storage to control and optimize electric propulsion systems. *CMC-Computers Materials and Continua*, 71(3), 6183–6200.

Harleen, B. (2016). A prediction technique in data mining for diabetes mellitus. *Apeejay Journal of Management Sciences and Technology*, 4(1), 1–12.

Hassan, S. A., Samsuzzaman, Md., Hossain, M. J., Akhtaruzzaman, Md., and Islam, T. (2017). Compact planar UWB antenna with 3.5/5.8 GHz dual band-notched characteristics for IoT application. In *2017 IEEE International Conference on Telecommunications and Photonics (ICTP)* (pp. 195–199). IEEE.

Hong, I., Park, S., Lee, B., Lee, J., Jeong, D., and Park, S. (2014). IoT-based smart garbage system for efficient food waste management. *The Scientific World Journal*, 2014, 646953. https://doi.org/10.1155/2014/646953.

Huang, J., Rathod, V., Sun, C., Zhu, M., Korattikara, A., Fathi, A., Fischer, I., Wojna, Z., Song, Y., Guadarrama, S., and Murphy, K. (n.d.). Speed/accuracy trade-offs for modern convolutional object detectors. *arXiv*. https://doi.org/10.48550/arXiv.1611.10012.

Huiyu, L., Ganiyat, Owolabi, and Kim, S.-H. (2019). Automatic classifications and recognition for recycled garbage by utilizing deep learning technology. In *Proceedings of the 2019 7th International Conference on Information Technology: IoT and Smart City* (pp. 1–4). ACM. https://doi.org/10.1145/3377170.3377190.

Jajoo, P., Mishra, A., Mehta, S., and Solvande, V. (2018). *Smart Garbage Management System*. https://doi.org/10.1109/ICSCET.2018.8537390.

Karadimas, D., Papalambrou, A., Gialelis, J., and Koubias, S. (2016). An integrated node for smart-city applications based on active RFID tags; use case on waste-bins. In *2016 IEEE 21st International Conference on Emerging Technologies and Factory Automation (ETFA)* (pp. 1–7). IEEE. https://doi.org/10.1109/ETFA.2016.7733532.

Kaur, J., Bhambri, P., and Gupta, O. P. (2013). Distance based phylogenetic trees with bootstrapping. *International Journal of Computer Applications*, 47, 6–10.

Kumar, R., Rani, S., and Awadh, M. A. (2022). Exploring the application sphere of the internet of things in industry 4.0: A review, bibliometric and content analysis. *Sensors, 22*(11), 4276.

Mamun, Md. A., Hannan, M. A., and Hussain, A. (2014). A novel prototype and simulation model for real time solid waste bin monitoring system. *Jurnal Kejuruteraan, 26,* 15–19. https://doi.org/10.17576/jkukm-2014-26-02.

Mao, W.-L., Chen, W.-C., Wang, C.-T., and Lin, Y.-H. (2021). Recycling waste classification using optimized convolutional neural network. *Resources, Conservation and Recycling, 164,* 105132. https://doi.org/10.1016/j.resconrec.2020.105132.

Nowakowski, P., and Pamuła, T. (2020). Application of deep learning object classifier to improve e-waste collection planning. *Waste Management, 109,* 1–9. https://doi.org/10.1016/j.wasman.2020.04.041.

Pardini, K., Rodrigues, J., Diallo, O., Das, A. K., Albuquerque, V. H. C., and Kozlov, S. (2020). A smart waste management solution geared towards citizens. *Sensors, 20,* 1–15. https://doi.org/10.3390/s20082380.

Rani, S., Arya, V., and Kataria, A. (2022a). Dynamic pricing-based e-commerce model for the produce of organic farming in India: A research roadmap with main advertence to vegetables. In *Proceedings of Data Analytics and Management* (pp. 327–336). Springer.

Rani, S., Kataria, A., and Chauhan, M. (2022b). Cyber security techniques, architectures, and design. In *Holistic Approach to Quantum Cryptography in Cyber Security* (pp. 41–66). CRC Press.

Rani, S., Kataria, A., and Chauhan, M. (2022c). Fog computing in industry 4.0: Applications and challenges—A research roadmap. In R. Tiwari, M. Mittal., and L. M. Goyal (Eds.), *Energy Conservation Solutions for Fog-Edge Computing Paradigms* (pp. 173–190). Springer.

Rani, S., Kataria, A., Chauhan, M., Rattan, P., Kumar, R., and Sivaraman, A. K. (2022d). Security and privacy challenges in the deployment of cyber-physical systems in smart city applications: State-of-art work. *Materials Today: Proceedings, 62*(7), 4641–4676.

Rani, S., Kataria, A., Sharma, V., Ghosh, S., Karar, V., Lee, K., and Choi, C. (2021). Threats and corrective measures for IoT security with observance of cybercrime: A survey. *Wireless Communications and Mobile Computing, 2021,* 1–30.

Rani, S., and Kumar, R. (2022). Bibliometric review of actuators: Key automation technology in a smart city framework. *Materials Today: Proceedings, 60*(3), 1800–1807.

Rani, S., Mishra, R. K., Usman, M., Kataria, A., Kumar, P., Bhambri, P., and Mishra, A. K. (2021). Amalgamation of advanced technologies for sustainable development of smart city environment: A review. *IEEE Access, 9,* 150060–150087.

Robinson, H. (2007) The composition of leachates from very large landfills: An international review. *Communications in Waste and Resource Management, 8,* 19–32.

Shahidul Islam, M., Islam, M. T., Almutairi, A. F., Beng, G. K., Misran, N., and Amin, N. (2019). Monitoring of the human body signal through the internet of things (IoT) based LoRa wireless network system. *Applied Sciences, 9*(9). https://doi.org/10.3390/app9091884.

Sheng, T., Shahidul Islam, M., Misran, N., Baharuddin, M. H., Arshad, H., Islam, Md. R., Chowdhury, M., Rmili, H., and Islam, M. (2020). An internet of things based smart waste management system using LoRa andtensorflow deep learning model. *IEEE Access, PP,* 1. https://doi.org/10.1109/ACCESS.2020.3016255.

Sreelakshmi, K., Akarsh, S., Vinayakumar, R., and Soman, K. P. (2019). Capsule neural networks and visualization for segregation of plastic and non-plastic wastes. In *2019 5th International Conference on Advanced Computing Communication Systems (ICACCS)* (pp. 631–636). IEEE. https://doi.org/10.1109/ICACCS.2019.8728405.

Wentao, C. H. U., Kuok-Tiung, L. E. E., Wei, L. U. O., Bhambri, P., and Kautish, S. (2021). Predicting the security threats of internet rumors and spread of false information based on sociological principle. *Computer Standards and Interfaces, 73,* 103454.

White, G., and Clarke, S. (2020). Urban intelligence with deep edges. *IEEE Access, 8,* 7518–7530. https://doi.org/10.1109/ACCESS.2020.2963912.

Yusof, N. M., Jidin, A. Z., and Rahim, M. I. (2017). Smart garbage monitoring system for waste management, In *MATEC Web of Conferences* (Vol. 97, p. 01098). EDP Sciences.

Zavare, S., Parashare, R., Patil, S., and Rathod, P. (2013). Smart city waste management system using GSM. *International Journal of Computer Science Trends and Technology (IJCST)*, 5. www.ijcstjournal. org

Zheng, C., Yuan, J., Zhu, L., Zhang, Y., and Shao, Q. (2020). From digital to sustainable: A sciento-metric review of smart city literature between 1990 and 2019. *Journal of Cleaners Production*, 258, 120689. https://doi.org/10.1016/j.jclepro.2020.120689.

15

An IoT-Based Emotion Analysis and Music Therapy

Keerthik Dhivya Rajakumar, Jagannath Mohan and Adalarasu Kanagasabai

CONTENTS

15.1 Introduction

Cognitive radio is a paradigm for wireless communication in which either a network or a wireless node changes its transmission or reception parameters to communicate effectively avoiding interference with licensed or unlicensed users (Bhambri and Gupta, 2014). The issue of the energy shortages is affecting the entire planet (Shrivastava et al., 2021). IoT-based healthcare technologies are a recent trend in the medical industry. Healthcare devices engage with patients and physicians to provide remote monitoring of vital physiological data of patients (Rani et al., 2022c, 2022d). It can be used in different forms, which include diagnosing a patient's vitals, analyzing patient data on the physician's end, and treating a patient by prescribing medicines and therapeutic treatments (Chhabra and Bhambri, 2021; Rani et al., 2021a).Previously, a patient monitoring system was arranged at the central nurse station to monitor the physiological parameters of intensive care unit patients inside the hospital, but remote monitoring could be done only for the shorter range, that is,

DOI: 10.1201/9781003298335-15

inside the hospital (Abbasi-Kesbi et al., 2020; Lee and Park, 2000). Also, the patients recovering from surgery or patients with implants need to be monitored, so wearable devices with Bluetooth, wireless Local Area Network (LAN) (Ahmed et al., 2016), or web services (Agarwal and Lau, 2010) have emerged to collect information from patients and transfer it to the physician, wherein the physician analyzes the physiological data, provides suggestions for the treatment, and sends them to the patient (Bhambri et al., 2021). These healthcare technologies avail the use of the internet to transfer and receive the patient's data, but the processing of data could only be achieved on the physician's end. Today, an IoT solution is implemented in this healthcare technology, which transfers patient data, processes them on a cloud server, and send them to the physician (Sakr and Elgammal, 2016; Wu et al., 2020; Juyal et al., 2021). It can be accomplished by using sensor networks, cloud servers, smartphones or smart devices, and the internet (Rani et al., 2021b, c). These kinds of passing vital patient data provide real-time monitoring, are easy to access remotely, consume less time, reduce the cost of bulk devices, treat patients in minimal time, keep patients' history on memory, and help in those in critical conditions. Patients who are affected by brain disorders (Maggioni et al., 2021), post-surgery trauma (Aris et al., 2021), cancer (Chen et al., 2021; Lynch et al., 2021; Yang et al., 2021), and developmental disorders (Bompard et al., 2021) are treated using music therapy. The patients experience negative thoughts and anxiety due to diseases and surgery, which would affect their emotions (Chen et al., 2021; Banerjee et al., 2022). The patients undergo music therapy sessions to alleviate their emotions and achieve a relaxed mood and positive thoughts. This relaxation can relieve stress about diseases and surgery, which eventually helps patients recover faster from the diseases. Therefore, the physician initially analyzes the emotions of patients using any physiological signals, such as electroencephalogram (EEG), electrocardiogram (ECG), and heart rate (HR), or by providing questionnaires followed by a therapeutic session based on their mood. The music therapeutic session involves in providing any kind of music for patients, which includes classical, instrumental, and the favorite music of patients. Some patients (if not in a critical condition) prefer to stay home or other preferred places after their surgery or during their treatments. As music therapy requires that appropriate music should reach the patient, it can be even achieved remotely without visiting the hospital to attend the music therapy session (Dhanalakshmi et al., 2022). Thus, this study focuses on an IoT solution to deliver real-time music therapy to patients remotely by processing their physiological data such as EEG, ECG, and HR on a cloud server (Siddiqui et al., 2020). The patient's emotions can be identified by utilizing a machine learning architecture from the cloud, and the results from the machine learning can be transferred to a patient's mobile phone application that is enabled with the internet. This mobile application is provided with music files for each emotion type. Hence, this application collects the information about the type of emotion from the cloud and plays music according to that emotion for the patient to listen.

15.1.1 Emotions

Human emotions are moods that can be expressed or felt. Human emotion varies in different types such as happy, excitement, wonder, fear, angry, annoyed, bored, sleepy, sorrow or sad, relaxed, peaceful, and calm. Thayer's (1990) emotional plane describes the arousal, valence, positive mood, and negative mood as shown in Figure 15.1. According to him, the x-axis from left to right is negative to positive mood which is known as valence whereas the y-axis from bottom to top is low to high mood, which is known as arousal.

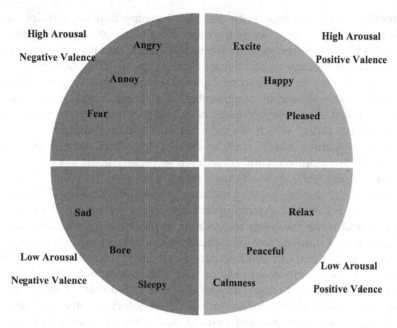

FIGURE 15.1
Thayer's emotional plane.

15.1.2 Music Therapy

Music is an ancient art that is involved in humans' social activities in the form of listening, chanting, and playing. Music enters the human body as an acoustic stimulus through the auditory path. Music varies in different forms based on its tone, timbre, tempo, rhythm, pitch, and harmony. Each form of music gets processed in the cortices of the brain. The processing of pitch and tone is carried out by the auditory cortex of temporal lobes, whereas the processing of timbre, syllable, and type of musical instrument involved is handled by the planum temporale that is posterior to the temporal lobe (Warren, 2008; Kothandaraman et al., 2022). The right and left anterior superior temporal gyri are associated with processing tempo and rhythm (Hernandez-Ruiz, 2019). Harmony is handled by the frontal lobe while rhythm is handled by the parietal lobe according to Warren (2008), and these lobes are correlated with working memory and behavioral response. It is obvious from these studies that all lobes of the brain are involved in processing a single piece of music; hence, music can create structural and functional changes in the brain, and this ability is what creates the basis for music therapy.

Music therapy is a non-pharmacological, alternative treatment that utilizes the advantages of music to deal with patients' emotional, physical, and cognitive activity. Music therapy is considered to be, by Stegemann et al. (2019) and Kumar et al. (2022), 'a systematic process of intervention wherein the therapist helps the client to promote health, using music experiences and the relationships that develop through them as dynamic forces of change'. According to a survey Kern and Tague (2017) performed, professional music therapists (n = 2495) from Australia, Europe, Latin America, North America, Southeast Asia, and the western Pacific revealed that music therapy has been delivered widely to patients affected by developmental disorders, depression, autism, emotional disorders, behavioral disorders, mental health issues, dementia, intellectual disability, Alzheimer's disease, anxiety, attention-deficit/hyperactivity disorder, learning deficits, multiple deficits, and speech or language impairment, while the other disorders like cancer and traumatic brain injury are second in the list of patients treated by music therapy. This study proved the significance of music therapy on the emotions of a patient. They said that the period for delivering music therapy to a patient probably takes from weeks up to a few months, so the data of each session should be documented, stored, and assessed yearly based on the severity of the deficit. The primary goals of music therapists are to make and observe changes in patient skills, which include communication, emotions, and socialism. Accordingly, other patient skills, such as music, cognition, movement, and spiritual requirements, are also monitored and considered secondary goals in each session of music therapy (Ekman et al., 1969). In each music therapy session, the patient undergoes all or few of the sessions on singing, playing musical instruments, dancing, listening, and composing as shown in Figure 15.2. A singing and composing session involves choosing songs to learn to sing and write the lyrics to or songs or pieces of instrumental music, respectively, by the patient. A dancing session typically includes playing a music piece or song so that, accordingly, the patient can make up dance movements. A session on listening encompasses playing any pre-composed music or song that the patient listens to. A session on playing a musical instrument adopts any kind of music genre and musical instrument as per the patient's desire. In healthcare, music-based interventions are categorized into music medicine, music therapy, and general music–based interventions according to Stegemann et al. (2019). Music therapy is applied for treating different disorders that are described in the Sections 15.1.2.1 through 15.1.2.4.

15.1.2.1 Music Therapy on Brain Disorders

Brain disorders like Parkinson's disease, Alzheimer's disease, and others affect a large population globally per the report by the World Health Organization in 2017. Parkinson's

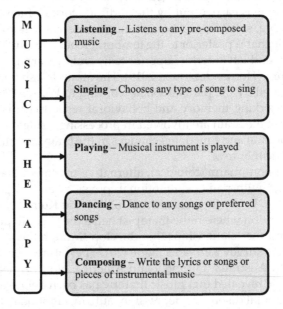

FIGURE 15.2
Schematic diagram of music therapy methods.

disease impacts the patient's locomotive activities along with cognitive activity and sleep deprivation (Maggioni et al., 2021). A study (Maggioni et al., 2021) using three pieces of music, such as Bach's Keyboard Concerto in D Minor, Mozart's piano sonata, and the song "Dona Dona Yiddish" Are used in the current research. EEG signals from 14 Parkinson's affected patients are acquired using Brain Vision Analyzer 2.2 and MATLAB R2019a.

The preprocessing stage of EEG signals incorporates a Butterworth bandpass filter with a passband frequency range between 0.5 and 70 Hz and a notch filter cutoff frequency of50 Hz. Fast Fourier transform is applied to attain power spectral density followed by the estimation of relative power spectral density during music and rest periods in alpha and theta bands. The connective pattern of EEG nodes is later computed using Granger causality analysis (GCA). The results from the GCA shows increased connectivity after listening to music in the frontotemporal region of Parkinson's disease patients (Sangwan et al., 2021).

15.1.2.2 Music Therapy on Traumatic Patients

Postoperative traumatic patients in recovery experience emotional imbalances and difficulties due to pain and stress on their bodies (Kaur and Bhambri, 2019). These patients require a system or technique to relieve their pain and reduce their stress so their emotions can be positively enhanced, which would help in a faster recovery. Music therapy can increase the arousal in such patients by offering sessions on listening to music, singing, composing, or dancing. Patients who had total knee arthroplasty surgery (Aris et al., 2021) have shown improvement in their physiological parameters such as diastolic blood pressure, respiratory rate, and oxygen saturation after listening to music. It is inferred that the pain and anxiety experienced by these patients can be reduced with the help of music therapy. Postoperative pain can be controlled by music therapy, which is evident in a study (Neda et al., 2019) in which participants were categorized as control and experimental (patients having undergone open heart surgery) groups. The experimental group listened to music while the immediately after the surgery. Systolic blood pressure, pulse rate, and oxygen saturation measured from the experimental group showed significant improvement in recovery times; thus, the pain of the postoperative traumatic patients can be reduced by listening to music while there is no significant change in diastolic blood pressure and heart rate.

15.1.2.3 Music Therapy on Cancer

The depression faced by cancer patients can be relieved by five-element music therapy (Yang et al., 2021), but its effect on anxiety is not well defined. A systematic review study (Yang et al., 2021) on cancer patients regarding their anxiety, sleep, quality of life, and depression provided evidence that the clinical application of music therapy can enhance the positive mood of cancer patients so that difficulties with depression, quality of life, and sleep can be reduced and controlled. A randomized controlled trial on cancer patients using EEG to find the effects of music therapy showed increased valence and arousal in the group that underwent music therapy sessions (Ramirez et al., 2018). The arousal of EEG signal is given as ratio of beta waves to alpha waves, and it is expressed by Ramirez et al. (2018):

$$\text{Arousal of EEG} = \frac{\beta F3 + \beta F4 + \beta AF3 + \beta AF4}{\alpha F3 + \alpha F4 + \alpha AF3 + \alpha AF4},$$

(15.1)

where $\beta F3$, $\beta F4$, $\beta AF3$, and $\beta AF4$ are beta waves and $\alpha F3$, $\alpha F4$, $\alpha AF3$, and $\alpha AF4$ are alpha waves from prefrontal lobes F3, F4, AF3, and AF4, respectively.

The valence of the EEG was also calculated in the study performed by Ramirez et al. (2018), and it is given as

$$\text{Valence of EEG} = \alpha F4 - \alpha F3. \tag{15.2}$$

The anxiety, fatigue, and breathing issues of the experimental group were reduced with improved emotional health.

15.1.2.4 Music Therapy on Developmental Deficits

Children with developmental deficits were participants in a study (Bompard et al., 2021) in which their parents' levels of stress and the children's quality of life were measured. They attended music therapy sessions at their home, and the outcomes showed an increased quality of life in the children and reduced stress in their parents.

15.2 Machine Learning Architecture for Healthcare Applications

Machine learning is a data analyzing technique for reading the information of data and making decisions from the data. In healthcare, patient data are stored in huge quantities, such as patient history, number of patients affected by disease, number of patients treated by disease, and others. These data are required to be stored and managed to predict the diseases or find the probability of impact on the patients. In such a case, a machine learning algorithm is used that usually obtains the patient data, processes the data to collect features, labels the data to train the data for classification or prediction, and tests the data to understand the result of the algorithm. It uses statistical analysis methods to find the probability and advanced methods to predict the data. Machine learning is mainly classified into three different categories based on the data and their awaited results: supervised learning, unsupervised learning, and reinforcement learning (Dhillon and Singh, 2019) as shown in Figure 15.3. Singh et al. (2021) cover the actual implementation upshots, data taken from the user, and the way they are stored in the database. Supervised learning requires training data to learn, and from that trained model, the algorithm predicts or classifies the data. The algorithm in supervised learning consists of training data and testing data, which are divided from the given patient data. Initially the supervised learning model trains the data by providing labels. For example, class A and class B are labeled as 0 and 1 to train the data that contain class A and class B. Once the model receives the training, it enters the testing phase in which another set of data is given. The testing phase should classify the data into 0 as class A and 1 as class B. Later the performance metrics are applied to evaluate the accuracy, precision, sensitivity, and specificity of the outcome.

Some of the available supervised learning machine learning algorithms are ensemble learning, K-nearest neighbor, decision tree, support vector machine, naïve Bayes, and neural network (Alpaydın, 2010). Unsupervised learning consists of training data and testing data but without labels. This algorithm encompasses the grouping or clustering of the data

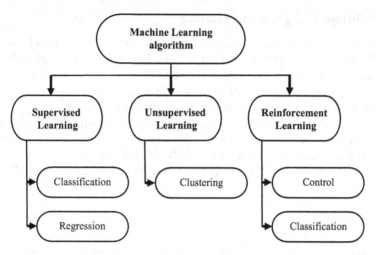

FIGURE 15.3
Basic categories of machine learning algorithms.

or features by similarity measures of natural association such as Euclidean distance. Examples of unsupervised learning algorithms include K-means and K-medoids clustering, in which the clusters are arranged based on the K-value of the algorithm. A reinforcement machine learning algorithm involves learning from the feedback or reinforcement network. It does not contain training data or labeled data. It uses number of iterations to learn about the data in a sequential manner.

15.2.1 Emotion Analysis Using Machine Learning

Six types of basic emotions, namely, fear, joy, sad, surprise, disgust, and anger (Ekman et al., 1969), are classified using different machine learning algorithms and deep learning networks, and the results are compared to define the best technique for classifying emotions (Bălan et al., 2020). It has been observed that physiological signals and a dataset for emotion analysis using EEG and physiological and video signals (DEAP) database are used for the analysis process. Features were extracted from the EEG, vertical electrooculography (vEoG), zygomaticus electromyography (zEMG), trapezius electromyography (tEMG), galvanic skin response (GSR), respiration rate (RR), plethysmography (PPG), and temperature. Other features included fractal dimensions (Higuchi's and Petrosian) and approximate entropy of EEG. The emotion is labeled as 1 whereas no emotion was labeled 0. Training these data was carried out using various machine learning techniques, including support vector machine, K-nearest neighbor, random forest, linear discriminant analysis and deep learning techniques. In the performance metric, classification accuracy for emotion is measured. Another study (Alhalaseh and Alasasfeh, 2020) on a machine learning algorithm for emotion classification encompassed only the EEG signal. The features extracted in the study by Bălan et al. (2020) were fractal dimension and entropy. These features are used for classification, and some of the machine learning they used were naïve Bayes, K-nearest neighbor, convolutional neural network (CNN), and decision tree, among which CNN provided the highest accuracy of emotional classification.

15.2.2 Music Therapy Using Machine Learning

A huge research study including 320 participants listened to music in which three categories are made so for participants who experience low relaxation, high relaxation, or no relaxation (Raglio et al., 2020). The emotional state of participants after the music listening session has been analyzed using a machine learning algorithm – a decision tree. The performance metric showed good accuracy in predicting emotions. While listening to music, physiological data such as electrodermal activity, pupil dilation, blood volume pulse, and skin temperature were acquired from 24 subjects (Rahman et al., 2021). A neural network was applied to the extracted features to classify the subject's emotion, which eventually showed good accuracy. This method can be adopted to improve mental health using music therapy.

15.3 IoT Solutions in Healthcare

The IoT connects healthcare devices, such as wearable sensors or those embedded in the internet and mobile applications, to monitor patients (Pradhan et al., 2021). These sensors can be ECG, EEG, HR, PPG, and temperature sensors. Physiological data from these sensors are recognized by the physician to analyze, diagnose and, in some cases, treat via the cloud. The patients and physicians can be provided with a mobile application. To achieve the IoT in healthcare requires combining an IoT solution and a cloud with the biomedical data. According to Oryema et al. (2017), the IoT in healthcare consists of three main blocks: publisher, broker, and subscriber. The publisher involves in acquiring the physiological data using wearable sensors or other sensing devices. It acquires the data continuously and passes it to the broker block through a network. In the second block, the broker processes the collected physiological data and stores the data in the cloud. The processing can be signal processing or machine learning in the cloud. In the final block, the subscriber analyzes and diagnoses the processed patient data via any information and communication technology ICT tool, such as a mobile phone, a smartwatch, a tablet, a computer, and others. According to Pradhan et al. (2021), the IoT in healthcare consists of different methods such as ambient assisted living, mobile IoT, wearable devices, community-based healthcare, cognitive computing, and so on, among which ambient assisted living utilizes a machine learning approach for healthcare information transmission, and a mobile IoT encompasses the user interface or application to communicate and transfer the patient data (Rani et al., 2022d). It should be noted that in a machine learning approach, the data get processed, analyzed, and stored in the cloud rather than waiting for the physician to analyze. However, IoT-enabled mobile phones require a good-quality internet connection and a mobile application along with the cloud server. A basic architecture of the IoT in healthcare is shown in Figure 15.4.

15.3.1 Machine Learning–Enabled IoT

Machine learning as discussed in Section 15.2; it requires input data that are then used to extract informative features for analyzing. The feature sets are later divided into training data and testing data, which are further labeled as per the data samples. It is followed by testing the machine learning algorithm using another set of data, and finally, it requires a

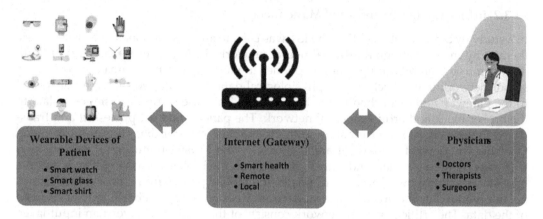

FIGURE 15.4
Basic Architecture of IoT in Healthcare. (source courtesy: freepik https://www.freepik.com/free-vector/wearable-technology-icons-set_4411695.htm;pixabay https://pixabay.com/vectors/medical-doctor-health-hospital-5459630/.)

performance metric to measure the performance of the algorithm. In the machine learning–enabled IoT, the data are acquired from the sensor network; that is, ECG, EEG, HR, and PPG data are acquired from the respective sensors. The acquired is initially preprocessed to remove physical and physiological artifacts. The features such as energy, entropy, relative power, pulse arrival time, HR variability, and blood pressure can be extracted. Then, the features are considered as dataset that is later divided into training and testing data (Rani et al., 2022b). The training set is labeled according to the target value. After the training, the machine learning algorithm learns about the data and learns to classify or predict the target. The algorithm is tested using the testing data followed by the measuring of sensitivity, specificity, accuracy, and precision. From data processing to performance metrics, the cloud is used followed by data storage and data transmission. The physiological data are either transferred to the physician or directly to the patient based on the severity of the disease, the patient's condition, and the patient's requirements. The complete architecture of machine learning–enabled IoT is shown in Figure 15.5.

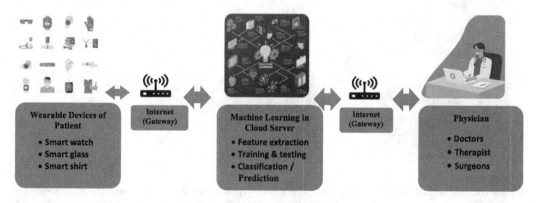

FIGURE 15.5
Machine learning enabled IoT. (source courtesy: freepikhttps://www.freepik.com/free-vector/isometric-data-analysis-flowchart_5971941.htm#page=1&query=machine%20learning&position=18&from_view=keyword.)

15.3.2 IoT for Emotion Analysis and Music Therapy

In a study by Siddiqui et al. (2020), the IoT was used to analyze emotions to provide music therapy by incorporating an artificial neural network. They proposed an architecture to deliver music therapy through mobile phones to patients. The body area network is the sensor network that collects all the physiological data. The acquired data are transferred to the gateway node and then to the base station. The base station transfers the data to the broker block and artificial neural network. The patient data get processed and transferred to the medical server for storage and to the physician for diagnosis and treatment. Once the emotions of the patient are analyzed by the physician, music for that emotion is chosen by the physician and transferred back to the broker network, followed by the base station, the gateway node, and, finally, the mobile phone. In this work, the features are not required as the artificial neural network does not rely on labeled data or features of the data. The artificial neural network consists of three different layers: an input layer, a hidden layer, and an output layer. The hidden layer again consists of two sublayers for disease and music. Figure 15.6 shows the process of emotion analysis by the physician and delivering music therapy through IoT solutions.

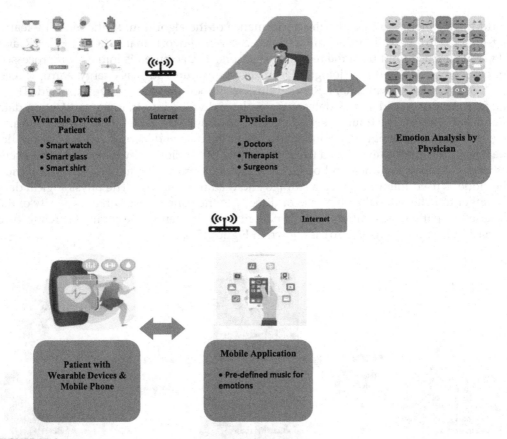

FIGURE 15.6

IoT for emotion analysis and music therapy. (source courtesy: freepik https://www.freepik.com/free-vector/emoji-emoticons-set-face-expression-feelings-collection_2610009.htm#page=1&query=emotions&position=6&from_view=search; https://www.freepik.com/free-vector/smartphone-flat-design_765774.htm#page=2&query=mobile%20application&position=16&from_view=search; https://www.freepik.com/free-vector/healthcare-trackers-wearables-sensors-abstract-concept-illustration_12291156.htm#page=1&query=human%20with%20wearable%20device&position=1&from_view=search.)

15.4 Proposed Architecture

The proposed architecture, which is illustrated in Figure 15.7, includes the acquisition of physiological signals such as EEG, ECG, and HR from the human body. They can be acquired using a sensor network such as wearable sensors or smartwatches. The acquired physiological data are subjected to transfer to the machine learning architecture, which is maintained in the cloud server (Pradhan et al., 2021). The machine learning in the proposed chapter initially requires the features from acquired data for which fractal dimension from EEG (Alhalaseh and Alasasfeh, 2020; Bălan et al., 2020), HR variability from ECG and HR can be extracted.

Classifiers such as support vector machine, decision tree, and k-nearest neighbor can be used as these algorithms are supervised learning. Supervised learning involves labeling the classes for which the change in arousal or valence of emotion (Ramirez et al., 2018) captured by these features can be labeled as 0 for arousal and 1 for valence (Bălan et al., 2020).

Training and testing the data are followed by the performance metrics in which classification accuracy, sensitivity, precision, and specificity can be evaluated. When the emotions get distinguished into arousal or valence, the scale of arousal or valence can be measured

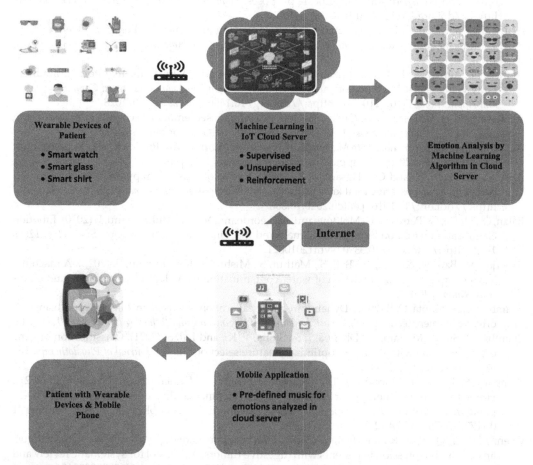

FIGURE 15.7
Proposed architecture of IoT-based emotion analysis and music therapy.

using the DEAP database. The main distinction of this machine learning algorithm between general machine learning is it works in real time in the cloud server, and the proposed architecture does not require a physician to analyze the physiological data. Later, the emotions, such as fear, angry, sad, happy, excited, and so on, as mentioned in Thayer (1990), are distinguished, and according to that distinction, music will be stored in the Android application of the patient's mobile phone. For example, if the emotion is classified as fear, a motivational song will be played on the mobile, or if the emotion is happy, hard rock music or beat songs will be played in the mobile. Whenever the patient opens the designed Android music application, the internet should be enabled so that the wearable sensors acquire the data immediately and transfer them to the cloud server for processing and classification using a machine learning algorithm. Finally, the predefined music or songs plays for the respective emotions.

References

Abbasi-Kesbi, R., Asadi, Z., and Nikfarjam, A. (2020). Developing a wireless sensor networkbased on a proposed algorithm for healthcare purposes. *Biomedical Engineering Letters*, 10(1), 163–170. https://doi.org/10.1007/s13534-019-00140-w.

Agarwal, S., and Lau, C. T. (2010). Remote health monitoring using mobile phones and Web services. *Telemedicine Journal and E-Health: The Official Journal of the American Telemedicine Association*, 16(5), 603–607.

Ahmed, N., Ajmal, M., Hai, M., Khuzema, A., and Tariq, M. (2016). Real time monitoring of human body vital signs using bluetooth and WLAN. *International Journal of Advanced Computer Science and Applications*, 7(10), 210–216. https://doi.org/10.14569/ijacsa.2016.071028.

Alhalaseh, R., and Alasasfeh, S. (2020). Machine-learning-based emotion recognition system using EEG signals. *Computers*, 9(4), 1–15. https://doi.org/10.3390/computers9040095

Alpaydın, E. (2010). *Introduction to Machine Learning Second Edition*. MIT Press. https://kkpatel7.files.wordpress.com/2015/04/alppaydin_machinelearning_2010.pdf.

Aris, A., Sulaiman, S., and Che Hasan, M. K. (2021). Effects of music therapy on physiological outcomes for post-operative total knee arthroplasty (TKA) patients. *Enfermeria Clinica*, 31, S10–S15. https://doi.org/10.1016/j.enfcli.2020.10.006.

Bălan, O., Moise, G., Petrescu, L., Moldoveanu, A., Leordeanu, M., and Moldoveanu, F. (2020). Emotion classification based on biophysical signals and machine learning techniques. *Symmetry*, 12(1), 1–22. https://doi.org/10.3390/sym12010021.

Banerjee, K., Bali, V., Nawaz, N., Bali, S., Mathur, S., Mishra, R. K., and Rani, S. (2022). A machine-learning approach for prediction of water contamination using latitude, longitude, and elevation. *Water*, 14(5), 728.

Bhambri, J., and Gupta, O. P. (2014). Dynamic frequency allocation scheme of mobile networks using priority assignment technique. *International Journal of Engineering and Technology Innovation*, 1(1), 9–12.

Bhambri, P., Singh, M., Jain, A., Dhanoa, I. S., Sinha, V. K., and Lal, S. (2021). Classification of gene expression data with the aid of optimized feature selection. *Turkish Journal of Physiotherapy and Rehabilitation*, 32(3), 1158–1167.

Bompard, S., Liuzzi, T., Staccioli, S., D'Arienzo, F., Khosravi, S., Giuliani, R., and Castelli, E. (2021). Home-based music therapy for children with developmental disorders during the COVID-19 pandemic. *Journal of Telemedicine and Telecare*. Advanced online publication. https://doi.org/10.1177/1357633X20981213.

Chen, X., Wei, Q., Jing, R., and Fan, Y. (2021). Effects of music therapy on cancer-related fatigue, anxiety, and depression in patients with digestive tumors: A protocol for systematic review and meta-analysis. *Medicine*, 100(22), 1–4. https://doi.org/10.1097/MD.0000000000025681.

Chhabra, Y., and Bhambri, P. (2021). Various approaches and algorithms for monitoring energy efficiency of wireless sensor networks. In *Sustainable Development through Engineering Innovations* (pp. 761–770). Springer, Singapore.

Dhanalakshmi, R., Anand, J., Sivaraman, A. K., and Rani, S. (2022). IoT-based water quality monitoring system using cloud for agriculture use. In *Cloud and Fog Computing Platforms for Internet of Things* (pp. 183–196). Chapman and Hall/CRC, Singapore.

Dhillon, A., and Singh, A. (2019). Machine learning in healthcare data analysis: A survey. *Journal of Biology and Today's World, 8*(6), 1–10. https://doi.org/10.15412/J.JBTW.01070206.

Ekman, P., Sorenson, E. R., and Friesen, W. V. (1969). Pan-cultural elements in facial displaysof emotion. *Science (New York, N.Y.), 164*(3875), 86–88. https://doi.org/10.1126/SCIENCE.164.3875.86.

Hernandez-Ruiz, E. (2019). How is music processed? Tentative answers from cognitive neuroscience. *Nordic Journal of Music Therapy, 28*(4), 315–332. https://doi.org/10.1080/08098131.2019.1587785.

Juyal, S., Sharma, S., and Shankar Shukla, A. (2021). Smart skin health monitoring using AI-enabled cloud-based IoT. *Materials Today: Proceedings, 46*(20), 10539–10545. https://doi.org/10.1016/j.matpr.2021.01.074.

Kaur, J., and Bhambri, P. (2019). Various DNA sequencing techniques and related applications. *International Journal of Analytical and Experimental Model Analysis, 11*(9), 3104–3111.

Kern, P., and Tague, D. B. (2017). Music therapy practice status and trends worldwide: An international survey study. *Journal of Music Therapy, 54*(3). https://doi.org/10.1093/jmt/thx011.

Kothandaraman, D., Manickam, M., Balasundaram, A., Pradeep, D., Arulmurugan, A., Sivaraman, A. K., … Balakrishna, R. (2022). Decentralized link failure prevention routing (DLFPR) algorithm for efficient internet of things. *Intelligent Automation and Soft Computing, 34*(1), 655–666.

Kumar, R., Rani, S., and Awadh, M. A. (2022). Exploring the application sphere of the internet of things in industry 4.0: A review, bibliometric and content analysis. *Sensors, 22*(11), 4276.

Lee, H., and Park, D. (2000). Bio-medical FM-FM-FSK radiotelemtry system for multi-signal transmission. In *Proceedings of the 22nd Annual International Conference of the IEEE Engineering in Medicine and Biology Society* (pp. 1553–1555). IEEE. https://doi.org/10.1109/IEMBS.2000.898038.

Lynch, K. A., Emard, N., Liou, K. T., Popkin, K., Borten, M., Nwodim, O., Atkinson, T. M., and Mao, J. J. (2021). Patient perspectives on active vs. passive music therapy for cancer in the inpatient setting: A qualitative analysis. *Journal of Pain and Symptom Management, 62*(1), 58–65. https://doi.org/10.1016/j.jpainsymman.2020.11.014.

Maggioni, E., Arienti, F., Minella, S., Mameli, F., Borellini, L., Nigro, M., Cogiamanian, F., Bianchi, A. M., Cerutti, S., Barbieri, S., Brambilla, P., and Ardolino, G. (2021). Effective connectivity during rest and music listening: An EEG study on Parkinson's disease. *Frontiers in Aging Neuroscience, 13*, 1–16. https://doi.org/10.3389/fnagi.2021.657221.

Neda, M. A., Abouzar, M., Hamed, N., and Shala, K. (2019). Effect of music on postoperative physiological parameters in patients under open heart surgery. *Journal of Research and Health, 9*(3), 195–202. https://doi.org/10.29252/jrh.9.3.195.

Oryema, B., Kim, H. S., Li, W., and Park, J. T. (2017). Design and implementation of an interoperable messaging system for IoT healthcare services. In *2017 14th IEEE Annual Consumer Communications and Networking Conference, CCNC 2017* (pp. 45–51). IEEE. https://doi.org/10.1109/CCNC.2017.7983080.

Pradhan, B., Bhattacharyya, S., and Pal, K. (2021). IoT-based applications in healthcare devices. *Journal of Healthcare Engineering, 2021*, 6632599. https://doi.org/10.1155/2021/6632599.

Raglio, A., Imbriani, M., Imbriani, C., Baiardi, P., Manzoni, S., Gianotti, M., Castelli, M., Vanneschi, L., Vico, F., and Manzoni, L. (2020). Machine learning techniques to predict the effectiveness of music therapy: A randomized controlled trial. *Computer Methods and Programs in Biomedicine, 185*, 105160. https://doi.org/10.1016/j.cmpb.2019.105160.

Rahman, J. S., Gedeon, T., Caldwell, S., Jones, R., and Jin, Z. (2021). Towards effective music therapy for mental health care using machine learning tools: human affective reasoning and music genres. *Journal of Artificial Intelligence and Soft Computing Research, 11*(1), 5–20. https://doi.org/10.2478/jaiscr-2021-0001.

Ramirez, R., Planas, J., Escude, N., Mercade, J., and Farriols, C. (2018). EEG-based analysis of the emotional effect of music therapy on palliative care cancer patients. *Frontiers in Psychology*, 9(MAR), 1–7. https://doi.org/10.3389/fpsyg.2018.00254.

Rani, S., Arya, V., and Kataria, A. (2022b). Dynamic pricing-based e-commerce model for the produce of organic farming in India: A research roadmap with main advertence to vegetables. In *Proceedings of Data Analytics and Management* (pp. 327–336). Springer.

Rani, S., Bhambri, P., and Chauhan, M. (2021a). A machine learning model for kids' behavior analysis from facial emotions using principal component analysis. In *2021 5th Asian Conference on Artificial Intelligence Technology (ACAIT)* (pp. 522–525). IEEE.

Rani, S., Kataria, A., and Chauhan, M. (2022c). Cyber security techniques, architectures, and design. In *Holistic Approach to Quantum Cryptography in Cyber Security* (pp. 41–66). CRC Press.

Rani, S., Kataria, A., and Chauhan, M. (2022d). Fog computing in industry 4.0: Applications and challenges—A research roadmap. In R. Tiwari, M. Mittal., and L. M. Goyal (Eds.), *Energy Conservation Solutions for Fog-Edge Computing Paradigms* (pp. 173–190). Springer.

Rani, S., Kataria, A., Chauhan, M., Rattan, P., Kumar, R., and Sivaraman, A. K. (2022a). Security and privacy challenges in the deployment of cyber-physical systems in smart city applications: State-of-art work. *Materials Today: Proceedings*, 62(7), 4671–4676.

Rani, S., Kataria, A., Sharma, V., Ghosh, S., Karar, V., Lee, K., and Choi, C. (2021b). Threats and corrective measures for IoT security with observance of cybercrime: A survey. *Wireless Communications and Mobile Computing*, 2021, 5579148. https://doi.org/10.1155/2021/5579148.

Rani, S., Mishra, R. K., Usman, M., Kataria, A., Kumar, P., Bhambri, P., and Mishra, A. K. (2021c). Amalgamation of advanced technologies for sustainable development of smart city environment: A review. *IEEE Access*, 9, 150060–150087.

Sakr, S., and Elgammal, A. (2016). Towards a comprehensive data analytics framework for smart healthcare services. *Big Data Research*, 4, 44–58. https://doi.org/10.1016/j.bdr.2016.05.002.

Sangwan, Y. S., Lal, S., Bhambri, P., Kumar, A., and Dhanoa, I. S. (2021). Advancements in social data security and encryption: A review. *Nveo-Natural Volatiles and Essential Oils Journal| NVEO*, 8(4), 15353–15362.

Shrivastava, A., Rizwan, A., Kumar, N. S., Saravanakumar, R., Dhanoa, I. S., Bhambri, P., and Singh, B. K. (2021). VLSI implementation of green computing control unit on Zynq FPGA for green communication. *Wireless Communications and Mobile Computing*, 2021, 4655400. https://doi.org/10.1155/2021/4655400.

Siddiqui, S., Nesbitt, R., Shakir, M. Z., Khan, A. A., Khan, A. A., Khan, K. K., and Ramzan, N. (2020). Artificial neural network (ANN) enabled internet of things (IoT) architecture for music therapy. *Electronics (Switzerland)*, 9(12), 1–24. https://doi.org/10.3390/electronics9122019.

Singh, A. P., Aggarwal, M., Singh, H., and Bhambri, P. (2021). Sketching of EV network: A complete roadmap. In *Sustainable Development Through Engineering Innovations: Select Proceedings of SDEI 2020* (pp. 431–442). Springer, Singapore.

Stegemann, T., Geretsegger, M., Phan Quoc, E., Riedl, H., and Smetana, M. (2019). Music therapy and other music-based interventions in pediatric health care: An overview. *Medicines*, 6(1), 25. https://doi.org/10.3390/medicines6010025.

Thayer, R. E. (1990). *The Biopsychology of Mood and Arousal - Robert E. Thayer - Google Books*. Oxford University Press.

Warren, J. (2008). How does the brain process rhythm? *Clinical Medicine*, 8(1), 32–36.

World Health Organisation. (2017). Depression and other common mental disorders: Global health estimates. https://apps.who.int/iris/handle/10665/254610.

Wu, T., Wu, F., Qiu, C., Redoute, J. M., and Yuce, M. R. (2020). A rigid-flex wearable health monitoring sensor patch for IoT-connected healthcare applications. *IEEE Internet of Things Journal*, 7(8), 6932–6945. https://doi.org/10.1109/JIOT.2020.2977164.

Yang, T., Wang, S., Wang, R., Wei, Y., Kang, Y., Liu, Y., and Zhang, C. (2021). Effectiveness of five-element music therapy in cancer patients: A systematic review ands meta-analysis. *Complementary Therapies in Clinical Practice*, 44(101416), 1–10. https://doi.org/10.1016/j.ctcp.2021.101416.

16

Complete Low-Cost IoT Framework for the Indian Agriculture Sector

Ashish Verma and Rajesh Bodade

CONTENTS

16.1 Introduction

India is a developing country whose economy is based on industry and agriculture; India's agriculture sector generates 18% of the country's gross domestic product. The agriculture industry is the economic backbone of India. It can also be said that agriculture has an important contribution to the economy of developing countries because having a good economy helps meet the basic needs of the population for food, wages, and employment. India's agriculture industry, directly and indirectly, employs more than 50% of the population. To improve the accuracy of paddy production, the hybrid classifier will be designed based on k-mean clustering and naive Bayes classifier (Kaur et al., 2019; Dhanalakshmi

DOI: 10.1201/9781003298335-16

et al., 2022). Iris images can be easily taken while taking photographs or selfies through mobile phones and misused in later stages (Sinha et al., 2020).

Smart agriculture or smart farming is an emerging technology, because IoT sensors can provide data about agricultural fields and then operate based on human input (Adam et al., 2019). The Internet of Things (IoT) is a cloud-based technology that allows for scalable management, data management, data security, data analysis, and more (Heble et al., 2018).

Show Figure 16.1 IoT smart farming solutions with cloud connectivity and data analysis, sensor technology, field status on a mobile app, field irrigation and water management, insect and pest and disease detection, crop and animal monitoring, and insect and pest and disease detection. Increased productivity, less waste, real-time data and production insight, greater production quality, and enhanced animal management were all a result of these important characteristics (Math and Dharwadkar, 2022). The present IoT solutions are not suitable for the Indian agriculture sector due to being very complex and not cost-effective, meaning not applicable to the reality on the ground (Rani et al., 2022d). The present IoT solutions, which are suitable only for economy developed countries, are not applicable for developing countries. Paika and Bhambri (2013) developed a method for automatic edge detection of a digital image. Most of the existing IoT solutions employ paid network GSM/NB-IoT/4G/5G for sensor networks, which are not suitable for IoT slow-speed networks, and the main challenge is network coverage in internal Indian rural areas, remaining existing (Rani et al., 2021a, 2022c). The solution uses unmanned aerial vehicle (UAV)– or drone-based farming that cannot be easily adopted by the Indian farmer (Rani et al., 2022a). The Indian government is currently focusing on modern farming methods. Presently Indian government also announced a certification program for agricultural drones on January 26, 2022, which allows them to carry a payload that does not contain pesticides or other

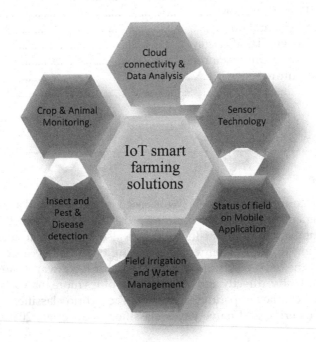

FIGURE 16.1
Key features of IoT-based farming.

liquids used in drone spraying (Tetila et al., 2020; webTropoGo. 5 feb.2022). Peer-to-peer networks have to stream videos on the internet (Bhambri and Gupta, 2013). Today, with the wide use of various communication technologies and the internet, it has become extremely easy to reproduce, communicate, and distribute digital content (Kaur and Bhambri, 2015).

This chapter proposes an economic architecture to help farmers overcome their limitations through proposed holistic affordable IoT framework focused on the agriculture Indian scenario (Rani et al., 2021b, 2022b). Farmers need a network that is free of cost to access local wireless sensor networks for which only internet connections at the center node with very low maintenance costs are required. The IoT infrastructure for agricultural monitoring should be low-cost and low-powered (Chopra et al., 2011; Kumar et al., 2022). Monitoring of crops and fields requires a sensor-based network. This infrastructure should be low-cost and low-power usage and can also be connected to the internet and the cloud with the help of a gateway at the center node (Rani and Gupta, 2016). Since it is observed that most of the IoT end devices are battery-powered, there is a need to adopt a low-power wide-area network (LPWAN) to keep the power consumption down (Mekki et al., 2019).

This framework provides better area and resource management through crop and field monitoring sensors. This framework connects all the necessary and related things, including the weather department and the agriculture research organization Indian Council of Agricultural Research (ICAR). The quality and quantity of crop production can be improved with the help of cloud-based services, including e-mandi, Indian market, nearest point of sale, current price position with location, and internet connectivity with agricultural scientists. It also includes monitoring of temperature, humidity, soil moisture and crop conditions, field irrigation, insect and pest detection, animal monitoring, actuator intervention, message notification for disastrous weather warnings, and expert advice for farmers (Uviase and Kotonya, 2017). The most important thing in crop monitoring is the detection of crop diseases, with the help of cameras, advanced images can be extracted using image-processing techniques. The research in bioinformatics has accumulated large amount of data (Bhambri and Gupta, 2012; Rani and Kumar, 2022). Advanced image-processing techniques are based on machine learning techniques (Singh et al., 2021). Image processing can be further enhanced by using deep learning algorithms, enabling camera images to detect crop diseases and pests (Raj et al., 2019; Kothandaraman et al., 2022).

In this chapter, a compressive study of the existing IoT technique/framework has been presented as well as an affordable economical, suitable IoT architecture for the Indian scenario (Arunachalam et al., 2021). Many crops are grown in India, but our research area is in Madhya Pradesh, where wheat and soybean cultivation is more prevalent. The second reason is ICAR's Soybean Research Center in Indore, Madhya Pradesh, which is the primary reason for selecting soybean crops for this study.

16.2 Proposed Model

This proposed methodology is focused on the Indian situation, where so many IoT solutions have failed to overcome issues at the ground level. After reading the literature, it turned out that most of the IoT solutions, which are expensive to adopt in farming, were not affordable for every farmer, and some technical solutions are too complex for every farmer to understand. This proposed model has most of the things automated, as well as analysis and decision-making on a cloud platform so that even a non-technical person can easily adopt it after some training, such as handling mobile applications.

This model combines all the cloud's features and capabilities with IoT to create a smart agriculture system. Under this IOT system, there is the use of an embedded board that is based on a microcontroller; in most cases, we use Arduino UNO in which we provide internet connectivity and wireless sensor network connectivity. Agricultural data were collected from agricultural field areas using a combination of several sensors (Ahmed and Nabi, 2021). LoRa module with wireless sensor network and LoRa gateway microcontroller-based system for internet access. It can transfer agricultural field data to the cloud with the help of an internet connection. The IoT-based agricultural system architecture depicted in Figure 16.2 incorporates everything described in the introduction to provide service to this architecture while keeping the Indian situation in mind (Heble et al., 2018; Verma and Bodade 2022).

16.2.1 Elements of the Proposed Model

This architecture is divided into four broad categories:

 a. Wireless sensor network spread on agriculture field
 b. Microcontroller embedded section
 c. Cloud service section
 d. Application user interfacing section

The architecture is shown in Figure 16.3. Sensor networks comprise multiple sensors for humidity, temperature, soil, and so on. The sensor network is maybe wired, and wireless connections depend on sensor type that is spread on field. The microcontroller interfaces

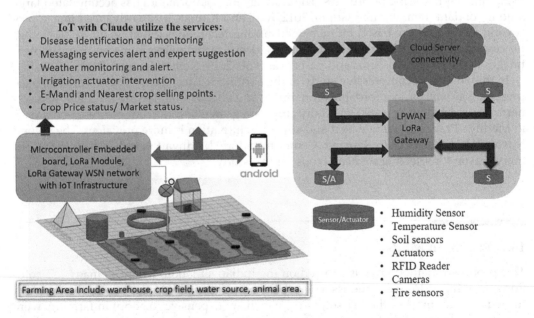

FIGURE 16.2
Proposed model of IoT-based agriculture system.

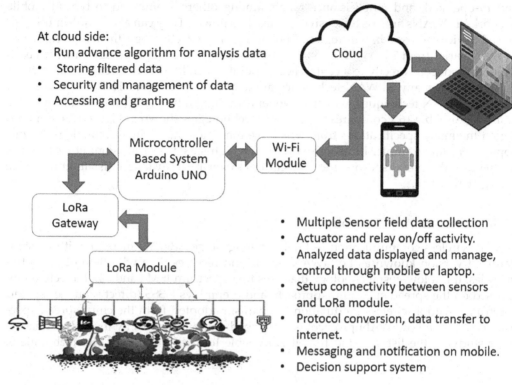

At cloud side:
- Run advance algorithm for analysis data
- Storing filtered data
- Security and management of data
- Accessing and granting

Cloud

Microcontroller Based System Arduino UNO

Wi-Fi Module

LoRa Gateway

LoRa Module

- Multiple Sensor field data collection
- Actuator and relay on/off activity.
- Analyzed data displayed and manage, control through mobile or laptop.
- Setup connectivity between sensors and LoRa module.
- Protocol conversion, data transfer to internet.
- Messaging and notification on mobile.
- Decision support system

FIGURE 16.3
Architecture of IoT-based agriculture system.

with the LoRa gateway, LoRa module, and Wi-Fi in the embedded system. The LoRa gateway and modules provide connectivity between the transmitter and the receiver for long-distance communication. The Wi-Fi model is interfaced due to providing internet; if we replace Arduino UNO with ESP32, then we will not need to interface the Wi-Fi module. Using cloud features and advanced algorithm techniques, smart agriculture decision support systems will be able to monitor crops for diseases and pests, allowing for better disease and pest detection. The Android app includes a number of features, including sector-specific weather monitoring and data display, system control, messaging expert assistance, climate change notifications, crop-selling locations near you, and showing e-mandi centers. All features and services use the IoT cloud with a central controller (MPU or MCU) attached to the sensor network via an LPWAN LoRa module and a gateway (Verma and Bodade, 2022).

16.3 LPWAN Techniques

LPWAN works on low-power and node networks with internet connectivity, hence the name low-power wide-area network. It is a category of networks that follow its own merits, and they are all referred to as LPWAN category networks because of their main characteristics such as low power consumption, low bandwidth for data transmission, battery-operated, and long-distance range, among others. Compared to typical mobile networks, LPWANs are less expensive and use less power. They can also handle more connected devices across a bigger region. Depending on the technology, the long range of an LPWAN varies from 2 km to 1,000 km. LPWANs often use a star topology, in which each endpoint connects directly to a central access point, much like Wi-Fi (Mekki et al., 2019).

Globally so many LPWAN techniques are available, but Figure 16.4 shows different types of LPWAN techniques, which are generally adopted by the IoT and M2M (machine to machine). Table 16.1 compares the LPWAN technologies shown in Figure 16.4, depending on the many specifications from which we may pick the optimal technology for our application, for example. Bluetooth is ideal for high-speed transmission; however, it is unable to link several sensors and transfer data over large distances (Islam et al., 2020; Zhang et al., 2020).

16.3.1 LoRa/LoRaWAN Technology

LoRa is wireless communication technology; long-range LPWAN method, with its standardized version known as LoRaWAN, sends and receives data with help of radio frequencies. It is a low-cost technology that uses free-spectrum ISM bands. LoRa technology is based on the spread spectrum approach, and it employs DSSS (direct sequence spread spectrum), with a wireless modulation mechanism adopted from the chirp spread spectrum (CSS). The LoRaWAN protocol is developed and maintained by the LoRa Alliance. After studying the list in Table 16.1, it is possible to justify that the LoRa technique is

TABLE 16.1

List of Specifications of Various LPWAN Technology

Technology	DataRate	Power Usage (Battery-Life)	Security	Range	Remark
LoRa	≤50 kbps	Very low (8–10 years)	High	2–50 km	LAN and MAN formation, Range very on urban–rural area, ISM band used
Zigbee	250 kbps	Very low (5–10 years)	LOW	~100m	LAN formation and better than BLE for IoT, ISM used
BLE	1 Mbps	Low few months	HIGH	~50m	LAN formation, Speed is high to other LPWAN technique
Sigfox	≤1kbps	Very low(5–10 years)	HIGH	~50km	LAN, MAN formation, Long distance covered, ISM band used.
Weightless	≤24 MB	Low(very long)	HIGH	~5km	LAN, MAN formation, non-ISM band used.
NB-IoT	~250 kbps	High (1–2 years)	HIGH	~50km	LAN, MAN formation WAN at cell network, non-ISM band.

Note: LAN and MAN form the sensor network only, and with internet connectivity, the system can connect to the WAN. The range of the network varies according to the urban and rural areas. The speed of the network varies according to the frequency spectrum.

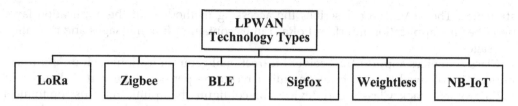

FIGURE 16.4
Different types of LPWAN techniques.

superior to all other LPWAN techniques, is low cost, uses an unpaid spectrum, and is easy to implement over a long range (Perković et al., 2021).

LoRa communication enables for the use of a variety of spread factors (SFs) to achieve a balance between communication range and data transfer rate. It also employs a forward error correction technique that, in combination with LoRa modulation, improves receiver sensitivity. Messages transmitted by LoRa end devices are received by all gateway devices, resulting in the creation of star-to-star network architecture.

The LoRa network infrastructure may adjust the data rate and RF output for each end-device separately via an adaptive data rate approach to optimize both end-device battery life and overall network capacity. All Gateway devices receive messages delivered by LoRa end devices, creating a star-of-stars network structure. Time difference of arrival is a mechanism that employs gateway synchronization. To avoid collisions, the CSMA (carrier sense multiple access) technique was employed. The LoRaWAN protocol employs an ALOHA-style communication mechanism, with varying packet lengths. All these parameters affect LoRa performance and its responsible for the speed of data transmission, the number of connected nodes, and the distance between the node and the gateway (Magrin et al., 2020).

16.3.1.1 LoRaWAN Specification

- LoRaWAN specification focus on Indian region (Farooq et al., 2019):
  - Speed: Bit rates from 0.3 to 5 Kbps
  - Range: 2 km–15 km
  - Band: India 865–867 MHz ISM Band of frequencies 865.0625 MHz, 865.4025 MHz, 865.985 MHz
  - Spreading Factor: 7–12
  - Bandwidth (125 KHz)
  - Spreading Technique: CSS spread spectrum
  - Digital Modulation Technique: FSK
  - Mode of operation class A, B, C
  - Deceive hand link 100s of devices at the same time.

16.3.1.2 LoRa Protocol Stack

LoRa wireless protocol stack includes a four-layer radiofrequency (RF) layer, a physical layer, a medium access control (MAC) layer, and an application layer. The RF layer describes the signaling RF standard, and the physical layer describes modulation strategies. The MAC layer describes the accessing methods, and the application layer describes the application interface LoRa frames contain uplink messages and downlink messages.

Class A devices support transceiver bidirectional communication; each uplink transmission is followed by two brief downlink reception periods. Figure 16.5 depicts the LoRa protocol stack. Class A end devices can configure the uplink transmission to meet their specific requirements with just mild jitter (random variation before transmission). Class A devices consume the least power, but they also have the least flexibility in downlink transmission (Magrin et al., 2020). LoRa class operating functionality is shown in the Figure 16.6.

Bidirectional class B has allotted slots. Class B end devices open additional windows at specified times. As a result, the network server will require a synchronized beacon (synchronization frame) from the gateway to determine whether the endpoint device is

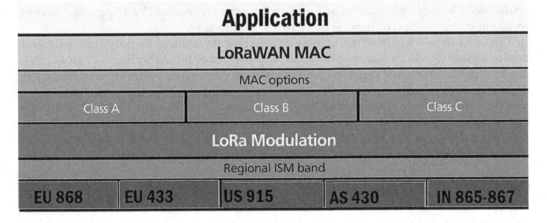

FIGURE 16.5
LoRa protocol stack.

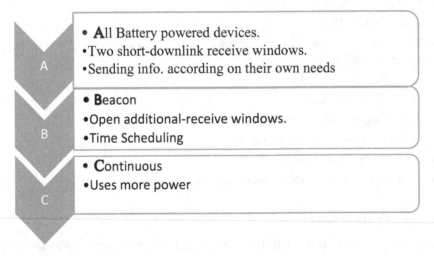

FIGURE 16.6
LoRa class operating functionality.

listening. Bidirectional class C maximum receiving slots and getting Windows on Class C end devices are continuously involved in transmission. As a result, they use the greatest amount of energy (Gupta et al., 2011; Perković et al., 2021).

16.4 Computer Vision Technology

Image processing is the process of executing features on pictures in order to enhance them or extract useful information from them. However, unlike the human brain, it is incapable of making decisions. Image data processing is a subfield of computer vision (CV). The goal of computer vision is to extract information from incoming images or videos so that they can be completely comprehended. Visual input can be predicted in the same way that the human brain does. In CV, machine learning is used to detect patterns in images for interpretation. The computer's visual prediction is analogous to the human vision process. Neural networks are designed to follow the way the human brain functions. Figure 16.7 represents the Computer Vision Process. The CV process ranges from image acquisition in the actual visual data to decision-making via image processing (Dai et al., 2020). CV tries to replicate human vision using digital pictures by conducting three important processing steps:

- Image acquisition
- Image processing
- Image analysis and understanding

16.4.1 Image Acquisition

The process of converting object information into binary data, which are subsequently interpreted as digital images, is known as image acquisition. The sources are webcams and cameras, among others.

16.4.2 Image Processing

In this section, we apply algorithms to the obtained binary data to estimate deep-level information on parts of the image. Complex computational modeling methods and approaches are frequently included in the second level.

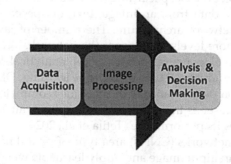

FIGURE 16.7
CV process.

This procedure is divided into the following sections:

Edge detection

Segmentation

Classification

16.4.2.1 Edge Detection

Edge detection is a critical technique in image processing, machine vision, and computer vision, notably in feature detection and extraction. Edges are curved line segments formed by points in an image that have fast variations in brightness.

16.4.2.2 Segmentation

Segmentation is the technique of segmenting a digital image into various segments or sections is known as image segmentation. Segmentation is generally used to simplify or transform an image's representation into something that might create more meaning or make analysis easier.

16.4.2.3 Image Classification

Image classification is a CV method that can categorize an image based on its visual information. With a large number of labeled images, an artificial neural network should be able to detect if an object is present in the image.

16.4.3 Analyzing and Understanding

In this block, an information analyzer using advanced algorithms states information and processes to make decisions. The end result of image analysis operations is a numerical output rather than a picture, which distinguishes it from other forms of image-processing methods like as enhancement or restoration.

Machine learning is a data analysis approach that trains machines to accomplish things that people and animals naturally do (Jasmine and Gupta, 2012). Machine learning algorithms do not rely on predetermined equations and are instead used directly as a model, employing a computational approach to "learning." It is now used to solve complex issues including image recognition, natural network processing, image classification, image segmentation, and object detection. Deep learning (DL) is a form of machine learning in which a model learns to classify data from an image, text, or speech. DL is frequently implemented using a neural network architecture. The number of layers in a network determines how deep it: the more levels, the deeper the network. DL is a subclass of machine learning that aims to develop neural networks for analytical learning that mirror the human brain. DL is a more advanced type of machine learning. DL requires a large training dataset as the classification performance of the classifier completely depends on the quantity and quality of the dataset as the number of examples available for learning increases as the algorithm improves its performance (Tetila et al., 2020).

Convolutional neural networks (CNNs) area type of neural network technology. It is a DL system that can take an input image and apply learnable weights and biases to various features of the image, allowing it to distinguish between them. Shown in Figure 16.8 is an internal block of a CNN, which shows the processing steps of a CNN.

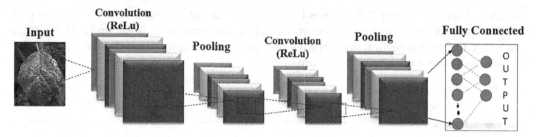

FIGURE 16.8
Internal block of convolution neural network.

Convolution is the initial layer, which extracts characteristics from the input image and uses kernels or filters to learn the relationship between them. A rectified linear unit for nonlinear operation is referred to as a ReLU (rectified linear unit) layer. Downsampling employs the pooling layer to decrease the number of parameters and retain only the most important data for further processing.

Max pooling is divided into two types, that is, average and sum pooling (Bhupal et al., 2021). We convert our complete matrix to a vector, similar to a vertex that can be provided to the input layer. The flattened vector is passed to the input layer by fully connected layers. A literature study and expert persons suggest that DL is the better outcome compared to machine learning; for crop and plant disease detection, CNN is the best technology for disease and pest detection. Some researchers suggest hybrid technology (Zhang et al., 2019; CNN Explainer, n.d.).

16.5 Conclusion and Future Scope

Today, as new technology is being discovered, new dimensions are emerging to make agriculture better, then it can be said that it is not easy to adopt new technology, it depends on many parameters, the country's economy, literacy rates, government organization funding, research, adaptability of new technology by farmers, and much more. The present IoT solutions are not suitable for the Indian agriculture sector due to being very complex and not cost-effective, meaning it is not applicable to the reality on the ground. Most of the existing IoT solutions employ a paid network GSM/NB-IoT/4G/5G for sensor networks. In this chapter, a compressive study of the existing IoT framework was presented as well as a holistic, affordable IoT framework, a suitable IoT architecture for the Indian scenario. By apply new technologies like machine learning and DL in the IoT decision support system in the cloud, an automation-based system can handle production and management in a smart way. To make the system low cost, we used an Arduino board and a LoRa module, which will be an affordable device for the farmers. All the sensors, such as those for temperature, humidity, soil moisture, and camera, will play a major role in telling crop and field status. Due to the crop information being in the cloud, we can know the status of the crop anytime, anywhere, and this is the strongest feature of IoT. With the help of this information, the decision support system, which is in the cloud, which includes algorithms, is able to make decisions. Farmers can make decisions about irrigation, expert suggestions, e-mandi information, the nearest crop-selling point, and insect pest control. This framework for crop disease detection recommends using a CNN methodology with DL, whose

Decision Support System (DSS) gives better output. In future work, this framework can adopt edge and fog computing to improve data management more securely. The results for insect and pest detection are improved by the increasing number of data sets and the adaptation of more improved algorithms.

References

Electronic Journal/Conference

Adam, A. H., Tamilkodi, R., and Madhavi, K. V. (2019). Low-cost green power predictive farming using IOT and cloud computing. In *2019 International Conference on Vision Towards Emerging Trends in Communication and Networking (ViTECoN)*. doi:10.1109/vitecon.2019.8899500.

Ahmed, L., and Nabi, F. (2021). Agriculture 5.0—The future. In *Agriculture 5.0: Artificial Intelligence, IoT, and Machine Learning* (pp. 187–203). Routledge. doi:10.1201/9781003125433-9.

Arunachalam, P., Janakiraman, N., Sivaraman, A. K., Balasundaram, A., Vincent, R., Rani, S., … Rajesh, M. (2021). Synovial sarcoma classification technique using support vector machine and structure features. *Intelligent Automation and Soft Computing*, 32(2), 1241–1259.

Bhambri, P., and Gupta, O. P. (2012). A novel method for the design of phylogenetic tree. *International Journal of Information Technology, Engineeringin Applied Science Reserach*, 1(1), 24–28.

Bhambri, P., and Gupta, O. P. (2013). Design of distributed prefetching protocol in push-to-peer video-on-demand system. *International Journal of Research in Advent Technology (IJRAT)*, 1(3), 95–103.

Bhupal, D. S., Ramakrishna Sajja, V., Jhansi Lakshmi, P., and Venkatesulu, D. (2021). Smart farming using IoT. In D. Bhattacharyya and R. N. Thirupathi (Eds.), *Advances in Intelligent Systems and Computing* (pp. 409–418). Springer. doi:10.1007/978-981-15-9516-5_34.

Chopra, S., Bhambri, P., and Singh, B. (2011). Segmentation of the mammogram images to find breast boundaries. *International Journal of Computer Science and Technology*, 2(2), 164–167.

Dai, Q., Cheng, X., Qiao, Y., and Zhang, Y. (2020). Crop leaf disease image super-resolution and identification with dual attention and topology fusion generative adversarial network. *IEEE Access*, 8, 55724–55735. doi:10.1109/access.2020.2982055.

Dhanalakshmi, R., Anand, J., Sivaraman, A. K., and Rani, S. (2022). IoT-based water quality monitoring system using cloud for agriculture use. In *Cloud and Fog Computing Platforms for Internet of Things* (pp. 183–196). Chapman and Hall/CRC, Singapore.

Farooq, M. S., Riaz, S., Abid, A., Abid, K., and Naeem, M. A. (2019). Undefined. *IEEE Access*, 7, 156237–156271. Doi:10.1109/access.2019.2949703.

Gupta, O., Rani, S., and Pant, D. C. (2011). Impact of parallel computing on bioinformatics algorithms. In *Proceedings 5th IEEE International Conference on Advanced Clomputing and Communication Technologies* (pp. 206–209). IEEE.

Heble, S., Kumar, A., Prasad, K. V., Samirana, S., Rajalakshmi, P., and Desai, U. B. (2018). A low power IoT network for smart agriculture. In *2018 IEEE 4th World Forum on Internet of Things (WF-IoT)*. doi:10.1109/wf-iot.2018.8355152.

Islam, N., Ray, B., and Pasandideh, F. (2020). IoT based smart farming: Are the LPWAN technologies suitable for remote communication? In *2020 IEEE International Conference on Smart Internet of Things (SmartIoT)*. doi:10.1109/smartiot49966.2020.00048.

Jasmine, B. P., and Gupta, O. P. (2012). Analyzing the phylogenetic trees with tree-building methods. *Indian Journal of Applied Research*, 1(7), 83–85.

Kaur, J., Bhambri, P., and Sharma, K. (2019). Wheat production analysis based on naïve Bayes classifier. *International Journal of Analytical and Experimental Model Analysis*, 11(9), 705–709.

Kaur, P., and Bhambri, P. (2015). To design an algorithm for text watermarking. *The Standard International Journals (The SIJ)*, 3(5), 62–67.

Kothandaraman, D., Manickam, M., Balasundaram, A., Pradeep, D., Arulmurugan, A., Sivaraman, A. I., ... Balakrishna, R. (2022). Decentralized link failure prevention routing (DLFPR) algorithm for efficient internet of things. *Intelligent Automation and Soft Computing, 34*(1), 655–666.

Kumar, R., Rani, S., and Awadh, M. A. (2022). Exploring the application sphere of the internet of things in industry 4.0: A review, bibliometric and content analysis. *Sensors, 22*(11), 4276.

Magrin, D., Capuzzo, M., and Zanella, A. (2020). A thorough study of LoRaWAN performance under different parameter settings. *IEEE Internet of Things Journal, 7*(1), 116–127. doi:10.1109/jiot.2019.2946487.

Math, R. M., and Dharwadkar, N. V. (2022). Early detection and identification of grape diseases using convolutional neural networks. *Journal of Plant Diseases and Protection.* doi:10.1007/s41348-022-00589-5.

Mekki, K., Bajic, E., Chaxel, F., and Meyer, F. (2019). A comparative study of LPWAN technologies for large-scale IoT deployment. *ICT Express, 5*(1), 1–7. doi:10.1016/j.icte.2017.12.005.

Paika, E. V., and Bhambri, E. P. (2013). Edge detection-fuzzy inference system. *International Journal of Management and Information Technology, 4*(1), 148–155.

Perković, T., Rudeš, H., Damjanović, S., and Nakić, A. (2021). Low-cost implementation of reactive jammer on LoRaWAN network. *Electronics, 10*(7), 864. doi:10.3390/electronics10070864.

Proceedings of International Conference on frontiers in computing and systems. (2021). *Advances in Intelligent Systems and Computing.* doi:10.1007/978-981-15-7834-2.

Raj, S., Sehrawet, S., Patwari, N., and Sathiya, K. C. (2019). IoT based model of automated agricultural system in India. In *2019 3rd International Conference on Trends in Electronics and Informatics (ICOEI)* (pp. 84–93). IEEE. doi:10.1109/icoei.2019.8862749.

Rani, S., Arya, V., and Kataria, A. (2022a). Dynamic pricing-based e-commerce model for the produce of organic farming in India: A research roadmap with main advertence to vegetables *Proceedings of Data Analytics and Management* (pp. 327–336). Springer.

Rani, S., and Gupta, O. P. (2016). Empirical analysis and performance evaluation of various GPU implementations of protein BLAST. *International Journal of Computer Applications, 151*(7), 22–27.

Rani, S., Kataria, A., and Chauhan, M. (2022b). Cyber security techniques, architectures, and design. In *Holistic Approach to Quantum Cryptography in Cyber Security* (pp. 41–66). CRC Press.

Rani, S., Kataria, A., and Chauhan, M. (2022c). Fog computing in industry 4.0: Applications and challenges—A research roadmap.In R. Tiwari, M. Mittal., and L. M. Goyal (Eds.), *Energy Conservation Solutions for Fog-Edge Computing Paradigms* (pp. 173–190). Springer.

Rani, S., Kataria, A., Chauhan, M., Rattan, P., Kumar, R., and Sivaraman, A. K. (2022d). Security and privacy challenges in the deployment of cyber-physical systems in smart city applications: State-of-art work. *Materials Today: Proceedings, 62*(7), 4671–4676.

Rani, S., Kataria, A., Sharma, V., Ghosh, S., Karar, V., Lee, K., and Choi, C. (2021a). Threats and corrective measures for IoT security with observance of cybercrime: A survey. *Wireless Communications and Mobile Computing, 2021.* doi:10.1155/2021/5579148.

Rani, S., and Kumar, R. (2022). Bibliometric review of actuators: Key automation technology in a smart city framework. *Materials Today: Proceedings, 60*(1). doi:10.1016/j.matpr.2021.12.469.

Rani, S., Mishra, R. K., Usman, M., Kataria, A., Kumar, P., Bhambri, P., and Mishra, A. K. (2021b). Amalgamation of advanced technologies for sustainable development of smart city environment: A review. *IEEE Access, 9*, 150060–150087.

Singh, M., Bhambri, P., Singh, I., Jain, A., and Kaur, E. K. (2021). Data mining classifier for predicting diabetics. *Annals of the Romanian Society for Cell Biology, 25*(4), 6702–6712.

Sinha, V. K., Jeet, R., Bhambri, P., and Mahajan, M. (2020). Empowering intrusion detection in IRIS recognition system: A review. *Journal of Natural Remedies, 21*(2), 131–153.

Tetila, E. C., Machado, B. B., Menezes, G. K., Da Silva Oliveira, A., Alvarez, M., Amorim, W. P., ... Pistori, H. (2020). Automatic recognition of soybean leaf diseases using UAV images and deep Convolutional neural networks. *IEEE Geoscience and Remote Sensing Letters, 17*(5), 903–907. doi:10.1109/lgrs.2019.2932385.

Uviase, O., and Kotonya, G. (2018). IoT architectural framework: Connection and integration framework for IoT systems. *Electronic Proceedings in Theoretical Computer Science, 264*, 1–17. doi:10.4204/eptcs.264.1.

Verma, A., and Bodade, R. (2022). Low-cost IoT framework for Indian agriculture sector: A compressive review to meet future expectation. In *Proceedings of Data Analytics and Management* (pp. 241–258). Springer. doi:10.1007/978-981-16-6289-8_21.

Zhang, X., Zhang, M., Meng, F., Qiao, Y., Xu, S., and Hour, S. (2019). A low-power wide-area network information monitoring system by combining NB-IoT and Lora. *IEEE Internet of Things Journal*, 6(1), 590–598. doi:10.1109/jiot.2018.2847702.

Online Documents/Web

CNN explainer. (n.d.). Retrieved from https://poloclub.github.io/cnn-explainer/

World population projected to reach 9.8 billion in 2050, and 11.2 billion in 2100. (2017, October 23). Retrieved from https://www.un.org/development/desa/en/news/population/world-population-prospects-2017.html

Index

Printed in the United States
by Baker & Taylor Publisher Services

Printed in the United States
by Baker & Taylor Publisher Services